THE SEARCH FOR WEALTH AND STABILITY

© Ailsa Maxwell, J. R. Ward, Alan Milward, Michael Palairet,
George Hammersley, R. J. Morris, S. B. Saul, Wray Vamplew,
chael Cullen, Roger Davidson, Rosalind Mitchison, T. C. Smout,
Stephanie Blackden, Ian Levitt 1979

First published 1979 by
THE MACMILLAN PRESS LTD
London and Basingstoke
Associated companies in Delhi Dublin
Hong Kong Johannesburg Lagos Melbourne
New York Singapore and Tokyo

Typeset by Santype International Ltd., Salisbury, Wilts

Printed in Great Britain
by J. W. Arrowsmith Ltd., Bristol BS3 2NT

British Library Cataloguing in Publication Data

The Search for Wealth and stability
  1. Great Britain – Social conditions – Addresses,
essays, lectures
  I. Smout, Thomas Christopher   II. Flinn, Michael
Walter
309.1'41   HN385.5

ISBN 0-333-23358-1

THE SEARC
WEALTH
AND STABIL

Essays in Economic and Social History presented to M. W. Flinn

Edited by
T. C. SMOUT

Contents

List of Tables

List of Figures

List of Contributors

STEPHANIE BLACKDEN teaches history and economic history at George Heriot's School, Edinburgh.

MICHAEL CULLEN is Senior Lecturer in History, University of Otago, New Zealand.

ROGER DAVIDSON is Lecturer in Economic History at Edinburgh University.

G. HAMMERSLEY is Senior Lecturer in History at Edinburgh University.

IAN LEVITT is Lecturer in Sociology, Plymouth Polytechnic.

AILSA MAXWELL was formerly Research Associate in the Department of Economic History at Edinburgh University.

ALAN MILWARD is Professor of European Studies at the University of Manchester Institute of Science and Technology.

ROSALIND MITCHISON is Reader in Economic History at Edinburgh University.

R. J. MORRIS is Lecturer in Economic History at Edinburgh University.

MICHAEL PALAIRET is Lecturer in Economic History at Edinburgh University.

S. B. SAUL is Vice-chancellor of the University of York.

T. C. SMOUT is Professor of Economic History at Edinburgh University.

WRAY VAMPLEW is Senior Lecturer in Economic History at the Flinders University of South Australia.

J. R. WARD is Lecturer in Economic History at Edinburgh University.

List of Abbreviations

(for Notes to Chapters)

AICP	Association for the Improvement of the Condition of the Poor
APS	*Acts of the Parliaments of Scotland*
BAJ	Business Archives Jowitt (Brotherston Library Leeds)
BL	British Library
East.	Easter
EHR	*Economic History Review*
FA	Football Association minute books
FL	Football League minute books
Glos. RO	Gloucestershire Record Office
HMC	Historical Manuscripts Commission
Hil.	Hilary
Here. RO	Herefordshire Record Office
JRSS	*Journal of Royal Statistical Society*
JSSL	*Journal of the Statistical Society of London*
Mich.	Michaelmas
MRC	Medical Research Council
Mon. RO	Monmouthshire Record Office
NLS	National Library of Scotland
OECD	Organisation for European Co-operation and Development
PP	Parliamentary Papers
PRO	Public Record Office
R & D	Research and Development
SRO	Scottish Record Office
Trin.	Trinity

Introduction

T. C. SMOUT

Michael Flinn arrived as a lecturer at Edinburgh University in the autumn of 1959, from holding a teaching position at Isleworth Grammar School, Middlesex: he was appointed by Professor A. J. Youngson, who had himself recently become the first holder of a chair of economic history in the university. Mr Flinn (as he then was) came, however, with an established reputation as a scholar of the iron industry whose revision article in the *Economic History Review* for 1958 (24)* was in many respects the starting point for our modern understanding of the industry in the eighteenth century. Three years later he published his monograph on the north-eastern iron-masters the Crowley family; this remains a remarkable illustration of what can be done in business history in the absence of a central set of business records.

With the publication in 1961 of an introductory school textbook which continues to be widely used (1), he had already accepted the challenge of reaching a wide audience. Perhaps, however, it was expounding to a large Scottish first-year class the historical mechanisms of economic growth and social change which brought him to develop on a broad front the two other main research interests which he has pursued throughout his academic career: population and public health on the one hand, and the Industrial Revolution on the other. His interest in population and public health led successively to the classic edition of Chadwick's 1842

---

* The figures in parenthesis refer to items in Ailsa Maxwell's bibliography of Professor Flinn's works (see following this Introduction).

Report on the Sanitary Condition of the Labouring Population (10) – the Introduction is unsurpassed as a model of how to place a great Parliamentary Paper in context; to the Economic History Society pamphlet *British Population Growth, 1700–1850* (6); to two important articles on famine and plague for the *Journal of European Economic History* (41 and 48); and, finally, to the planning and execution, with the help of Social Sciences Research Council funds and the labour of five colleagues, of a pioneer study of Scottish historical demography, culminating after seven years in the publication of *Scottish Population History from the Seventeenth Century to the 1930s* (7), described as 'the greatest single contribution to Scottish social history in this decade'. His approach to the question of population was different from that in the schools of Cambridge and Paris, in so far as it laid less emphasis on pure methodology than on solidly relating change to the economic history of the societies under study. In the case of Chadwick, he was a firm believer in the influence of personality in history: as he was wont to say to tutorial classes studying the McDonagh thesis, 'But somebody had to make it all happen.'

His second major interest, in the dynamics of the Industrial Revolution, issued in *The Origins of the Industrial Revolution* (4), a paperback widely used in universities throughout Britain. This interest itself diverged in various particular directions. In 1967 he contributed a remarkable paper to an Edinburgh social-science seminar on the psychological roots of the Industrial Revolution (37), which has perhaps not had the follow-up it deserved. In 1966 he published a criticism of the John–Jones thesis on cheap grain as a factor in the demand for industrial goods (34), a comment that has been brushed aside more often than met. In 1974 his analysis of the statistical series measuring trends in real wages in the 1750–1850 period (40) was an attempt to put the standard-of-living debate on a more rigorous plane than had been evident in the Hobsbawm–Hartwell exchanges.

If Michael Flinn did not, then, shun controversy in the search for more satisfactory historical explanations, neither did he lose the trust and respect of the profession. He served the Economic History Society as editor of twenty-four pamphlets (1968–77) in the series 'Studies in Economic and Social History' (14), which he built up from scratch to become a major teaching tool in the discipline, and in 1978 he headed the local organising committee of the

Seventh International Economic History Congress, held at Edinburgh, with exemplary good nature and efficiency. His own university awarded him the degree of D. Litt. in 1965 and appointed him to a personal chair of Social History in 1967. He also had a notable career as chairman of his department, principal warden of the halls of residence and dean of his faculty. It is a measure of the breadth of his interests that he served a term as chairman of the music committee of the Scottish Arts Council.

His colleagues miss him most, however, not for his administrative skills but for his academic ability. He commenced his university career at the same time as Edinburgh got under way as an effective teaching department, and over two decades under his benign influence, his standards as a teacher and a scholar percolated down to us all. Perhaps above all we miss his enormous intellectual appetite, his satisfaction with good scholarship and indignation over bad, and his enthusiasm for economic history (as for life), which made him such fun as a friend. He has now moved to retirement and to further research in his house in Gloucestershire.

It is to honour this most distinguished economic and social historian, therefore, that we present these essays by past colleagues and former students at Edinburgh. Some of the chapters connect closely with themes he followed himself (the charcoal iron industry, the problems of public health under urbanisation); others (the control of English football crowds, Slav emigration) are in very different fields from those in which he made his own reputation.

The editor imposed only one condition on his contributors: that they should write something exciting and important to themselves, for only such work would really please the recipient. Nevertheless, when the thirteen chapters were assembled, it turned out that the book did indeed have a kind of coherence. We have called it *The Search for Wealth and Stability*, because that is what so much of economic and social history is about. The search for wealth is both the social quest for a growing GNP and the private hunt for enrichment – which in this book comprehends, for example, both Milward's essay on European paths to agricultural modernisation and Saul's study of technological factors in British growth, on the one hand, and Palairet's Slav migrants, on the other. The search for stability is less often acknowledged as a central topic of social history, but the search for wealth was a disequilibrating, nervy business, both privately and publicly. Ward's planter disciplining his slaves yet ruling with their help was seeking private stability; so was Morris's middle class, with their rhythms of borrowing and lending designed to conserve and hand on wealth. A concern for stability *pro bono publico* was clearly behind Charles Booth's anxiety over London (studied here by Cullen) and Davidson's civil servants intervening in industrial disputes; even more obviously it was the concern of those who (in Vamplew's paper) were attempting to control the crowds in England's great new mass-spectator sport, Association football. The book ends with four essays on the Scots' attempts to provide for those who had lost in the search for wealth and whose failure endangered stability: studies of the highly distinctive nineteenth- and twentieth-century Scottish poor relief have been very neglected, and it is appropriate to include them in a volume for a scholar who contributed much to the study of Scottish as well as British history. In a way, a division between wealth and stability is artificial, for several of the essays can be said to deal with both: there is a sense in which the ruling classes in all European countries over the last 300 years have assumed 'No wealth, no stability; no stability, no wealth' as a motto to justify and explain their direction of affairs.

Ailsa Maxwell has prefaced the book with a bibliography of Professor Flinn's works, exclusive only of reviews, because there were too many to enumerate or even to trace, and completed it with an index.

We must acknowledge the surreptitious help of Grace Flinn, who knew what we were up to before he did. To both Michael and Grace, therefore, we offer this book with our admiration and love, and our wishes for a very happy retirement and many learned works to come.

Publications of Professor M. W. Flinn, BA, Dip. Ed., MA, D. Litt.

AILSA MAXWELL (compiler)

BOOKS

1   1961 *An Economic and Social History of Britain, 1066–1939* (London: Macmillan).
2   1962 *Men of Iron: The Crowleys in the Early Iron Industry* (Edinburgh: Edinburgh University Press).
3   1963 *An Economic and Social History of Britain since 1700* (London: Macmillan, 2nd edn 1975).
4   1966 *The Origins of the Industrial Revolution* (London: Longmans). Translated into Spanish as *Orígenes de la Revolución Industrial* (Madrid: Instituto de Estudios Politicos, 1970).
5   1968 *Public Health Reform in Britain* (London: Macmillan).
6   1970 *British Population Growth, 1700–1850* (London: Macmillan, for the Economic History Society).
7   1977 (Editor, and co-author with Judith Gillespie, Nancy Hill, Ailsa Maxwell, Rosalind Mitchison and Christopher Smout) *Scottish Population History from the Seventeenth Century to the 1930s* (Cambridge: Cambridge University Press).

SOURCE MATERIAL EDITED WITH INTRODUCTIONS

8   1957 *The Law Book of the Crowley Ironworks*, Surtees Society vol. CLXVII (Durham and London).

9   1964 *Readings in Economic and Social History* (London: Macmillan).

10   1965 Edwin Chadwick, *Report on the Sanitary Condition of the Labouring Population of Great Britain, 1842* (Edinburgh: Edinburgh University Press).

11   1969 A. P. Stewart and E. Jenkins, *The Medical and Legal Aspects of Sanitary Reform, 1867* (Leicester: Leicester University Press).

12   1973 E. T. Svedenstierna, *Tour of Great Britain, 1802–3* (Newton Abbot: David and Charles).

ESSAYS AND OTHER CONTEMPORARY WORK EDITED

13   1974 (With T. C. Smout) *Essays in Social History* (Oxford: Clarendon Press for the Economic History Society).

14   1968–77 'Studies in Economic and Social History', 24 vols (London: Macmillan for the Economic History Society).

15   1978 *Proceedings of the Seventh International Economic History Congress*, 2 vols (Edinburgh: Edinburgh University Press).

ARTICLES IN BOOKS AND PERIODICALS

16   1951 'The Iron Industry in Sixteenth-century England', *Edgar Allen News.*

17   1953 'Sir Ambrose Crowley, Ironmonger, 1685–1713', *Explorations in Entrepreneurial History*, v 162–80. Reprinted in *Explorations in Enterprise*, ed. H. G. J. Aitken (Cambridge, Mass.: Harvard University Press, 1965) pp. 241–58.

18   1954 'Samuel Schröderstierna's "Notes on the English Iron Industry" (1749)', *Edgar Allen News.*

19   1954 (With A. Birch) 'The English Steel Industry before 1856, with Special Reference to the Development of the Yorkshire Steel Industry', *Yorkshire Bulletin of Economic and Social Research*, VI 163–77.

20   1954 'Scandinavian Iron Ore Mining and the British Steel Industry, 1870–1914', *Scandinavian Economic History Review*, II 31–46.

21   1955 'British Steel and Spanish Ore, 1871–1914', *Economic History Review*, 2nd ser., VIII 84–90.

22   1955 'The Marriage of Judith Crowley', *Journal of the Friends' Historical Society*, XLVII 71–7.

23 1958 'Industry and Technology in the Derwent Valley of Durham and Northumberland in the Sixteenth Century', *Transactions of the Newcomen Society*, XXIX (1953–5) 255–62.

24 1958 'The Growth of the English Iron Industry, 1660–1760', *Economic History Review*, 2nd ser., XI 144–53.

25 1959 'Abraham Darby and the Coke-smelting Process', *Economica*, new ser., XXVI 54–9.

26 1959 'Timber and the Advance of Technology: A Reconsideration', *Annals of Science*, XV, 109–20.

27 1969 'The Lloyds in the Early Iron Industry', *Business History*, II 21–31.

28 1960 'Sir Ambrose Crowley and the South Sea Scheme of 1711', *Journal of Economic History*, XX 51–66.

29 1961 'The Travel Diaries of Swedish Engineers of the Eighteenth Century as Sources of Technological History', *Transactions of the Newcomen Society*, XXXI (1957–9) 95–109.

30 1961 'The Poor Employment Act of 1817', *Economic History Review*, 2nd ser., XIV 82–92.

31 1961 'The Industrialists', in *Silver Renaissance: Essays in Eighteenth-century English History*, ed. Alex Natan (London: Macmillan).

32 1964 'William Wood and the Coke-smelting Process', *Transactions of the Newcomen Society*, XXXIV (1961–2) 55–71.

33 1966 'The Overseas Trade of Scottish Ports, 1900–60', *Scottish Journal of Political Economy*, XIII 220–37.

34 1966 'Agricultural Productivity and Economic Growth in England, 1700–1760: A Comment', *Journal of Economic History*, XXVI 93–8.

35 1967 'Consommation du bois et développement sidérurgique en Angleterre', in *Actes du colloque sur la forêt*, ed. C. Fohlen (Paris: Les Belles Lettres), pp. 107–28.

36 1967 'Population in History', *Economic History Review*, 2nd ser., XX 140–4.

37 1967 'Social Theory and the Industrial Revolution', in *Social Theory and Economic Change*, ed. T. Burns and S. B. Saul (London: Tavistock), pp. 9–34.

38 1971 'A Policy of "Public Works"', *New Society*, 18 Nov., pp. 977–9.

39 1972 'Friedrich Engels's Manchester', *Listener*, 3 Feb., pp. 140–2.

40 1974 'Trends in Real Wages, 1750–1850', *Economic History Review*, 2nd ser., XXVII 395–413.

41 1974 'The Stabilisation of Mortality in Pre-industrial Western Europe', *Journal of European Economic History*, III 285–317.

42 1976 'Real Wage Trends in Britain, 1750–1850: a reply', *Economic History Review*, 2nd ser., XXIX 143–5.

43 1976 'Medical Services under the New Poor Law', in *The New Poor Law in the Nineteenth Century*, ed. Derek Fraser (London: Macmillan), pp. 45–66.

44 1976 'The English Population Scare of the 1930s', in *Historisch-Demographische Mitteilungen*, ed. J. Kovacsics (Budapest: Eotvos Lorand University) pp. 60–76.

45 1977 'Malthus, Emigration and Potatoes in the Scottish Northwest, 1770–1870', in *Comparative Aspects of Scottish and Irish Economic and Social History, 1600–1900*, ed. L. M. Cullen and T. C. Smout (Edinburgh: John Donald), pp. 47–64.

46 1977 'Exports and the Scottish Economy in the Depression of the 1930s', in *Trade and Transport, Essays in Economic History in Honour of T. S. Willan*, ed. W. H. Chaloner and B. M. Ratcliffe (Manchester: Manchester University Press), pp. 279–93.

FORTHCOMING

47 'Public Support for the Arts in Scotland', in *The Scottish Government Yearbook, 1979*, ed. H. M. Drucker and M. G. Clarke (Edinburgh: Paul Harris).

48 'Plague in Europe and the Mediterranean Countries', *Journal of European Economic History*.

49 'Technological Change as an Escape: England, Seventeenth and Eighteenth Centuries', conference paper presented at Bellagio, Italy, in 1977 to a seminar on 'Escapes from Resource Scarcity', due for publication under the editorship of W. N. Parker.

Part I
The Wider World

1 A Planter and His Slaves in Eighteenth-Century Jamaica

J. R. WARD

The British West Indian sugar colonies of the eighteenth century were marked by the institution of slavery to a degree which has never been matched elsewhere. The sugar plantations established a virtual monoculture and they worked most profitably on a large scale, with hundreds of black slaves supervised by a handful of white men. So in all of these islands by the middle of the century the white colonists were a minority, often a very small minority, among their slaves. They accounted for about a quarter of the population in Barbados, and about a tenth in the Leeward Islands and Jamaica. How then did they maintain their authority? What measures did they take and what effects did they have? We must answer such questions if we are to understand these societies, but reliable information that might allow us to do so is scarce. There are many surviving collections of plantation papers, but these are concerned mainly with business matters – so much sugar made and sold, so many supplies bought – and they have little to say about the relations of the masters with their slaves. Most contemporary descriptions of West Indian society are those of travellers or casual visitors to the islands, and even if they observed and wrote dispassionately they were outsiders, likely to record what was striking or curious, but uncertain guides to the daily routine. In any case, most visitors were not dispassionate: by the later eighteenth century the ethics of slavery had become controversial and most reporters came with strong preconceptions, sometimes in favour of the slave-owners, but usually against them. On the other hand, what little was written by the white West Indians themselves is open to suspicion as self-exculpation and special pleading.

Most later historical writing has given a very harsh view of West Indian slavery, taken largely from its contemporary critics: a greedy and fearful white minority maintaining its authority by the most savage discipline; the black masses demoralised and cowed, erupting spasmodically in elemental outbursts of fury and despair. But more recently less thoroughly pessimistic interpretations have evolved. Accompanying the undoubted brutalities there was also, it is claimed, a measure of accommodation on both sides. The slaves could develop styles of behaviour – evasion, passive resistance, and so on – to adjust to the demands made upon them, to mitigate their sufferings and maintain their self-respect. Their masters acquiesced more or less in these subterfuges and so developed a common culture, a society based not just on coercion but also on a kind of co-operation and shared experience, an implicit understanding on each side of what could be expected from the other. How far can this argument be carried? The degradation of the slaves may not have been complete, but there can be no denying the cruelties that they often suffered. What was the true balance between these elements in West Indian society? Because of the nature of the sources available to us the problem is particularly difficult. More evidence is needed and that is what is offered here. It is taken from the diaries kept by Thomas Thistlewood, who between 1750 and 1786 worked in Jamaica as a plantation overseer. During this time Thistlewood was able to become more familiar with local life than any casual visitor. Also he kept his diaries purely for his own satisfaction; he had no wish to entertain the public with the curious or sensational, and he never troubled himself with doubts about the rights or wrongs of slave-ownership. There was no reason for him deliberately to colour his account; he simply recorded things as they happened, as they seemed to him.[1]

Thomas Thistlewood was born in 1721, a younger son of a Lincolnshire farmer; he left home at the age of eight to attend school, and after finishing his education passed a few rather futile years spending his modest patrimony and dealing in livestock.

In 1746 he sailed as a supercargo on an East India Company vessel, returned to England in 1748, spent some months of idleness in Lincolnshire and London, made a short pleasure trip to France and the Austrian Netherlands, and then early in 1750 took ship for Jamaica. He carried with him a chest of clothes, a library of 180 volumes, a small set of pornographic pictures acquired on his Continental travels, and hopes for a new life on the colonial frontier as a surveyor, the profession in which he had been trained. But when he reached his destination prospects seemed better as a salaried estate-manager, and this is how he began – on the Vineyard Pen, a cattle ranch in the western parish of St Elizabeth.

As a newcomer to Jamaica, work on a pen suited Thistlewood well. It was easy enough to look after cattle, but slaves were rather more difficult; here he had leisure to study their ways and practise the arts of management. However, before long he wished to progress to a sugar plantation, technically more exacting, but offering greater prestige and rewards, and soon his chance came. In September 1751 he was offered the post of overseer at Egypt plantation in the adjacent parish of Westmoreland. Egypt was a peninsula of firm land among the swamps of the Cabarita River, about three miles along the main road running west from Savanna-la-Mar, the main town of the parish. Plagued by mosquitoes, with about 150 acres of cane land and ninety slaves in 1751, it was certainly not the most distinguished of Jamaican estates; but, as to obtain the post of overseer might still be thought a respectable achievement for a man who had been on the island for little more than a year, Thistlewood accepted the offer. He was to remain at Egypt, with two short interruptions, for the next sixteen years, usually as the only white man among his slaves, apart from a single assistant book-keeper. In 1767 he retired to pass the last twenty years of his life on a small provision estate nearby. This essay deals only with Thistlewood's life at Egypt, for Jamaican society revolved round sugar and it is on the plantations that its most characteristic features are to be found.

Thistlewood could expect that slave-management would present more problems at the plantation than at the pen. In growing sugar, with its remorseless annual cycle of planting, harvesting and consignment, the gang had to be disciplined more tightly and stretched much closer to the limits of its strength. But there was a further difficulty, which he may not have expected. At the pen Thistlewood had been given a free hand by his employer, who is a faceless figure in the diaries, living at a distance and rarely visiting his property. But his new employer, William Dorrill, was interfering and opinionated, imagining himself to be a great expert in the management of slaves, and often favouring his overseer with advice. Moreover, he lived only ten miles away, at Salt River, another of his plantations, and so he could see whether or not his advice was followed. Slaves from Egypt in need of specially careful treatment – women about to give birth, for example – were to be sent to Salt River, bearing tales if they wished. From the start Thistlewood's authority was compromised:

[15 November 1751.] Sad murmuring amongst our negroes. Perceive they have private encouragement at Salt River.

At the pen he had taken up his command in a very decisive way. A few days after his arrival:

[16 July 1750.] This afternoon Dick (the mulatto [driver]) for his many crimes and negligences, was bound to an orange tree in the garden, and whipped to some purpose (given near 300 lashes).

The man did not emerge from his hut again until nine days later. But at Egypt, with Dorrill's restraining influence, there was no such spectacular beginning; in general punishments were less frequent and less severe, and clearly this greater leniency made the task of management more difficult. Thistlewood met with impertinence and truculence of a kind that he had not experienced before. Often an offender would not submit meekly to punishment. There were some undignified scuffles in which Thistlewood himself had to drag the slave to the whipping post, or on other occasions he simply ran away, returning of his own accord a few days later, apparently with impunity.

To make matters worse, in June 1752, after the year's crop had been completed, Dorrill took it into his head that Egypt was unsuited to sugar and should be converted into a pen. Thistlewood and most of the gang were to be shifted to another plantation that Dorrill owned, adjacent to Salt River. The move itself was unsettling for the slaves, and now Dorrill had even more opportunities to interfere:

> [3 August 1752.] Received from Guy six dung baskets. Had him whipped, which made a great uproar and confusion, Mr Dorrill as usual with him sending to know who was whipping, etc., etc.

There were some unpleasant new developments. Quashie, the driver, took to making sarcastic remarks in front of the gang about Jenny, Thistlewood's principal mistress among the slaves at this time. This lady was exempt from field labour and it seems to have been her custom to saunter about in the finery that she received as the reward for her position. Finally, Thistlewood suffered a bout of venereal disease. Eventually he was to learn how to endure such attacks and at the same time supervise the routine of a sugar estate (to be able to do so was evidently one of the planter's most essential skills in eighteenth-century Jamaica), but for the moment it was beyond his strength. So in August 1752 he left Dorrill, left his gang and returned to Egypt, with the intention of staying there until his health had recovered; then he would leave to look for work with some other employer. For the next four months he rested, taking the mercury pills prescribed by his doctor, and supervising in a perfunctory way the handful of watchmen and invalids who had been left on the estate.

But early in December Thistlewood changed his plans. His symptoms had abated, and he could even contemplate working for his old employer once more, after four months without seeing him. Dorrill in the meantime had decided to continue sugar production at Egypt, so the gang was sent back there and Thistlewood was hired once more as overseer, with a salary of £60 a year and strict instructions that the negroes should not be ill treated. But within a few days of their return the old troubles had started once more:

> [21 December 1752.] Last night negroes very impudent when throwing grass.

> [22 December 1752.] Quashie extreme impudent and saucy, threaten my life, etc.

The latter incident was recorded more fully a few days later:

> [27 December 1752.] Last Friday in the field, Quashie told
> me (before all the negroes) that I should not eat much more
> meat here! I asking if he meant to poison or murder me, after
> a pause he replied neither, but he intended to mount some
> great lie, and go tell his master, to get me turned away.
> He further said, that his master would believe a negro before
> a white man and gave an instance of the same at Bowens,
> where Mr Dorrill said he would take a negro's word before
> Robert's though he had a white face, etc. About some peas!

But worse was to follow, for this recollection had been provoked
by an even more alarming episode, which had occurred earlier
on the day that Thistlewood had made this entry in his diary.
Three weeks before, he had quarrelled with Congo Sam, one of
the watchmen guarding the estate, and the man had run away.
Now, on the evening of 27 December, while walking about the
estate, Thistlewood met up with the runaway and tried to seize
him, but he would not submit.

> Attempting to take him, he immediately struck at me with a
> backed bill he had in his hand, and repeated his chops with
> all vehemence, driving me back into the morass towards the
> river twenty or thirty yards from the road, but through the
> great mercy of God, his blows either fell short of me or were
> warded off with a pimento stick I had in my hand, with which
> I sometimes got a good stroke at him, and although he hit
> on my jacket several times yet as pleased God I received no
> harm; the bill being new was not very sharp. But what the
> most showed his intention was when I kept him off from me
> with my stick, saying, 'You villain runaway, away with you',
> etc., he answered in the negro manner, 'I will kill you, I will
> kill you now', etc., and came upon me with greater vigour.

As the struggle continued, Thistlewood appealed to two of his
other slaves standing nearby, but they refused to help; Sam 'spoke
to them in his language and I was much afraid of them'. A
party of slaves from another estate passed by and they too would
do nothing, 'neither for threats nor promises: one saying he was

sick, the other that they were in a hurry'. Only after London, one of the more amenable of the Egypt gang, and then two white men had arrived was the runaway finally subdued, dragged home and locked up. Thistlewood was left to brood alone. He recalled driver Quashie's threats of a few days before; he doubted how London would have acted if the white men had not appeared so providentially.

Titus with great reason may also be suspected. Have also reason to believe that many of the negroes, as Quashie, Ambo, Phibbah, etc., knew that Sam had an intent to murder me, when we should meet, by what I heard them speak one day in the cook room, when I was in the back piazzo reading.

According to Jamaican law, a slave striking a white man could suffer death, and for what seemed so clearly to be a case of attempted murder it might have been expected that the punishment would be exemplary. But Sam was tried at Savanna-la-Mar early in the new year, and if he was punished at all he could have got no more than a flogging, for he was back at Egypt within a few days and before long had even taken to running away again. Thistlewood does not make clear why he should have been treated so leniently, except to say that the three magistrates who tried him were 'old women'. Also it seems that London refused to testify.

[5 January 1753.] At night London refuses to go with me to Sam's trial! Told me, he would not go.

Evidently, for whatever reason, Thistlewood could expect no more support from the public authorities than he had got from his employer.

After such an unfortunate beginning it might have been doubted whether he would ever establish himself as a plantation manager at Egypt or anywhere else, but it is a measure of his undoubted courage and strength of character that eventually he succeeded. Perhaps his ordeal gave him some new authority, or perhaps it made Dorrill realise the danger that his overseer was in. At least, there are no more episodes as menacing as this, no more complaints of Dorrill's interference, and even some rather equivocal hints of a new warmth in his relations with his slaves:

[17 May 1753.] The negroes one and all declare they will not move to Bowens except I go with them to take care of them. . . . They are instigated to it by Philip [the book-keeper] for certain ends.

So Thistlewood survived and before long he had a new employer. In April 1753 Dorrill gave his daughter in marriage to John Cope, the son of a neighbouring planter, and a year later he handed over to his son-in-law control of his estates. Cope had little of Dorrill's concern for the slaves; for him the purpose of a sugar plantation was to make money, and so long as it did this his overseer was safe from interference. But the change of master was not without its difficulties, for Cope wished to raise production at Egypt and to make this possible the gang was to be treated more rigorously and enlarged.

New slaves came onto the plantation in batches – about forty-five in 1754, and ten the following year. Some were brought from other estates, while the rest were fresh from Africa; but all presented Thistlewood with new problems of management and discipline. Under Dorrill, it seems, his troubles came from his employer's interference, and possibly from his own uncertainty and inexperience. The slaves had responded with truculence and insubordination. But, for all this, as most of them had been at Egypt for many years, they were at least inured to their labours and bound to the plantation by habit and personal ties. Among the new arrivals, those coming from other estates had old connections that they wished to keep up, while the new imports from Africa had to be broken in to a life of toil. They were all particularly difficult to control, and very liable to run away.

Thistlewood took some pains to reconcile the newcomers to Egypt, especially those from Africa. They were issued with suits of clothes made by the estate's sempstresses. For their first week they were usually kept on light work before being sent out to join the main gang in the fields. They were allocated provision grounds and given special daily rations until these were properly established. But Thistlewood was exasperated that all this seemed to have so little effect, and, with Dorrill's restraining influence removed, punishments became more frequent and more severe. During his time at Egypt under Dorrill, Thistlewood had ordered a whipping about once a month on average, but from 1755 he records three or four a month, and they are now supplemented with various other refinements, detailed with a new venom and relish:

[8 August 1754.] Today Nero would not work, but threatened to cut his own throat. Had him stripped, whipped, gagged, and his hands tied behind him, that the mosquitoes and sand flies might torment him to some purpose.

[30 July 1756.] Punch catched at Salt River and brought home. Flogged him and Quacoo well, and then washed and rubbed in salt pickle, lime juice and bird pisses.

[1 August 1756.] Plato brought home Hazat, catched him in the morass near Bluff Point. Put him in the bilboes both feet. Gagged him, locked his hands together. Rubbed him with molasses and exposed him naked to the flies all day, and to the mosquitoes in the night without fire. Run away 7 April last.

This intensification of discipline, affecting the old slaves as well as the new, continued through the first two or three years of Cope's ownership; however, after this things improved a little. Whippings were always to be more common than they had been under Dorrill, but the frequency reached in 1756 was rarely matched again. It seems also that the new regime eventually brought about a real change in the slaves' behaviour, for episodes of insubordination became much rarer than they had been before 1754, and at the same time there was another development that made Thistlewood's life easier. Under Dorrill offences on the plantation usually were punished only if Thistlewood detected them himself, and most runaways came back either of their own accord or after they had been caught by outsiders. But by the later 1750s several of Egypt's slaves were regularly employed to hunt for runaways (in the past this had been much less common) and the estate's watchmen were reporting cases of theft or cane-breaking in a way that they had not done before. Discipline was being maintained with the active co-operation of the slaves themselves. So the particular severity of the first two or three years of Cope's ownership seems to have been a temporary crisis of adjustment between the laxity allowed by Dorrill and the harsher climate that followed, but it had finally established Thistlewood's command at Egypt.

If his first ordeal in Jamaica was to learn his trade as overseer, his second, much briefer but more intense, was the rebellion of 1760. Through the early years of settlement, insurrection had been endemic in the island. After the conquest in the 1650s, many of the slaves of the Spanish colonists remained to fight the English invaders after their masters had fled, offering a dangerous example to the fresh contingents subsequently brought in from Africa. Gangs rose as a body, massacred their masters and escaped to the densely wooded mountains of the interior. But as time passed disturbances became rarer, particularly after the rebel bands had been tamed by the military campaigns of the 1730s. Thistlewood records some moments of alarm soon after his arrival.

[17 July 1751.] Much fear of the negroes revolting in this island. Never such liberties allowed, and so little precautions used before.

[31 July 1751.] In the evening we heard a shell blow twice (at Smithfield) as an alarm. Could see no appearance of fire. Mr Dorrill greatly feared it was an insurrection of the negroes, they being very ripe for it, almost all over the island.

But after this there is no hint of trouble until 1760, when on 6 April, Easter Sunday, rebellion broke out in St Mary's parish at the eastern end of the island.[2] Even so, Thistlewood does not mention it, and, when some slaves in Westmoreland followed this example on the evening of Sunday, 25 May, their insurrection seems to have been almost completely unexpected. That afternoon Thistlewood had gone to dine with a neighbour, and while he was there a visitor had come with a rumour that an uprising in the parish was planned for the next day. But he returned home and went to bed without taking any special precautions.

[26 May 1760.] Soon after midnight Messrs Say, Brown, Walker and Rumbold called me up and told me of Mr Smith at Captain Forest's being murdered by the negroes. Mr Smith shot about a quarter before ten o'clock. Captain Hoar sadly chopped etc., Captain George Richardson and Thomas Barnes etc. running to the Bay on foot, a narrow escape they had. When we reached Colonel Barclay's, I galloped back immediately to Egypt, and secured my keys, writings, etc., which had before neglected in my fright, because those who called me were some almost without clothes, and rode bareback, telling me I should probably be murdered in a short time, etc., etc. Soon returned after I had put my things in order as well as I could, and was down at the Bay about two o'clock. Did duty till day light, then was set at liberty by Mr Antrobus to go home and take care of the estate.

John Graves [the current book-keeper at Egypt] like a madman, shot at several negro boys, wounded Oliver, Mr John Cunningham's waiting boy. Went to the Bay without my orders, etc., but in the evening he returned.

The days that followed were confused and terrifying. One report followed another of plantations risen; 3000 negro men from Westmoreland and Hanover were said to have met secretly to launch the insurrection, and, although it had begun on estates at some distance from Egypt, by 27 May a party of rebels was reported at the Salt Savanna, less than a mile away; two days later the neighbouring plantation was attacked. In Westmoreland with its 10,000 slaves there was a force of about 400 white militia and a few regular soldiers. There were also the seamen from the merchantmen that were loading the season's crop and waiting to take convoy, but they were very doubtful reinforcements once they had got their hands on rum. Egypt lay between Savanna-la-Mar and one of the main centres of the uprising along the road to the west, so it was regularly used as a staging post.

[25 May 1760.] Sailors and militia halted at Egypt, gave them six or eight pails of grog. Had a silver spoon stole in the hurry, etc., etc.

That evening Thistlewood was obliged again to entertain one of these sailors; he had fallen asleep nearby, no doubt overcome by the effects of Jamaican hospitality, and had lost his weapons. Two days later the party returned.

[27 May 1760.] The sailors commanded by Captain Watson returning called, and had grog again. Gave the Captain and officers punch and bread and cheese. The sailors drunk, etc.

Obviously there was no question of troops being available to guard individual plantations; each owner or overseer had to shift for himself, and many of them fled. But Thistlewood stayed at his post after the first night of panic. If he could present an appearance of composure to his gang and keep up the plantation routine, then old habits of obedience might carry him through. When he returned from Savanna-la-Mar on the morning of the outbreak he had let the slaves off work, but by the next day they were back to their usual duties, although so far as possible he tried to keep them under his eye at tasks round the estate buildings. At night four slaves stood armed guard about the works while Thistlewood and his book-keeper took turns to sleep, and when danger was closest the other men were armed too.

[29 May 1760.] About 2 p.m. a mulatto boy and two negro men boys came running from Jacobsfield, the late Mr Allen's, and reported that some negroes came with a shout, and fired four or five guns, and began to tear the great house in pieces, before they escaped. I immediately wrote to the commanding officer at Savanna-la-Mar, and sent Job on horseback express with it. A party of fourteen horsemen were soon sent there.

Immediately armed our negroes and kept a strict guard, and sharp lookout all the afternoon and night, being under dreadful apprehension, as Mr Jacob Johnson told me for God's sake to take care of myself, and Colonel Barclay told me we had but bad success, being defeated and several of our people killed, of which perceive our negroes have good intelligence, being greatly elevated, and ready to rise, now we are in the most imminent danger. Saw Mr John Jones' house burnt tonight, etc.

Thistlewood depended on his slaves but he could not trust them:

[28 May 1760.] When the report was of the Old Hope negroes being rose, perceived a strange alteration in ours. They are certainly very ready if they don't, and am pretty certain they were in the plot, by what John told me on Sunday evening, what they had said in the field on Saturday in the Papah Tree piece, that he, what signified him, he would dead in a Egypt, etc., etc., and from many other circumstances, Lurie being over at Forest's [the plantation where the rebellion had started] that night, also Dover and Lincoln etc. Coffee and Job also very outrageous.

With these fears preying on their minds, and with nights passed keeping watch, both Thistlewood and his book-keeper were soon exhausted. At first no progress was made to put down the rising; plantations followed each other into rebellion while the colonists' forces were in confusion. Only after a week did the tide begin to turn. Many of the rebels had fortified themselves within a stockade and this was taken by 2 June; groups of prisoners passed along the road through Egypt on their way to torture and execution at Savanna-la-Mar; by the end of the month Thistlewood felt safe enough to reduce the nightly watch. There were some further alarms and the struggle was continued into the next year by a few small bands up in the mountains, but the worst of the emergency had passed and the white population could begin to take stock.

It seemed clear to contemporaries that the uprising was not a spontaneous or incoherent outburst but a thoroughly organised conspiracy. Arms had been collected, leaders appointed, and the date chosen. Perhaps the French or the Spaniards were behind it, for this was a time of war, and strangers with suspicious accents had been seen; some believed that many of the Jewish distillers brought in to improve the rum manufacture were Jesuits in disguise, or that there were black Jesuits at work in the island. It was said that all the slaves in the island were to have risen on Whitsunday, when the white community, not usually conspicuous in its observance of the church calendar, would be off its guard. But instead the rebels of St Mary's had begun prematurely, at Easter, possibly because of a mistake in that year's edition of the *Spanish Town Almanac*, which they had been using to prepare their timetable. Alternatively, the colonists owed their deliverance to the astuteness of the captain of a slave ship: a conspirator had been rallying support for the cause by carrying in procession a standard decorated with parrot's feathers, but the captain recognised this as an African war standard, had the man seized, and the plot was revealed. Or a touch of domesticity was added to an account of the Westmoreland uprising. It was planned to take place after the ships had sailed with the last of the sugar crop, when the seamen were no longer at hand to give the colonists their support, for what it was worth; but Wager, the local leader, had a quarrel with his wife at their provision ground, she threatened to reveal the plot, and so they had to begin early. It is difficult to judge how much truth, if any, there is in all this. Such stories, of the artfully contrived plot, of the lucky accident that foiled it at the last moment, circulated after every West Indian rebellion. Some of the details are plausible – for example, 25 May, the day of the uprising in Westmoreland, was in fact Whitsunday – but others are improbable or mutually contradictory.

Whatever the truth may have been, the colonists certainly believed that an elaborate plan had been made for their extermination, and yet they had noticed nothing, although with the benefit of hindsight the warning signs seemed obvious enough. Thistlewood in his diary gives no premonition of the Westmoreland rising, but beside the entries for some of the days that preceded it are marginal additions, apparently made later, recording small incidents that he had overlooked at the time but the significance of which he now understood.

> [22 May 1760.] Two of Captain Forest's negroes at our negroes' houses. Come to see Jackie.

The rebellion had begun at Forest's plantation.

> [25 May 1760.] About 9 p.m. heard a blast of a horn at our negro houses.

This was the night of the outbreak. There were other signs that he recalled later:

> [19 October 1760.] Note: at the beginning of the rebellion, a shaved head amongst the negroes was the signal of war. The very day our Jackie, Job, Achilles, Quasheba, Rosanna, etc., had their heads remarkably shaved. Quasheba's brother fell in the rebellion. He had feasted away some time before.

The rebellion had come after a long period of apparent calm during which the white population had grown relaxed and careless about security. In the dangerous early years of the colony, planters had built their houses like fortresses, with gunloops for windows and formidable armouries. The laws passed for controlling the slaves were strict and the penalties for any indiscipline were ferocious. But the atmosphere of Thistlewood's diaries in the 1750s is casual, apart from his personal difficulties with the gang at Egypt. He was in the habit of walking about unarmed; he notices as a curiosity a house built with portholes for defence; and he clearly shows that many of the regulations prescribed for the slaves were dead letters. According to law, no slave was to travel off his plantation without a ticket signed by his master, there were to be no unauthorised gatherings, and the negroes' houses were to be regularly searched for weapons. But in practice Thistlewood very rarely issued tickets, slaves met freely at their markets and celebrations, and, perhaps most remarkable of all, they were allowed to own guns. Often this may have begun with their master's authority, in connection with estate business: trained marksmen were used to shoot game; watchmen and the hunters sent out after runaways often carried guns. In 1756 a slave from Egypt was shot and then hacked to pieces while robbing provision grounds on a neighbouring plantation. But slaves also had guns for their own purposes:

[28 April 1752.] This morning in the still house, Ambo playing with a gun (that our negroes brought with them from Salt River, with intent to shoot the monkey that troubles their grounds at Hill) she unexpectedly went off in his hands, and it was a great mercy that no harm was done, for he never examined whether she was loaded or not.

[8 September 1755.] Last night, Salt River negroes being in liquor, one of them left a pistol upon our store-house steps, Ambo found and gave it me.

[14 March 1760.] Sold Old Sharper the gun I bought from driver Quashie many years ago. He gives me only 10s. for her but paid ready money. He will soon shoot alligators etc. enough at Hill.

So it is not surprising that, at its first meeting after the risings, the Jamaican House of Assembly busied itself with measures to make the white population more careful. It repeated the old laws against slaves' travelling without tickets, against unauthorised assemblies and the negroes' music and drumming. The deficiency tax on estates with an insufficient proportion of white men was increased, with a higher rate where the owner was not resident: most of the rebellious plantations had belonged to absentees. There were new clauses against magical practices, against overseers' leaving their plantations on Sundays or holidays, and for the first time slaves were specifically prohibited from owning guns. The 1696 act which ordered masters to search their slaves' houses every fortnight for 'clubs, wooden swords, or other mischievous weapons' did not admit this possibility, although it was implicitly recognised by some later laws, to regulate the sale of gunpowder and curb the colonists' enthusiasm for 'squibs, serpents, rockets, or other fireworks'.[3] Also the Governor tried to strengthen the island militia, which had shown itself to be lamentably ill disciplined and ill trained. By law all able-bodied men were bound to serve and they were supposed to muster in each parish to exercise at least once every two months. But in practice attendance had often been irregular and the exercises perfunctory.

[15 December 1752.] In the morning rode to Savanna-la-Mar and although I had not arms, stood in rank, by Colonel Barclay's advice till my name was called over, that I might not be fined. Were dismissed for a month.

[4 April 1753.] Morning to Savanna-la-Mar to exercise, but few people there. Dismissed till May 4th next.

Now orders were issued to the local commanders to enforce attendance more strictly, particularly about the Christmas holidays, when the danger of disturbance seemed greatest.

Thistlewood's diaries show that in the immediate aftermath of the crisis security was tightened. He began to issue tickets to his slaves when they went off the plantation to the Sunday markets. Their houses were searched for guns and half a dozen were found and thrown into the river. They were given strict instructions to work their provision grounds, for food had been scarce about the time of the rebellion and the planters imagined that this was the result of deliberate neglect by the slaves in anticipation of their freedom. The driver was flogged for allowing drums to be played. Two of Egypt's possible trouble-makers were shipped off the island, along with many more from other plantations. Militia patrols became a regular feature of the Christmas holidays and there were occasional visits by companies specially organised to hunt for rebels or runaways.

[18 November 1760.] Forsythe stays night with two white men, twenty rangers (mulattoes and negroes) and six or eight baggage negroes. Rangers served gallon rum, drunk. Tried to break negro house doors to come at girls. I was obliged to get out of bed, take my pistols and go to quiet them, which soon effected. But fought each other till near midnight.

However, even before the rebellion had been properly suppressed, Thistlewood and his fellow whites were sliding back to the casual habits of the past:

[27 July 1760.] Negroes begin to ride and walk about in the night again, without tickets, and suspect something more a-brewing amongst them.

[26 October 1760.] Gave tickets to our negroes, but only two come for any – rest gone without.

[9 November 1760.] But one negro come to me for a ticket, the rest go without, no person questioning them! 500 negroes in the road to leeward every Sunday with plantains etc.; few have tickets.

Then the law was applied more rigorously for a time: slaves without tickets were picked up by militia men and flogged, and through the following year Thistlewood issued about twenty tickets each week. But by 1762 the slaves usually felt free once more to travel without written authority, although there was another enforcement campaign after some further disturbances in Westmoreland in 1765.

On other points also, the story is one of growing laxity as memories of the rebellion faded. Militia service is an example. Through the latter part of 1760 Thistlewood or his overseer attended quite regularly, but in 1761 he appeared only for the Christmas patrols, and he secured a promise from Cope, one of the principal officers in the parish, of a commission that would be superseded. This was the recognised means of evading service and something that the Assembly had particularly legislated against. Two years later Thistlewood was joined at Egypt by his nephew John Thistlewood, who also kept a diary that illustrates the casual way in which militia duties had come to be regarded once more:

> [10 February 1765.] Went to Savanna-la-Mar to keep guard this afternoon.... No company met. Stayed at the Bay till 10 p.m. Met in company with Mr Sparks, master of the *Best in Christendom*, a very good sort of man, and Mr Morris and Mr Pugh, all good sort of men. Was very merry. Spent four bits per piece in porter. A fine pleasant dry day with wind at north east. I here promise that if ever I be warned to attend their guard again I will not attend except that it be in wartime or in rebellion times, for I have been several times and nobody met.

Finally the slaves were again allowed to get their hands on guns. The act of 1760 prescribed the death penalty for any slave found with firearms, gunpowder or any other weapon, unless he was in the company of a supervising white man. Yet Thistlewood persisted in sending out slaves with guns to shoot game or look for runaways and none of his neighbours seem ever to have made any objection. Once John Thistlewood rather officiously apprehended a slave from another plantation who was passing by with a gun and pistol and threatened to prosecute, but at the request of the man's owner he relented. Shortly afterwards, on 17 December 1764, he also reported a search of the negro houses at Egypt for arms and ammunition which produced nothing. These are the only indications in the diaries that any heed at all was being paid to the new law.

Indeed, the episode that brings to a close John Thistlewood's brief career in Jamaica suggests that things had changed little since the 1750s. On 30 March 1765 he went out shooting in the morass, his canoe overturned and he was drowned. His body was found the following day and carried back to the plantation. Thomas Thistlewood was much moved, in spite of the trouble that his nephew had often given him.

[31 March 1765.] About 11 a.m. our white man discovered my kinsman floating down about 150 yards below the old barcadier. Soon made hands get him out. Oh! how strangely he looked. I rode and acquainted Mr Stone, but he thinks it needless to have an inquest over him. Flanders made coffin and Mr Hayward who spent day with me read prayers over him, when we buried him in the evening about fifteen yards N. E. of my house. Davie and Quashie here at his burial.

Evidently the slaves were also affected by this misfortune, and they wished to let their master know just how they felt:

[5 April 1765.] Last night between 8 and 9 o'clock heard a shell blow on the river, and afterwards in the night, two guns fired, with a loud huzza after each, on the river against our negroes' houses, for joy that my kinsman is dead I imagine. Strange impudence.

Thistlewood took no steps to punish his slaves' behaviour; it seems that he was surprised by their effrontery but not by the fact that they had guns.

Thistlewood's diaries leave no doubt about the characteristic harshness of Jamaican slavery; when this was restrained for some reason, as during the period of Dorrill's ownership, grave difficulties resulted. But it seems that the routine brutality was accompanied also by a degree of co-operation between the master and at least some of his slaves. It was only a minority of the gang who suffered from the worst severities. Of the 400 or so whippings that Thistlewood ordered while he was at Egypt, roughly half went to thirty of the 190 slaves who worked on the estate during this time. For the rest one of these punishments was a comparatively rare occurrence, although the field slaves were exposed also to the book-keepers and the black drivers, and Thistlewood mentions only incidentally the whippings that they gave. But for the slaves with special skills or positions – the craftsmen, the overseer's personal attendants, and some of the watchmen – plantation life was not without its compensations. On the evidence of the diaries, if the master was sufficiently assured in his command, and if the treatment of the minority of persistent offenders was sufficiently severe, the collaboration of the 'confidential negroes' could be secured without too much difficulty. These were the slaves upon whom Thistlewood came to rely to catch runaways and other offenders and who stood guard at Egypt during the rebellion of 1760. Whatever suspicions he may have had, they did in fact remain loyal through this crisis, and the remarkable liberties that they were commonly allowed at this plantation and evidently at others suggests that in general their behaviour was sufficiently accommodating to secure the trust or at least the complacency of their masters. Jamaican slave society was not based on fear alone.

Notes

1 Thistlewood's diaries are among the Monson MSS. at the Lincolnshire Archives Office (Mon. 31/1–37), with one volume for each of his thirty-seven years in Jamaica. Other volumes (Mon. 31/83–5) give details of Thistlewood's early life up to his arrival in the island. There is also the journal of his nephew John Thistlewood, who stayed with him in Jamaica between 1763 and 1765 (Mon. 31/38), and several commonplace books, weather journals and game books. Thistlewood sent two of his weather journals to Edward Long, the historian of Jamaica, and they survive among the Long MSS. in the British Museum (Add. MSS. 18275A and B). His diaries have been used by O. A. Sherrard in *Freedom from Fear: The Slave and his Emancipation* (London, 1959) ch. 9. I am grateful to Lord Monson for permission to cite them, to Mr George Tyson for telling me about them, and to the staff of the Lincolnshire Archives Office for making them available. In quotations from the diaries, spelling and punctuation have been modernised. Recent studies of British West Indian slave societies are:

E. Brathwaite, *The Development of Creole Society in Jamaica 1770–1820* (Oxford, 1971); O. Patterson, *The Sociology of Slavery* (London, 1967), also on Jamaica; and E. Goveia, *Slave Society in the British Leeward Islands at the End of the Eighteenth Century* (New Haven, Conn., 1965). For discussion of the issues raised here relative to slavery in the Western Hemisphere as a whole, see S. Elkins, *Slavery: A Problem in American Institutional and Intellectual Life* (Chicago, 1959); and A. J. Lane, *The Debate over Slavery: Stanley Elkins and his Critics* (Chicago, 1971).

2 For a general account of the 1760 rebellion, see E. Long, *The History of Jamaica* (London, 1774) vol. II, pp. 447–62.

3 For the main laws on internal security, see PRO, CO 139, Jamaica Acts of Assembly, VIII, no. 45 (1696); X no. 15 (1717); XXI, nos 5, 22 and 24 (1760).

2 Strategies for Development in Agriculture: The Nineteenth-century European Experience

ALAN MILWARD

As the historical evidence on the development of economies accumulates, so do the models of development which once found most favour with historians appear as simplifications of history too excessive even for use in formal argument. The chief cause of discontent is the failure of such models to encompass the vital and complex role of the agricultural sector in the early stages of sustained development. The evidence from those European economies which experienced sustained development in the nineteenth century shows that the most typical path of development was that of a period, usually of three or four decades, of balanced responses and interaction between the primary sector and the rest of the economy, which was then followed by a period of sustained growth and development. Without this period of balanced response, sustained development often proved unobtainable. This pattern could be assimilated into the models of balanced growth only by reducing such models to a level so low as to be meaningless.

Balanced growth in the proper definition of the phrase was as unusual an experience in Europe as the 'industrial revolutions', 'take-offs', and 'breakthroughs' on which the more cataclysmic accounts of development pivoted, with their emphasis on the power of change in the industrial sector to transform the rest of the economy. It is clear that the period of balanced response between agriculture and the other sectors must in many (perhaps in all) cases have been preceded by a more or less lengthy period of adaptation and change in the agricultural sector itself, that 'agricultural revolution' to which textbooks of British economic history almost always devoted a chapter. Nevertheless, there was in the nineteenth-century European experience of the successful most typically a shorter and more critical period, which is not to be defined by a sudden increase in the ratio of investment to gross national product, nor in the increase of the rate of growth of industrial output, nor by identification of the sudden major institutional and political changes implicit in Gerschenkron's 'breakthrough'. Rather is it to be defined by the successful response of the primary sector to pressures and stimuli coming from the other sectors, and a successful interaction between the agricultural and other sectors which, when it took place, permitted the faster rate of improvement of productivity in the industrial sector to continue, to drive the economy towards higher levels of income.

Before, however, any useful model can be developed from this historical generalisation it is necessary to pose a question to which the answer is still far from clear. What was it that determined whether or not the agricultural sector would respond in a satisfactory way? The answer to this question is, of course, important not only in relation to economies which did develop successfully. It is, perhaps, also the biggest part of the response to the question about what went wrong in those which did not.

At the moment research into this question might be roughly divided into three general tendencies. One is the tendency to concentrate on the international environment – on those economic forces, coming from outside national and regional economies, that encouraged, permitted or forced them to move to higher levels of productivity. Another is the tendency to concentrate on the details of farming techniques in the hope of isolating more exactly what technical response was possible and necessary at any particular moment to enable the agricultural sector to respond adequately. A third is to concentrate on the role of government policy and institutional change. Obviously all these strands of inquiry intermingle at important points. To take the first two, it may well emerge from current research that the main factor in the widely observable increase in the productivity of small farms after 1894 was the sudden availability of machinery suitable for use on smaller farms, enabling them at the same point in time to respond to particular shifts in international demand. Furthermore, it is usually argued in the case of Denmark, where both these phenomena were most observable, that this was possible only because of earlier government policies.

Most current development theory would place the emphasis firmly on government policy as the overriding factor, since actions of the government can themselves go far towards determining the extent to which outside influences are allowed to affect the agricultural sector and can also do much towards accelerating or retarding the spread of more productive farming methods. Government, it is argued, must intervene to secure an adequate rate of development in the agricultural sector. The largest sphere of government action is usually considered to be the regulation of the pattern of landholding and of tenures, since the capacity of the agricultural sector to respond is limited and supposedly defined by the pattern of distribution of farms by size. It is this factor which determines the scope and capacity of subsequent government intervention. If it can be determined which pattern of distribution of farms by size is most conducive to reproducing a satisfactory response in the primary sector, the government then has a clear policy goal to steer towards. The interest of this type of theory for nineteenth-century European development is that European governments were then almost all faced unavoidably with the need to make precisely similar strategic decisions.

The transition from the juridical and tenurial arrangements of the 'old régime' not only forced countries to make such a choice, but in addition this choice often coincided with an active government intention to stimulate the process of development. The growing consciousness of the penalties of economic backwardness coincided with the awareness of the political necessity for fundamental legal, social and economic changes in the primary sector – and even where these changes were carried out, as in France, by violent action from below, they were always shaped by government decisions. The much-studied debate in Soviet Russia in the 1920s on the role of the primary sector in industrialisation was in fact foreshadowed by the discussions of agricultural-reform legislation in Prussia after Jena a century earlier. This same issue underlay the turbulent debates on tenurial reform in the French Assembly and Convention between 1789 and 1794, as well as those on the last European 'Act of Emancipation', in Romania in 1864. The overriding issue was always what sort of acceptable society and government would emerge from the process of economic change, and this forced governments and reformers alike to seek to influence the outcome by a choice of strategy. So it is in the underdeveloped world now, because 'acceptable to whom?' rdmains the major question.

The obstacles to be overcome in the primary sector of less-developed European economies were also the same as those in the less-developed world now. In the first place came poverty, and beyond that, the necessary defences against starvation which themselves were also barriers to emancipation from poverty; the fact that farming could not be a high-risk activity directed towards the maximisation of output, but had to be a low-risk activity designed to provide safety in a society prone to harvest failure and other catastrophes; social systems and kinship networks in which low labour productivity was inherent; lack of specialisation of function, because it was too dangerous; and adherence to a tradition so valuable that it needed the absolute certainty of something permanently more valuable before it was likely to be abandoned. If the task of government intervention is to help remove these obstacles, within what framework of land distribution may this best be achieved? The possibilities are usually considered as stretched out along a line the extremes of which are at one end a perfectly unimodal pattern in which the size of farms is more or less equal, and at the other end a bimodal pattern in which the size of farms is very unequal by virtue of the existence of a restricted number of farms much larger than the rest. Increasingly the favoured opinion is that unimodal strategies are technically the most satisfactory, since they induce a more well-sustained positive response from the agricultural sector. They also appear, of course, as fairer, more humane and even more democratic.[1] From current development theory we might, therefore, put two questions about the nineteenth-century European experience, in the hope of solving the larger question. Does the experience of nineteenth-century European development bear out the suggestion that particular patterns of the distribution of farms by size were more conducive to producing a balanced response than others? Does the experience of nineteenth-century European development indicate that government intervention in the agricultural sector was necessary if a period of balanced response was to be obtained? The distribution of farms by size in nineteenth-century European countries might provide examples of almost every point on the continuum between unimodal and bimodal. The limitations of these examples must be borne in mind. The advantages of the international environment vary in every case of development and do not always favour the same strategy. The path of technological innovation can also make sudden alterations to the effective possibilities of different strategies. But the most serious objection is that the dichotomy between, on the one hand, unimodal and bimodal, and on the other, the concept of a continuum stretching between a perfectly unimodal and a perfectly bimodal pattern, is far too simple to fit the historical reality. Probably it is also too simple to fit contemporary reality. This, however, does not invalidate the usefulness of applying current theories to historical reality, for these theories have, of course, far wider implications, which are not invalidated by the simplistic definitions in which they are expressed. Nineteenth-century European economies did vary between those where decision-making in the primary sector was strongly affected by the power which farmers of small farms exercised and those where it was mainly influenced by owners or tenants of larger farms.

The main economic advantage of unimodal strategy is usually held to be its capacity to disseminate increases in farm incomes amongst a larger part of the rural population. It can of course only have this capability if the peasant farms provide a satisfactory framework for attracting capital into the sector and if investment is spread across the whole sector. If this does occur, improvements in productivity will also be widely disseminated rather than confined to a small number of farms or to certain specialised types of production, and this will encourage an active participation in the development process by the rural population as well as providing a larger domestic market for manufactures. That this might be so is an idea with an honourable lineage in Europe. The tax and tenure reforms of von Raab in Bohemia in the 1780s, intended as a pilot project for the Austrian Empire, were based on the assumption that correctly sized peasant farms would be the best base for the national revenue once the old régime was completely dissolved. The concept of a standard-sized peasant farm as the optimal basic unit of production and as the pillar of society and the state was persistent, strongly influencing legislation in places as different as Hanover and Serbia.

It is, however, the example of Denmark which is most frequently plucked from history as demonstrating the advantages of a unimodal strategy. Indeed, Denmark has become that European country in the mirror of whose history less-developed countries are now encouraged to see an image the fairest of them all. Yet Denmark, while its history does in one sense illustrate many of the advantages claimed for a unimodal strategy, had nevertheless a pattern of farm distribution by size which varied considerably from the unimodal ideal. Restrictions on the subdivision of land and also on the accumulation of land into holdings considered too large followed a similar pattern in Denmark to that in several north German states. These restrictions were part of the policies of peasant protection (*Bauernschutz*), which were thought to provide certain military safeguards while also providing a reliable taxation base for the central government. Their corollary in an age of rising population was the growth of a farming class whose members fell outside this framework of legal protection and were unable, except with great difficulty, to increase the size of their own, very small landholdings.

These policies in Denmark were sealed by the work of the Great Rural Commission after 1786, which carried through a thorough reconstruction of the pattern of landholding and tenures, working towards the principle of a peasant farm of fixed optimum size with a rationalised unitary layout and free from the obstacles which tradition and custom erected to the improvement of techniques. The class which emerged, the *bonder* or peasant farmers, was a relatively homogeneous group, farming about three-quarters of the land in 1870 but comprising only about 35 per cent of all landowners. The mean size of a *bonde* farm was about thirty-two hectares. 10 per cent of the land was farmed by 64 per cent of the landowners, the *husmænd* or smallholders, the mean size of whose holdings was roughly two and a half hectares. The rough equality of landholding amongst the *bonder* not only permitted the evolution of certain favourable patterns of agricultural development, but also provided at moments a positive stimulus towards them. Excepting the noble estates which remained, the rest of the landowning community was partly excluded from these benefits.

The relative homogeneity of the *bonder* meant that it was much easier to solve the problem of providing capital at sufficiently low interest rates through the operations of self-governing village mortgage and short-term loan banks. In Denmark this was a particularly severe problem because of the length and depth of the investment required to effect the change in emphasis from grain farming to animal farming on which the growth and prosperity of the agricultural sector after 1870 were based. In 1909 banks of this type, with a formal control from the central bank, were providing loans equivalent to more than one-fifth the value of all the farms in the country.[2] Furthermore, the same rough equality of landholding and the existence of these financial mechanisms provided a positive encouragement to the dissemination of new technologies and systems of management. The use of the cream-separator and of its surplus products for pig-rearing was seen to be feasible, provided that the economies of scale to be realised from agricultural co-operation could be obtained. Fewer differences of income, status and attitude stood in the way of such co-operation, and the *bonder* were involved in a simultaneous change of attitudes, farming techniques, final product, investment mechanisms and marketing arrangements the original basis of which was the drastic restructuring of rural society carried out earlier by the central government.

Even setting on one side, however, the social tensions which these reforms sustained by maintaining so large a class of dependent labour in the countryside, the lessons from this experience are almost always drawn in an unrealistically optimistic light. In the first place, the investment required to effect so massive a reconversion of the agricultural sector could in fact bear fruit only after a long period. In spite of the fall in the contribution of vegetable products to the total value of agricultural output from 26 to 14 per cent, a fall which must strongly have mitigated the tendency of steeply falling grain prices to reduce the overall level of agricultural prices, the value of total agricultural output in current prices did not increase over the period 1870–4 to 1885–9.[3] It was the continued investment throughout this period in new methods of producing and processing animal foodstuffs which saw the strategy finally justified by a 57 per cent increase in net agricultural production between 1900 and 1914 and an accompanying improvement in productivity and wages, to the point where productivity per employed person increased faster in agriculture than in urban concerns after 1894. The spectacular improvement in agricultural output and productivity came, therefore, roughly one decade later than the only statistically measurable comparable advance in the industrial sector, although of course the investment which permitted it had begun much earlier, as had the wholesale pattern of change in the countryside. In the intervening period the growth of the economy depended on a wide range of industrial and commercial developments, many of which were quite independent of the process of change in the agricultural sector. They were, rather, in the greater part, the outcome of a long and complex history of international commercial activity and a far-flung network of international connections

This was hardly true of the growing exports of foodstuffs. For these, the international markets on which the rapid surge of growth in the agricultural sector after 1900 depended were very restricted. Essentially there were only two, Britain and Germany, and the second was diminishing in importance as it became more difficult to penetrate. It is this which gives further pause for reflection. The capacity of foreign markets to absorb Danish exports of butter and bacon was finite, especially in a world where Britain was the only substantial importer not to erect protective tariffs against these goods. On the eve of the First World War Denmark was already supplying half the British butter market. Would a country with more than Denmark's 2·7 million inhabitants have been able to find a corresponding opportunity to raise per capita incomes in this way?

Further, the precise historical circumstances in which Danish agriculture changed have to be considered: although other essential elements of the Danish model – a small population, an active seaboard commercial sector and a large, easily accessible foreign market – could be and, indeed, have been reproduced, the effect of these circumstances was peculiarly, perhaps uniquely, favourable. The power acquired by the Crown over tenures and land law in the seventeenth century meant that in the next century enlightened despotism was able to enforce radical changes in the pattern of landholding and in the layout of farm and village and then relax the central power to allow market forces more play. Superimposed on the influence of the Enlightenment came the romantic

fervour of the national revival movement after the crushing defeat
by the German armies and the loss of Schleswig-Holstein in 1866.
The basis of the revival movement was important changes in rural
education, which are usually claimed to have produced a higher
level of literacy, knowledge and general awareness in the Danish
countryside than in most other rural areas of western Europe.

It is understandable that the extraordinary rapidity and relative
painlessness of the transition in Denmark from peasant society
to a pattern of living, a level of income, and an occupational
structure typical of developed countries should have focused attention on the elements which accounted for this success. The trick
was turned within forty years. But in Hungary, where the strategy
for agricultural development was what might be called exaggeratedly bimodal, and where the distribution of farms by size was
more akin to that of present-day Colombia or Brazil, agriculture
made a greater statistical contribution to the growth of the economy
than in Denmark and showed most of the attributes of an industrial
'leading sector'. Estates of 575 hectares or more farmed either
integrally or in very large units accounted for 39 per cent of
the land area and this proportion actually increased slightly between
1860 and 1914.[4] A significant proportion of the rural population
emerged from the tenurial reforms of 1848–52 either completely
without land or possessed of a holding so small as to be inviable
even in the sheltered conditions and relatively high prices of the
Austro-Hungarian common market; before 1914 this proportion
grew while that of farms in the middle range showed a slight
decline. From the dissolution of the old régime to 1914, however,
the rate of growth of agricultural output was higher than over
the comparable period in Denmark. The same massive problems
of conversion of final product had also to be overcome, in this
case in the opposite direction, because the heavily protected customs
union favoured the conversion of the hitherto undrained
swampy plains of central and eastern Hungary from an area devoted
almost entirely to stock-rearing to a major grain-growing region.

The central problem of investment was solved as effectively within
a framework dominated by the large noble estate as within the
framework of the Danish *bonder*. The mutual credit and support
which the estate-owners provided, on the basis of the value of
the capital stock of their estates, through the mechanism of the
Hungarian Land Institute was analogous to similar arrangements

from the previous century in Silesia and Prussia. What was more
important was the important help given first to this institution
by the Hungarian government and later to successive mortgage
institutions engaged in lending on smaller properties. As in Denmark, the development of the consciousness of separate nationhood
furthered the process of providing agricultural mortgage capital.
The Land Credit Institute could obtain loans from the government
on what, in Hungarian conditions, were relatively favourable terms,
because it was seen as an instrument of emancipation from Viennese
capital. The self-identification of the estate-owners with the Magyar
nation eased the way for the government to provide those special
privileges which enabled the Institute to overcome the legal difficulties caused by the vagueness of land titles and the slow pace
of land registration and verification of the post-1849 tenures, difficulties which the Vienna money market saw no reason to risk encoun-
tering. The same privileged status was accorded to the National
Smallholdings Land Mortgage Institute in 1879, and, with the
slow evolution of Raiffeisen and other forms of co-operative banking,
it proved an easy step to legislate in 1895 for a central organisation
of co-operative banks which would receive the same status. The
self-interest of the large estate-owners in Hungary produced as
good a framework for investment as the combined self-interest
of peasant farmers in Denmark. In 1911 the funds to the mortgage
institutions for smaller units of landholding were further increased,
so that the drive to industrialise would not deflect Government
capital from supporting the division, leasing and re-equipment
of large estates encumbered by bankruptcies and fettered by entails
and mortmain.

   Judged purely from the standpoints of investment and growth,
the strategy must be considered to have been a success. The lowest
estimate of the rate of growth of agricultural ouput in Hungary
between 1867 and 1913 is 1·8 per cent per annum, the highest
2·5 per cent.[5] Of course, these percentage increases were in the
early years achieved over low initial levels, and in terms of output
per employed person in agriculture even the highest figure is less
impressive. But the total volume of growth achieved from the
agricultural sector over this period appears nevertheless high in
any comparison. That standards of consumption remained comparatively low in the Hungarian countryside is hardly to be disputed,
but low standards of consumption are, for a period, a necessary

concomitant of bimodal strategies. In the Hungarian case it mattered less because Hungary had the market of the whole empire available. The predominance of the very large farm may, however, have impeded the downward spread of technology. Some of the technological innovation on the large estates in the 1860s, of which the steam-plough was the most spectacular, had no relevance to the numerous smaller farms, and in 1913 the incidence of far less stately machinery than the steam-plough still dropped away steeply from larger farms to smaller.

Lack of technological innovation in methods of cultivation is not, however, equivalent to a lack of technological stimulation from the agricultural sector. In this respect most models of interaction between agriculture and technology are far too simple by virtue of the fact that they omit what was one of the most striking possibilities of the European experience. It was possible for a very rapid increase in foodstuff processing to lead to a search for economies of scale in the process, and, in turn, a narrow but distinct technological leadership in the particular technique. Since such rapid concentrated increases were as likely, perhaps more likely, in a less-developed than in a developed economy, their consequences could be and were felt by engineering industries still at a relatively primitive level of production.

The conversion of the marshy Hungarian plains to grain farming was the most rapid and extensive conversion of this kind in nineteenth-century Europe, and is only to be compared with the opening up of southern Siberia in the decade before the First World War. The exceptional rate of growth of grain output after 1830, and the geographical situation of Budapest – controlling the grain and flour export trade by river and rail into Austria and Germany – together with the fact that it was then the only town and business centre of any importance in the country, brought a rapidly growing quantity of grain into the city for milling. The small mills of the 1850s were replaced in two decades by a more massive and more modern technology, and the rapidity of this change brought a temporary international primacy in milling technology. Indeed, it was the design and construction of milling machinery which laid the basis for the growth of the engineering industry in Budapest and in particular of the famous electrical-engineering firm of Ganz. No railway locomotives were constructed in Hungary until 1873.

A similar phenomenon may be observed in Bohemia. There

the pattern of landholding was less exaggeratedly dominated by the large estate, but, even so, in 1902 over a third of the land area was held in farms of more than 50 hectares. Farms of between 200 and 500 hectares composed about 18 per cent of the land area of Bohemia and Moravia, while, at the other end of the scale, over 70 per cent of the farms were of less than 5 hectares.[6] As in Hungary, the existence of the larger farms was crucial to inducing technological advance through a rapid growth of output over a short time in a food-processing industry. The estate-owners' rapid introduction of sugar beet as a root crop in fallow-reducing rotations, following the emancipation of 1848 and the cash payments which they received then, meant that the increase in beet output in Bohemia over the following two decades was faster than over comparable periods in western Europe. Production grew by 45 per cent between 1859 and 1873, which brought it temporarily to the same volume, on a much smaller area and in a shorter period, as German output. Landowners ploughed their profits back into the refining process and the same striving for rapid technological advance as in the Budapest milling industry made Bohemia for a short time the centre of novel technology in sugar refining. Before 1870 Czech machine-manufacturers had developed an export trade in refining – the foundations of the prosperity of Danek, one of the two major Austro-Hungarian engineering firms, were created by the large number of new refineries which it constructed between 1862 and 1872.[7] There was already an engineering industry in Bohemia, where the manufacture of textile machinery and railway equipment was established, but refining was a type of technological innovation different in important respects from the gradual early diffusion of new textile technologies through the Bohemian countryside from the late eighteenth century onwards, for the early technologies had all been derived from western Europe and were always lagging behind it.

Particular technological advances of this kind might well be more important in the shift of an economy towards sustained development than the more generalised demand for engineering products originating from a more widespread dissemination of machinery in the primary sector, although (to take a case where, by the standards of pre-1914 Europe, technology was more generally used in the primary sector) Sweden shows how high the demand from that sector could be. Output of agricultural machinery accounted for 25·7 per cent of the total value of engineering output in Sweden in 1906, including exports.[8] But the dynamic impact of agriculture on Swedish technology came through very similar mechanisms to those in Hungary and Bohemia. The sudden rise in demand for cream-separators after 1887 turned a small engineering firm, AB Separator, into a major multinational company in fifteen years. AB Separator satisfied a substantial part of the demand for separators which began to emanate from the Russian, German and Australian markets, and a wholly owned subsidiary company was the major producer of separators in the United States. Cream separators, like ball-bearings, were the type of specialised engineering export which could occupy a niche on world markets, and, although the manufacturing process was much simpler, it proved impossible to dislodge AB Separator from the niche it had been the first to occupy.

In the Swedish case this type of interaction took place in an economy where, since the eighteenth century, the influence of the protected peasant class, although not that of the cottars, on central government had been pervasive and the hope of development in the agricultural sector had lain (as in Denmark) in the rationalised peasant holding. Dynamic interactions of this kind were not dependent on any particular pattern of farm size. If the overall ability of the agricultural sector to meet the more fundamental demands on it be considered, precisely the same conclusion would appear to follow. No one could reasonably claim that French governments pursued any agricultural strategy. The revolutionary land settlement was the antithesis of strategy, since the major issues were settled from below; but it was part of the bedrock of the nineteenth-century State, its right to remain unchanged accepted by governments of all persuasions except that of Charles X, when the merest hint that the settlement might be questioned added strength to the forces that were to remove him.

The size of farms in France was more widely varied than in most European countries. Nor were peasant farms particularly small by European standards. But the country's history and political system placed it firmly in the category of those countries where investment decisions in the primary sector were dominated by peasant farmers in the aggregate. If the fundamental tasks of the agricultural sector are defined as increasing output to provide enough food to feed the growing population and to prevent food imports from rising at the same time as other imports on which development is based, these tasks were comfortably achieved. In spite of an increase of population between 1815 and 1870 of about 5·5 million, in good harvest years France was a net food-exporter until the end of that period, although on balance over longer periods she had become a net importer. Over the periods 1858–60 and 1864–6, French exports were an important addition to the European grain trade, and there were two years in the 1870s when there were substantial grain export surpluses.

These tasks, however, were achieved throughout western Europe (except in Spain) no matter in which direction the size of farms was skewed. In Prussia, where the government and investment in the agricultural sector alike rested on the large landed estate, the response seems, from the available evidence, to have been as satisfactory, or, given that the population grew more rapidly, better. The increase in grain output alone between 1816 and 1852 appears to have been about 50 per cent.[9] Nor are these figures out of line with the crude approximation for the whole of Germany, where the overall pattern of farm size in different states varied through every possibility. The population of Germany increased by 15·8 million between 1820 and 1870, but the country remained on balance a food-exporter until the 1860s. Over the period 1836–56, foodstuffs were on average between 18 and 22 per cent of the *Zollverein*'s exports.[10]

It does not, therefore, appear a tenable argument that any particular strategy of government intervention to control or alter the size of farms and the pattern of farm size throughout the economy was more successful than another. Nor, when the primary sector did not respond satisfactorily, is there any case where this was clearly owing to the failure to select one particular type of strategy. At the extremes of Europe, Russia and Ireland are often pilloried as examples of the defects of an agriculture dominated by the large estate. But, even supposing this to be a fair characterisation of Irish agriculture, what is to be said of the sad history of nineteenth-century agriculture in Belgium and, more particularly, in Flanders? Flanders came close to repeating the cruel experience of Ireland in 1846, and yet at the start of the century it was often singled out to exemplify the advantages of small peasant farms. Mann wrote,

The general result, which I have been able to form, from what I know of the Flemish agriculture, is, that they draw from their farms the best crops, and the most food for great and small cattle, fowl, etc. which the soil is capable of producing. The quantity thereof is certainly great, when compared to any extent of land in Germany, France, Spain, England or any other country I am acquainted with. The comparison, if made with due knowledge and impartiality, will certainly turn in favour of Flemish agriculture, whatever may be said in preference of the neatness and elegance of the methods used elsewhere, and of the usefulness of the new-invented machines employed therein.[11]

This very quality was to stand condemned, and in perfect justice, by Rowntree at the close of the century, as having long preserved a backward, low-productivity sector in an advanced, highly industrialised economy and having thus encouraged a distribution of income within that economy more unequal than it need have been, by comparison with that in its neighbour countries.[12]

The European experience does not suggest that any of the economic advantages now claimed for unimodal strategies were unique to such strategies, nor that success or failure in development was consistently owing to the selection of any particular strategy in the agricultural sector. On the other hand, it would be foolish to deny that differences in strategy in the agricultural sector could for a considerable time and throughout the formative stages of development deeply affect the structure of society in the country as a whole. The effects of such differences might linger in outlook long after the agricultural sector had ceased to be important. But it must also be accepted that the fate of most of the actively employed population in the agricultural sector, whatever their social status, was and is ultimately a common one – to leave it.

To what extent did the selection of a particular strategy encourage or retard the process of social and political modernisation? The terms on which serfdom was abolished in Russia, the retention of the *mir* and of redistribution, the tax and policy controls which retained labour in agriculture, and the large land surrenders made by most emancipated serfs all increased the instability of the Russian polity, whatever their immediate economic effects. In contrast, behold the educated, aware, independent, progressive, patriotic and democratic Danish peasant, the very bedrock of that modernised society which lures governments and development economists alike.

In reality the contrasts were far less stark and the contribution of the agricultural sector to political modernisation was determined more by the economic opportunities available than by the distribution of farms by size. In Silesia and on the large Prussian estates eastwards from the Elbe, noble landowners were early prepared to bring pressure to bear on central government in order to speed up the juridical changes which would enable them to use wage labour rather than the less efficient boon labour to which they were entitled, because wage labour provided a better means for the expansion of export sales. In Russia, noble estate-owners in the hinterland of Odessa pressed in the same direction in order better to exploit the growing export markets in western Europe which they could reach. Where such sentiments prevailed, the social tensions between modernisers and traditionalists could be resolved in agreement on a limited set of common economic and political causes. They did not lead to the explosive 'breakthrough' which Gerschenkron identifies both as a necessity for, and as the decisive moment in, the modernisation of European states.

Thus free trade, with its penumbra of liberal constitutional implications and its supposedly powerful modernising effects, received much support from conservative East Elbian Junkers in the 1850s. They were not, of course, in favour of universal male suffrage. But the French peasantry, who were, exercised it throughout the 1880s and particularly in 1889 to vote for high agricultural tariffs, which may well have been serious impediments to modernisation in France. Given the right economic circumstances, a rapidly growing market for food and a supply of investment capital, the tension between modernisers and anti-modernisers could be gradually released in the primary sector, irrespective of the particular strategy pursued, and, conversely, a unimodal strategy could be deeply conservative in its effects. Peasant farmers and the owners of large estates alike, provided that the circumstances were suitable, could be persuaded by force of economic conditions to put their trust in a freer flow of the factors of production and in the liberalisation of legislation to permit this. Indeed, it often was easier for larger landowners to accept such a policy, because they still controlled the greater part of the capital stock and often retained political control at a local level by controlling local courts; the real sacrifice of political power was much less than it seemed.

The conclusions pull in different directions. Agricultural systems dominated by the large farm could respond as satisfactorily as those dominated by a peasant sector. The importance of government intervention in the agricultural sector, however, emerges forcefully. It was only in those few, fortunate countries where a relatively high level of development and per capita income had been attained in the eighteenth century that government might have indulged the luxury of being a passive spectator of the agricultural sector. Even in those countries it did not entirely do so. In Britain the ease with which Bills of Enclosure could be passed through Parliament, and the readiness of Parliament to protect agriculture, and in France government's careful encouragement of enclosure in some regions after 1770 have nothing in common with the lofty indifference to agricultural problems in both countries after 1850.

It is only necessary to compare the wealth of barns, byres and other farm buildings in late eighteenth-century Britain and France with the lack of fixed capital in central and eastern European farms to see how much more important intervention was in the later developers. To create a responsive arable agriculture on the harsh plains of the Wallachian *bărăgăn* or the Hungarian *puszta* (Balkan prairies) was a sterner problem in capital investment and on a shorter timescale. There the friendly encouraging eye which French and British governments cast on the primary sector in the eighteenth century needed to be replaced in the nineteenth century by energetic and positive intervention. But, of what kind? If all, or any, patterns of farm-size could respond, how could government select the optimum strategy?

If one cause above all others be singled out for the success of economic development in Sweden and Denmark, it would have to be in both cases the prolonged, careful, yet forceful pressure which government began to apply to the agricultural sector in the eighteenth century and sustained until the long-delayed emergence of a significant industrial sector after the turn of the nineteenth century. There, the historical legacy encouraged such action. It was understandable that, in countries with so small a population and so unsophisticated a range of economic activity, agriculture should have remained in the forefront of government policy. To this extent both countries had a distinct advantage. In most of

Europe, until the close of the nineteenth century, development strategy in the primary sector was seen only as a permissive factor. The purpose of reform and intervention was to permit the primary sector to respond to the violent pressures for change which, it was assumed, would emanate from the other sectors. The debates on the winding-up of the old régime focused on the issue of how rapidly and how far the primary sector should be permitted to respond to these pressures. Should not the response of the primary sector be slowed down in the interests of social and governmental stability? It was rarely assumed that a restructuring of the agricultural sector could itself provide a powerful initial force for economic development. In Scandinavia, government was compelled, *faute de mieux*, to cling to the belief in agricultural improvement as the source of prosperity. The counterpart of the work of the Great Rural Commission in Denmark was the long history of Swedish agrarian legislation, beginning in 1757 with the granting of permission and facilities to landowners wishing to consolidate their holdings, and culminating in the acts of 1803 and 1827 which created a legal framework for progressive consolidation or enclosure according to region and custom. Pressure to rationalise the farm and financial assistance in the task were throughout the twin props of government policy and it was the long persistence with these policies which brought success.

In Hungary, by contrast, the large noble domain was the very basis of the Magyar national state and it was the strength of national allegiance to that state as nationalist sentiment grew which was enormously important in solving the central problem of investment by making capital available to farmers on easier terms. As in Sweden, government intervened to encourage and preserve what it considered essential in the national historical heritage and, given the nature of government and society, it is hard to see how success, measured in purely economic terms, could have come from any other course of action. In Prussia the investment role of the *Landschaften* in the eighteenth century was almost inseparable from the programmes of settlement and reconstruction in the east and was also designed to continue the crucial part played by the landed nobility in the state's history. It was separate national historical considerations of this kind also, it must be admitted, that weighed so heavily with Russian Slavophils and *narodniki* when they conceived their programme of 'going to the people'. From them the idea that Russian village society was uniquely valuable because uniquely and quintessentially Russian later passed into the justification of Tsarist policy that it, too, was in accord with the separate national historical legacy of Russia. This was partly a failure to interpret history correctly and partly a sad exception and exaltation of precisely those aspects of the national tradition which were likely to impede economic development and political modernisation.

Active intervention in the primary sector was indeed necessary if a balanced response was to be achieved – even Witte was to come to admit that – but, before it took place, a long, clear, accurate look at the historical legacy was also necessary. If the advantages in that legacy were identified and amplified, as they were by the Swedish government or by Bishop Grundtvig in Denmark or Raiffeisen in the Rhineland, an important, sometimes decisive, step forward in development could be taken. The trap to be avoided was to suppose that anything that seemed unique in that tradition was an advantage. Therein lay a growing danger in the nineteenth century, for the trap gaped the wider the stronger national sentiment grew. In Serbia the creation of inalienable peasant tenures, the political symbolisation of the ejection of the Ottoman landlords, became a severe barrier to obtaining mortgage capital on peasant farms. Further east, the revolutionary movement of 'going to the people' became ultimately the justification of any outmoded agricultural practice, in the name of 'holy Russia'. Unimodal strategies are particularly likely to induce a romantic wallowing in peasant traditions, which is more appropriate to a time of stability than to one of change.

From the onset of the process of sustained development in the late eighteenth century, countries sought a guiding path into the future from the history of the successful. From a wilfully simplified version of the French Revolution and of British history, mid-nineteenth-century Spanish and Italian liberals came to the conclusion that the imperatives of development would be met by removing the obstacles to the free movement of factors, simplifying the land law into a system of saleable rights of ownership and establishing a set of personal 'rights' for all citizens. Over large areas of both countries this made little difference to the performance of the primary sector, and the collapse of the railway boom in 1867 showed all too clearly that self-sustaining development had not been achieved. As the century advanced, the false historical images of the successful multiplied and policies in the unsuccessful became more eclectic. Free trade and emancipation in Romania were replaced by a protectionism the intellectual origins of which lay in Berlin, and this in turn was followed by a land reform similar to that in Russia. Soon countries outside Europe would eagerly study the Romanian land reforms. As images multiplied, the search for policy was conducted in a hall of distorting mirrors reflecting in ever more complicated fashion the falsifications of history produced by hope and desperate necessity.

The missing mirror was in most cases the clear mirror of national history, for only from a long and unflinching look therein was satisfactory guidance towards a correct strategy likely to be found. In the primary sector above all, the historical legacy was peculiarly national. Between sweeping land reform and linked sets of smaller, more detailed acts of intervention lay a wide choice of strategy. But the lesson of the European historical experience was that government must act and that the optimum strategy could only be derived from as finely sensitive an image as possible of the country's own historical legacy. The great and central problem was correctly to identify what was useful in that legacy and what could not be avoided. Lured by exaggerated aspirations, enmeshed in a political rhetoric of heroic peasants, sturdy yeomen and patriotic gentry, misled by oversimplified theories of development, an accurate assessment of the optimum strategy was hard to make. When it could be made, the likelihood of securing the necessary balanced response throughout the economy was greatly enhanced.

Of course, this was not all that was needed to achieve such a response. Nor would it necessarily produce it. Time, place, changes in the international environment, shifts in available technology, conflicts produced by other separate acts of government, war and even weather could all deflect and nullify even the most sensitive strategy, and some of these, it might transpire, should also be incorporated in any future model. Where, left to its own devices (as in nineteenth-century France), the agricultural sector did nevertheless achieve the main tasks of that sector with comparative ease, the attempt to show which factors were responsible for that response illustrates how much more must have been involved in poorer societies than merely a correct strategy of intervention by government.[13] Worse still, the historical legacy might offer very little hope. Nor would any such scheme of development have implications any more universal than those it would replace: clearly, there were quite different paths to development which could on occasions be followed. In spite of all these reservations it is still a forward step in constructing a historically more sensitive model of the development process in the nineteenth century to conclude that in most European economies government intervention in the agricultural sector was necessary to produce that short period of balanced response between the sectors which was itself usually necessary for sustained development to take place. Nor were governments in this the helpless prisoners of circumstance and chance. There were certain guiding lights by which an optimum strategy could be selected. They were not the guiding lights which current development theory suggests. Rather they were the hard, clear light of the history of the country itself.

Notes

1 The fullest and clearest advocacy of this view is in B. F. Johnston and D. Kilby, *Agriculture and Structural Transformation: Economic Strategies in Late-Developing Countries* (New York, 1975).

2 H. Faber, *Co-operation in Danish Agriculture* (London, 1918) p. 139.

3 The estimates are those of S. A. Hansen *Økonomisk Vækst i Danmark*, vol. 1: *1720–1914*, Københavns Universitet, Institut for Økonomisk Historie publication no. 6 (Copenhagen, 1972) pp. 185, 226.

4 See the calculations made by S. M. Eddie, 'The Changing Pattern of Landownership in Hungary, 1867–1914', *EHR*, 2nd ser., xx (1967).

5 The lower by L. Katus, 'Economic Growth in Hungary during the Age of Dualism, 1867–1918', in *Studia Historica*, no. 62 (1970); the higher by S. M. Eddie, 'Agricultural Production and Output per Worker in Hungary, 1870–1913', in *Journal of Economic History*, xxviii (1968). The higher figure gives an increase in output per employed person of 0·5 per cent annually. See also the estimates by I. Berend and G. Ranki, 'Nationaleinkommen und Kapitalakkumulation in Ungarn, 1867–1914', in *Studia Historica*, no. 62 (1970).

6 The figures are derived from the appendix to S. Pascu *et al.*, 'Einige Fragen der landwirtschaftlichen Entwicklung in der Österreichisch-ungarischen Monarchie', *Mitteilungen auf der Konferenz der Geschichtswissenschaftler, Budapest, 1964* (Bucharest, 1965).

7 See the figures given by J. Purs in 'Die Entwicklung des Kapitalismus in der Landwirtschaft der böhmischen Länder in der Zeit von 1849 bis 1879', in *Jahrbuch für Wirtschaftsgeschichte*, iii (1963).

8 J. Kuuse, *Interaction between Agriculture and Industry*, Meddelanden från Ekonomisk Historiska Institutionen vid Göteborgs Universitet, no. 34 (Göteborg, 1974) p. 22.

9 H. W. Graf Finck von Finckenstein, *Die Entwicklung der Landwirtschaft in Preussen und Deutschland* (Munich, 1960) esp. p. 313. The increase over the whole area of Germany could well have been greater, and Henning estimates an increase in real output per peasant family of between 15 and 20 per cent between 1800 and 1850 – F. W. Henning, 'Kapitalbildungsmöglichkeiten der bäuerlichen Bevölker-

ung in Deutschland am Anfang des neunzehnten Jahrhunderts', in *Beiträge zur Wirtschaftswachstum und Wirtschaftstruktur im 16 und 19 Jahrhunderts*, ed. W. Fischer (Berlin, 1971).

10 From the calculations of B. von Borries in *Deutschlands Aussenhandel 1836 bis 1856: Eine statistische Untersuchung zur Frühindustrialisierung* (Stuttgart, 1970).

11 T. A. Mann, 'On the Agriculture of the Netherlands', in *Georgical Essays*, vol. v (York, 1809) p. 33.

12 S. Rowntree, *Land and Labour* (London, 1910).

13 The discussion is carried on in M. Morineau, *Les Faux-semblants d'un démarrage économique: agriculture et démographie en France au XVIIIe siècle* (Paris, 1970); W. H. Newell, 'The Agricultural Revolution in Nineteenth Century France', *Journal of Economic History*, xxxiii (1973); and G. W. Grantham, 'The Diffusion of the New Husbandry in Northern France, 1815–1840', ibid., xxxviii (1978).

3 The 'New' Immigration and the Newest: Slavic Migrations from the Balkans to America and Industrial Europe since the Late Nineteenth Century

MICHAEL PALAIRET

How alike or unlike were the 'new' immigration from southern and eastern Europe to north America before 1914 and the temporary-worker migrations from the Mediterranean lands to western Europe in the 1960s and early 1970s? Was the 'new' immigration itself of the *Gastarbeiter* type? And, if so, what lessons may be learned from this analogous historical experience? In this study of the emigration history of the Balkans, we compare some aspects of migrational experience before 1914 and during the 1960s. For a long time this comparison was ignored, because it was supposed that the 1960s movement only involved the employment of temporary workers who retained their main domicile in the countries of their origin, and, thus, that the movement was not an immigration at all. By contrast, the 'new' immigration to America resulted for the greater part in permanent settlement, though it might be conceded that it also had a transitory component. However, the 'new' immigration was also thought by contemporaries to be a purely transient movement, for much the same reasons, and in the last few years western Europe has come to realise that, whatever the original expectations of its guest workers, this newest immigration has planted huge and probably irreversible demographic facts in its midst.

The aim in this essay is to discuss the basis for the assumption made twice this century that these migrations were only temporary, to assess its validity, and to try to discover why to so considerable an extent it was confounded by experience.

I

In the 1860s and 1870s news began to spread through the northern villages of Croatia of the opportunities of finding well paid work in the iron and copper mines of the American Midwest.[1] A new mass emigration movement was in the making, which was to spread gradually throughout the Balkans and would result in the USA opening its doors to about a million Balkan Slavs before World War I.[2] They came mostly from what is now Yugoslavia, but also included about 56,000 from the western marches of (subsequently) Greek Macedonia and about 29,000 from Bulgaria.[3] Of the Yugoslav immigrants about 60 per cent were Croats, 22 per cent Slovenes.[4] Most of the rest were Serbs, and about 10,000 were Slav Macedonians.[5] The largest contingent (about 310,000 arrivals between 1890 and 1910)[6] arrived from Croatia–Slavonia, especially from the villages of the densely populated but infertile limestone uplands in the western half of the territory.

The immigration of Balkan Slavs to the United States was a composite part of what came to be known as the 'new' immigration, from eastern and southern Europe, one notable characteristic of which was that a substantial percentage of arrivals failed to stay. Thus by 1920 high re-emigration as well as high mortality had reduced the residue of US residents who had been born in Yugoslavia to a mere 169,437 and those born in Bulgaria to 10,477. On the basis of the three-year stay which was supposed to be the normal sojourn of the returning migrant, the re-emigration rate for 1908–13/1905–10 may be estimated at 18·7 per cent for (so-called) Dalmatians and Bosnians, 38·4 per cent for Croats and

Slovenes and 45·8 per cent for Serbs, Bulgars and Montenegrins.[7]

Only recently have a few historians begun to pay much attention to the 'transient' character of the 'new' immigration, but it was a matter which exercised the lively attention of US public opinion at the time, for the migrants' practice of earning American wages, spending little and departing with their savings was resented as supposedly impoverishing the country.

This view – that the emigrants went out as temporary workers – was endorsed by informed opinion in the Balkans, and received approval for the same reason as it earned the disapproval of Americans. But expectations were of a virtual 100 per cent return, and in this respect they were highly exaggerated. Take for example the following (disastrously wrongheaded) judgement made in 1909.[8]

It is reckoned that about 60,000 men have recently emigrated from our small Dalmatia. Indeed this is a large number which would have alarmed us dreadfully, knowing that the emigrants are the strongest and healthiest of our youth, were we not influenced to some extent by the thought that our emigration is almost exclusively temporary.

This impression long persisted. In 1922 a writer on Dalmatia claimed a 95 per cent return rate. Something like the truth only dawned seven years later, when it was alleged that 95 per cent would *never* return to their homeland.[9] Thus, what was seen in retrospect as a massive movement of permanent resettlement was misinterpreted by contemporaries on both sides of the Atlantic as a temporary-worker migration. This was only too understandable, for the emigrants themselves thought the same. A survey conducted by B. Colakovic in 1972 among eighty-seven Yugoslav-born pre-1910 immigrants to the USA who had not subsequently returned (except on holiday) showed that fifty-three had originally expected to return, and only thirty-two to stay.[10] So, allowing for those who really did return, (assuming that was their original intention), about three-quarters intended to return, and the majority of stayers were people who believed they had changed their minds.

What gave rise to the belief that the emigrants were temporary workers? A large majority were young men from peasant families. While abroad they were regarded as temporarily away from home, earning money to assist their households, of which they remained, economically, as much a part as those who stayed to till the fields. On this basis, their transoceanic migrations were no more than the tip of an iceberg, the concealed bulk of which was represented by the hundreds of thousands of other migrant workers – *pečal-bari* – who customarily left home in search of wages with which to complement the subsistence afforded by their farms. Some *pečal-bari* were mere harvesters, but most were tradesmen, such as the foresters of Gorski Kotar (Croatia), the housebuilders and carpenters of south-east Serbia, and of the Tr'n and Gabrovo villages of Bulgaria, the dairymen, bakers and confectioners of Greek Macedonia, and the seamen and pedlars of Dalmatia.[11] Macedonia on its own sent out 85,000 migrant workers a year in the late nineteenth century.[12]

As most of the areas which sent migrants across the Atlantic were also familiar with these shorter-range migrations, the lesser movement was likely to be regarded as no more than part of the greater. Only an insignificant fraction of the Macedonian migration crossed the Atlantic. The same can be said of the emigration from Bulgaria, most of which came from a small area to the north of the Balkan range[13] which was much better known for its itinerant market gardeners, of whom about 12,000 left home each year.[14] It may even have been the market gardeners who started the emigration to the United States, and many of those who went to Latin America intended to pursue this vocation there.[15] Even the migration to the USA from Croatia is considered by one modern authority to have been secondary in magnitude to the huge internal movements from the same emigrant regions into the cities and the Slavonian plain.[16]

It could reasonably be assumed that these peasant workers would, as expected, save and remit their earnings to their villages, and therefore remain integrated with the rural economy. Neither the farm production of the smaller peasant holding nor the wages which could be earned by the peasant worker were adequate by themselves to provide a familial subsistence deemed tolerable by the standards of the day. But a family whose man went away to work while the rest kept the farm going could enjoy modest prosperity, the evidence of which was usually readily visible in villages which were well integrated into the market for migrant labour, especially if they possessed rich common pasture and woodland.[17] As Cvetko Kostić argued passionately in 1955, so as to dissuade the authorities from forcing workers to choose between their jobs and their land, both subsistence and wages were indispensable to the well-being of the peasant-worker family.[18] Even the income from a dwarf holding was as vital to such a family as that from wages. As late as the 1960s the average Yugoslav peasant-worker household with two or three hectares derived 55 per cent of its income from the holding itself.[19] In an earlier age, when employment tended to be more irregular and farms were larger, the contribution of the farm was probably still more decisive as a determinant of total income. The produce from his land was vital to the migrant worker's well-being, quite apart from its value in the event of unemployment, sickness or old age. So there was little incentive for him to cut the bonds which tied him to it.

As it was so important to retain the land, the journeys of the transoceanic emigrants were rarely financed by selling it. Indeed, it was not unknown for emigrants to buy land on credit before departure, to provide their families with an adequate income in kind, and to go abroad to earn sufficient to disencumber it.[20] Of 4048 property-owning Yugoslav emigrants in 1922, only 78 sold land before leaving.[21] And, of 100 unemployed Bulgarians in Chicago in 1908, it was discovered that seventy-eight had had their passages paid by the mortgaging of farms, but none, it seems, had sold them.[22] At least at their departure their financial links with their farms were unbroken.

The symbiotic dependence of the migrant on the farm and the farm on the migrant did not easily survive the crossing of the Atlantic. It became one-sided, and the mechanism which should have ensured the emigrant's return ceased to operate efficiently. Although immigrant earnings were poor by American standards, at about $1.70 for a ten-hour day of unskilled labour (in 1903), they compared with $0.43 in Belgrade or $0.30 in Dalmatia.[23] If the immigrant cared to do so, he could establish a family life for himself in the United States in greater comfort than he could hope to reattain at home, even with the farm and his wages together.

Such opportunities were only gradually perceived by the *pečalbari*, because, in the communities from which they came, consciousness of the possibility of utilising the foreign workplace as a place for permanent settlement was almost entirely lacking. And for many, especially the older emigrants, such a consciousness probably never even dawned. To them life in emigration could never be anything other than what they had anticipated on departure, an act of self-abnegation, of overwork and oversaving so as to return as soon as possible to the security, prestige, relative comfort, and idleness to be provided by the farm property and the 'bloodily earned dollars' in combination.

It may be doubted, however, whether the majority of younger emigrants viewed their prospects abroad in such terms, as an arid exile of self-denial. Superficially their prospects seemed similar: they too expected to have to remit and subsequently to return. Even in their own eyes they were also *pečalbari*, whose earnings abroad were considered the moral property of the head of their family.[24] Yet it may be doubted whether they gave much thought to their prospective return. Rather did they leave home with a profound sense of escape from the often futile hardships of peasant life, usually with great excitement and with boundless optimism, because of the impression of easy money conveyed by the remittances and letters sent home by earlier emigrants. It was a common pattern that distress – the destruction of the local vineyards by phylloxera, for example – would cause a few peasants in a district to emigrate to earn the money to restore their fortunes, and these would subsequently write and remit sums which seemed gigantic to their fellow villagers, telling also of the wages which were there for the taking. This could easily touch off an 'emigration fever', especially among the younger men, regardless of whether there were any 'need' for them to emigrate in an absolute sense. Such a sequence seems to have happened in Jastrebarsko (inland Croatia), where the first crop of remittances caused such a rush for the Adriatic ports that the railway could not cope with the traffic.[25] Children, it was frequently alleged, could hardly wait to leave school to go to America, and were unwilling to settle at employment locally.[26] Of 300 Yugoslavs 'polled' in the United States after the Second World War by G. Govorchin, 58 per cent instanced 'adventure' as one of the reasons why they emigrated.[27]

Such an attitude was utterly at variance with the patriarchal ethic of Balkan society. 'Lighthearted' emigration was frequently castigated, as it in effect meant emigration stimulated by pull influences, especially of those whom need did not drive away from home – 'on their stomachs for bread' as the saying went. Moralists never tired of forecasting the speedy demise of the 'lighthearted' emigrant, and the ruin of his family. Emigration controls were sometimes advocated to obstruct the departure of the discretionary emigrant – for his own good.[28] Experience no doubt had shown that 'lighthearted' emigration led to neither remittance nor return, and therefore threatened the interest of the home community.

Life in the United States, in the immigrant ghetto alongside the steel mill or the pithead, was grim, squalid and short, as countless writers have told us. But, if the subjective negative aspects of immigrant life could be surmounted, it was not difficult to live at a better standard than in the homeland. It was something of a shock for the publicist Tresić-Pavičić, who wanted to promote the ties between the emigrant and the old country, to learn of the reality that

> There are a large number who feel nothing for the homeland. . . . I have heard from the mouths of Croats [in America] these words: 'What have you come to tell us about the home-land? . . . The old homeland which bore us was a stepmother to us. . . . All our toil was taken from us by taxes, Jews, priests, and usurers. To us the homeland is where life is good to us, and that is here. . . . Tell your fairy tales in the old homeland but leave us here in peace for this is now our home.[29]

Even the emigrant societies, though they might profess a loyalty to the old country, could become irritated by the bland assumption made back in the Balkans that their life in America was only temporary, and not to be taken seriously,[30] and observers in the homeland, though they clung to the myth of return, were gradually forced to concede the paradox that it was on the whole the most successful emigrants who were least likely to return. This was difficult to reconcile with the idea that return marked the successful end of the emigration process, and that the majority of the emigrants who remained away did so because they were too poor to return.[31] As the standard of living of the home communities came increasingly to depend on emigrant earnings, so the failure of migrants to save, remit and return was regarded as betrayal, and even the expression of the intention not to return as heresy. Especially resented were the non-returning well-to-do, accused of 'trampling over their ancestral hearths seeking a more comfortable life beside their work – bothering only about their own souls and throats'.[32] In the literature there is complaint after complaint about emigrants who were deemed to have gone to the bad and neither remitted nor returned. 'Former Americans' told one writer that, of the Yugoslavs in America, the drunks, layabouts and gamblers accounted for 10 per cent, and that it was these, the good-for-nothings, and those who had married foreign women who would remain there.[33] To another writer it was 'only the sort of young men who abandoned themselves to drink and dice' who stayed for the long term, as they had no money to return with.[34]

The conclusion was clear. If – albeit for reasons imperfectly understood – remittance and return could no longer be counted on as a product of the emigrant's self-interest, then the emigrant's home community should take measures to protect itself. The kind of action which suggested itself to dissuade emigrants from behaviour which was regarded as antisocial was of the sort which governed the organisation of Montenegrin workers in Constantinople. Though lower than the wages that could be earned from unskilled labour in America, their pay was handsome by Balkan standards at four or five gold lira a month, from which it was possible to remit half or more – or to drink and gamble it away. The remittance of earnings was regarded as a formal obligation, and their community leaders were authorised to bring pressure to bear on those who failed to remit, or who frequented the cafés and spent their money. They even had the right, which was not infrequently used, of sending the unregenerate back to the homeland in irons. 'The lazy and the wastrels are not needed here. It is better that they perish of hunger over there.'[35] Such extreme measures could not be applied in America, but pressures were exerted through the emigrant community. A man who failed to support his wife would soon be informed upon by his fellows, who would 'write to her . . . about how he's earning money there, how he drinks with his companions, plays cards . . .'.[36] One writer advocated the establishment of 'some kind of committee . . . organised by our people abroad' which would among other things 'guide those who neglect their homeland, . . . and shame those who reduce their ancestral hearth to poverty'. He appealed 'to our patriotic pečalbari . . . to send back their brothers who . . . neglect and forget their ancestral hearth'.[37] It would be interesting to know to what extent this type of thinking affected the creation of emigrant organisations. It certainly affected emigration laws. Bulgaria in 1922 prohibited family emigration, and permitted only the departure of household heads, who had to put up caution money against their return within ten years.[38]

II

Soon after Balkan labour began to arrive in America, it also appeared on the western European labour markets. It is claimed there were half a million 'Yugoslav' industrial workers in western Europe on the eve of World War I, of whom 70,000, mainly Slovenes from Styria and Kranj, worked in the Ruhr coalmines and at other rough work which the Germans were beginning to leave to immigrant labour.[39] This movement continued during the interwar years, and, between 1930 and 1939, 132,000 Yugoslavs were recorded as migrating to European destinations, 41 per cent from Slovenia and 24 per cent from Croatia, while 82,000 returned.[40] In 1938 there were conservatively estimated to be 50,000 Yugoslavs in Germany and 35,000 in France.[41]

So there was nothing inherently new about the great migration wave of Yugoslav *Gastarbeiter* which took place in the 1960s, especially as the older Yugoslav communities in western Europe provided a bridge for new arrivals.[42] There was, however, a protracted postwar hiatus in work emigration from Yugoslavia, because, as with the rest of the Communist states, private travel abroad was virtually prohibited. Justification was provided for this prohibition by the claim that total planning would eliminate unemployment. The Bulgarian Government has never deviated from this standpoint, but in Yugoslavia a gradual departure was made both from full employment and from the total planning which was said to guarantee it. In time this was to temper the attitude of the Yugoslav Government towards emigration, from condemning it as 'desertion' to condoning it as a necessity. Unemployment first manifested itself in 1950–2 in consequence of job cutbacks occasioned by the Soviet blockade, and it continued persistently to rise. By 1957 'latent' unemployment, as manifested by the increasing number of street vendors and door-to-door job-seekers, was giving rise to official concern, and some thought was devoted to the possibility of sending surplus farm labour abroad to 'learn new work habits'.[43] Though the former policies of forced collectivisation and of treating the peasantry 'like the defeated side in a war'[44] had been dropped and discredited, the resulting air of uncertainty with which private farming was still attended, and the continued bias against farmers in the terms of trade, generated a *Landflucht* greater than industry could absorb. It became particularly difficult to find jobs for the so-called seasonal workers, peasants who worked for wages for part of the year, of whom the 1960 census showed there to be 516,000.[45] One observer even suggested that less care was being devoted to finding them work than before the war.[46] So it was this type of migrant, especially from the poor *karst* Dalmation–Bosnian borderlands, who began in the 1950s to filter illegally across the frontier for work in Austria and West Germany, for there was no work to be had locally.[47]

After a boom in 1957–9 the employment situation deteriorated to such an extent that in 1961 some Yugoslav employment exchanges were permitting workers to go out under their semi-official aegis, though nothing was said about this officially. A softening of the passport law in 1960 probably assisted. At any rate, in 1962 requests for permits lodged with exchanges in Croatia seem to have been attended with fair success, for their number leaped from 1850 in 1961 to 14,933 in 1962 and to 24,569 in the first half of 1963.[48] To the bureaucratic mind, the phenomenon was getting out of control, and this led to the first emigration law, the function of which was not to legalise employment abroad, but to crack down on it, for the provisions of the law were purely restrictive.[49] To comply with them was too difficult, applications for permits slumped, and, as it was easier to get a passport than a permit to work abroad, the majority went out on tourist visas – or fled the frontier without papers.[50] The authorities reacted by devising schemes such as for 'training' workers abroad in the catering trade, which, it was candidly admitted, was designed to channel and curtail the 'wild' (i. e. spontaneous) outflow of workers.[51] Despite the restrictions, between 1960 and 1963 the estimated stock of Yugoslav migrants in western Europe soared from 18,000 to 90,000.[52]

The equivocal policy of the State towards the departure of its citizens was largely abandoned in 1965, though for some while emigrants were to remain subject to the capricious vilification of local party zealots and harassment by the passport authorities.[53] Failure to sustain the growth rates of the late 1950s, inflation and intractable trade deficits gave increasing influence to the econo-

mic-reform movement. The reformers wanted an end to extensive
industrialisation, and the integration of Yugoslav industry within
the international division of labour. Firms would be forced to
respond to the disciplines imposed by application of market criteria.
Rather suddenly the reformers began to get their way in late
1965, competitive conditions were created, and an acute disinflation-
ary credit squeeze was applied. Firms were told to rationalise
and to cut back recruitment, especially of unskilled peasant labour.
The emigration of labour became a political necessity.

So now, with the floodgates open unemployment rising and
the demand for labour in western Europe as yet unsatisfied, the
number of workers going abroad – especially from Croatia, where
the effects of the squeeze were most severely felt – leaped yet again.[54]
By 1967 there were thought to be some 220,000 Yugoslav nationals
at work in western Europe. It was hoped that the tonic effect
of the reform on the balance of payments, and on the competitive
strength of Yugoslav industry, would soon diminish the need for
the export of labour, and that rapid employment growth could
soon be resumed. 'Economic emigration', it was now said, 'is only
a necessity of one stage in the growth of socialist society'.[55] The
emigration had thus been made temporary by definition. Officially
the emigrants were 'Yugoslav workers temporarily employed
abroad'. For predictive purposes this was a dangerous assumption
to make, for it depended on the triumph of emigration policy
over past experience of emigrant behaviour.

The consummation of this policy, the restoration of full employment, tended to recede into the future, extending the duration
of the transitional phase during which emigration was necessary.
Recovery, when it came in 1969–71, fell below expectations, and
synchronised with a strong upturn in the European economy, which
strengthened the forces attracting labour abroad. As emigration
flows responded more strongly to changes in the external demand
for labour than to changes in conditions in the domestic labour
market (according to one recent econometric analysis),[56] so the
emigration outflow continued to increase, despite the domestic recovery. In 1970 new arrivals in West Germany rose to a peak
of 238,502,[57] and the estimated stock of Yugoslav workers in western
Europe reached 550,000. A 'census' carried out by the Yugoslavs
in 1971 disclosed 672,000 persons 'temporarily' at work abroad
(as well as an estimated 190,000 written off as permanent emi-

grants). They were the equivalent of 22 per cent of the employed workforce of Yugoslavia, and, because of their regional bias, 38 per cent of that of Bosnia and 34 per cent of that of Croatia.[58] The net outflow to West Germany remained strongly positive till 1973, eight years after initiation of the reforms, a period which must have been far longer than any envisaged transition. Moreover, an increasing current of migration was now moving overseas, where, in 1971, 143,000 recent Yugoslav immigrant workers were to be found, rather more than half of them in Australia. The Yugoslav authorities formally designated even these emigrants as 'temporary' – a view widely accepted among the migrants themselves.

And this takes us to the heart of the conceptual difficulty. For, as with the earlier, transatlantic migration, the authorities were supported in their preconceptions as to the transience of the emigration by the apparent intentions of the emigrants. Of a large sample of migrant workers from Croatia who were interviewed on entry to Yugoslavia for the Christmas–New Year holiday of 1970–1, most declared an intention to return home permanently in the not too distant future, 47·9 per cent within the next two years, 13·8 per cent as soon as they could get a job. Only 9·6 per cent gave answers which suggested they were unlikely to return in the short or medium term.[59] But there are a number of reasons for treating these findings with reservation, quite apart from the fact that the sample was biased towards those with family connections in Yugoslavia. Earlier surveys of this type had produced wildly conflicting results. An inquiry carried out by the Yugoslavs in 1966 had elicited replies from 87 per cent of respondents that they intended to return, but an inquiry organised by a Swedish team at Malmö showed that only 13 per cent of their sample of 372 Yugoslav workers expected to return for sure, 47 per cent were undecided and 40 per cent said they would stay in Sweden. Z. Komarica interprets this divergence as arising from the attempt of the migrant workers to give answers pleasing to their questioners (knowing that the Swedes, unlike the Yugoslav authorities, favoured permanent settlement).[60] It also calls into question the strength of conviction underlying this expression of intent. Perhaps because of this, the principal instigator of the 1970–1 survey, Professor Baučić, seems to have entertained doubts as to the interpretative value of his findings, because he observed subsequently, if a trifle ambiguously, that migrants hesitated to cut themselves off from

their familiar surroundings for a long time and expressed the conviction that they would soon return home' – in so doing contributing
to 'the myth of the provisional character of the migration'.[61]

I should also contend that his interpretative difficulty arose primarily because asking people about intentions in respect of decisions
they are under no pressure to take is a methodologically questionable
procedure. The ambiguities which can arise from such a line of
questioning are well illustrated by the following dialogue between
a journalist and an emigrant departing for Australia:[62]

Q. Do you intend to return?

A. One day, but after many years. This is a long journey
and one should stick things out. I firmly believe in that.
Otherwise I should not have decided to leave home.

Q. Many before you have said the same, but have not returned
once they have set up home either abroad or in our cities. . . .

A. Life in the countryside, especially in inland Dalmatia, is
really hard. Perhaps the thought of returning from a satisfactory life and decent pay repels them. . . .

Q. What will you work at in Australia?

A. . . . I'll get a job in a factory as an unskilled worker. And
after that, I'll see; perhaps I'll buy some land and raise
cattle.

Thus, the follow-up to the answer expressing an intention to return
suggests, if anything, the reverse. One may wonder how many
answers by the respondents to the 1970–1 survey would have similarly been modified by further probing.

The most telling weakness of the exercise of seeking return intentions in abstract terms was also provided by the Baučić team
in the form of an experiment conducted as part of the 1970–1
survey. A total of 12,396 jobs were earmarked by the labour
exchanges to attract the return of workers to Croatia, and the
scheme was given media publicity. But only 134 of the vacancies
were filled. Since working abroad, emigrant notions of what constituted an acceptable wage had roughly doubled. So, to secure
the return of the emigrant, it now seemed that it was not enough
to solve the domestic unemployment problem: the gap between
Croatian and West German wage levels (then averaging $83·50
and $220 a month, respectively) had substantially to be closed.[63]

Like Yugoslavia, Bulgaria was also plagued by a growing problem of 'latent' unemployment in the 1950s. There the social war against the peasants was far more protracted and ruthless than in Yugoslavia, and caused a correspondingly massive *Landflucht* which neither industry nor the sketchy urban infrastructure could accommodate. The problem was eventually ameliorated by revitalisation of the private plots and by narrowing wage differentials between the collective farms and the factories,[64] but, as a palliative, labour was also exported. In 1957 Bulgarian labour was being sent to Czechoslovakia on farm and building work, and a few years later the practice began of sending workers to the Soviet Union. By the early 1970s, 12,000 Bulgarians were reported to be on forestry work in the far north of Russia and on construction.[65] But, as Bulgaria never risked a Yugoslav-style economic reform, covert unemployment was never shaken out, and continued to be paid for by low consumer incomes.

One reason which could not easily have been advanced in Yugoslavia for designating the emigration as purely temporary was that the migrants were peasants topping up the incomes from their farms, though in theory this is what they should have been. Before the economic reform they were mainly peasants, and according to the expectations of the reformers it was this sort of labour which would go abroad during the transitional years, because of the slowdown in recruiting of the lowly skilled. The already employed were supposed only exceptionally to lose their jobs, and the emigration of skilled labour was discriminated against, as it was considered to be in short supply. However, the peasants who blazed the emigrant trail were soon submerged numerically by an exodus of urban dwellers, often skilled. Among the *Gastarbeiter* migrations of the 1960s, the Yugoslav contingent was unusually well qualified. Of those sent abroad through the labour exchanges (whose skill level was below the average of the emigration as a whole), the proportion of pure peasants fell between 1964 and 1968 from 26 to 9 per cent, and that of skilled and non-manual emigrants rose from 6 to 28 per cent.[66] Also in 1968, 59 per cent of Yugoslav workers in West Germany were skilled or non-manual, compared with 15 per cent of those from Italy, 10 per cent of those from Greece and 18 per cent of those from Spain, all countries which had a higher per capita gross national product than Yugoslavia.[67]

The reasons for this have not yet been analysed convincingly. The explanation that income distribution was too egalitarian to hold the skilled worker is rendered suspect by frequent complaints that skilled workers were taking relatively low-grade work abroad. And although the majority of skilled emigrants probably left their work organisations of their own volition, it is nevertheless likely that many were also caught up in a wave of redundancies which convulsed Yugoslav industrial employment during the reform period. 19·6 per cent of the migrants from Croatia working abroad in 1970–1 (a number equal to 4·9 per cent of the employed labour force in 1968) had earlier been in employment in Yugoslavia but were unemployed at the time of their departure, and therefore had presumably lost their jobs. Conversely, new entrants to the labour market, about two-thirds of whom were farming peasants, who were supposed to make up the greater part of the emigration, amounted to only 22·8 per cent of the total.[68] This is not really surprising, as the peasantry stood to gain rather than lose from the economic reforms.

It was generally conceded that skilled workers and urban dwellers would have a lower propensity to return than unskilled workers and peasants, the reason usually given being the greater ease which the skilled–urban group enjoyed in adapting to and settling within the host community in a more advanced country, and the intense acculturation stress likely to be felt by the unskilled and peasants. But the relative failure to return of the urban and the skilled also reflected a probably weaker original motivation to return – first because so many departed because of acute frustrations in making progress within the system, and secondly because they had no farm ties of the sort which still motivated peasants to return to their land. So, other things being equal, there were grounds for thinking it possible that the 1960s emigration would even tend to be longer-term in character than its transoceanic predecessor. Moreover, the true demographic and social impact of emigration is also affected by the behaviour of the second generation and of family members brought over in their childhood, and it is for the hearts and minds of the emigrants' children abroad that the Yugoslav authorities wage their most energetic campaigns.[69]

Allied to this concern was a growing worry about youth emigration. The tendency observed before 1914 for the emigration to become increasingly youthful, and for the younger emigrants' hedonistic ethic and lack of commitment to the old country to replace the drudge philosophy of the older emigrants, still had force. V. Katunarić showed that the proportion of 'temporary' migrants under thirty had been rising steadily between 1968 and 1973, so that by 1973 77 per cent of those in Germany were under thirty. Among these, push structures were not of such importance in promoting emigration as among the older migrant workers. Indeed, once emigration had laid hold of a given area, then, long after its original cause had been alleviated, success in emigration became the locally used yardstick against which the performance of young people was measured. This caused them to turn their backs on domestic channels for advancement.[70] There were strident complaints that younger workers were going straight abroad from school without bothering to seek work in Yugoslavia.[71] Especially in peasant circles, emigration became a means for self-expression by young people who sought emancipation from patriarchal environments, and who were affected by 'the devalorisation of rural work, life and culture' which the régime has done so much to promote.[72] What was being observed was, surely, roughly the equivalent of the sense of 'adventure' noted by Govorchin, a sentiment which was unlikely to coincide with any strong commitment to return.

From the end of the 1960s, efforts were made to check youth and skilled-worker emigration, and, as there was still heavy unemployment, to spread foreign employment more evenly and to promote it in the least industrialised regions, for the emigration of peasants was officially conceded to be no great loss.[73] The labour exchanges were forbidden to arrange work abroad for those already in employment, or for those with skills in short supply, though there was little to prevent them from making their own arrangements. The result was a rapid increase in the outflow from rich but unindustrialised farming areas. This policy appears to have raised the participation rate of the less skilled and to have promoted the appearance of a new trend in the emigration of unaccompanied peasant women, who left their husbands to manage the farms. These tendencies probably improved return rates, but not sufficiently to alleviate disquiet. By 1972 sufficient evidence had accumulated for the claim to be made by M. Morokvašić that 'the expectation of return is an illusion'.[74]

The conclusion intended to be drawn from this was that something needed to be done about it: the tone of the literature became very hostile to emigration, though nothing overtly illiberal was planned, as in 1974 emigration was established as a constitutional right. Emphasis was given to informal methods of dissuasion: 'If somebody has work here', said Tito in 1972, 'and nevertheless goes abroad, he should have to explain why he is going in front of the League of Communists, and in front of his nation, his state . . . .' The comrades, 'especially you young ones', were admonished 'to enlighten the people . . . [as to] what sort of harm they can bring to our country'.[75] A new emigration law was promised in February 1973, and in a toned-down form was placed on the statute book in October. A plan was to be imposed on external migration, and, despite their longstanding reputation for incompetence, the labour exchanges were given a monopoly of recruiting with the task of diverting applicants for jobs abroad into jobs in Yugoslavia.[76] So, although they feared the nightmare of a mass return of unemployed former *Gastarbeiter*, the authorities were not wholly displeased when the oil crisis and unemployment in western Europe induced or compelled many to return, and when barriers were raised against the admission of new workers in the countries of immigration.

The extent to which measures taken to uphold the supposedly temporary nature of the migration in both Yugoslavia and in the immigration countries will fulfil the desire of the Yugoslav authorities for their *Gastarbeiter* emigration both to cease and to be reversed are still for the future to reveal. But, even in the two difficult years of 1974 and 1975, net repatriation from Germany was only 85,000 on a stock of half a million, and since then the net repatriation rate has sharply diminished.[77] And, taking account of the second generation, it is likely that the brave words of Chancellor Schmidt in February 1975, that 'we are not going to be burdened in the future with a nationality problem',[78] may prove wishful thinking.

The Bulgarians have also learned that it is not enough to designate skilled-labour emigration as temporary, under the title of training schemes and suchlike. Such workers who went to East Germany, Czechoslovakia and Poland mostly failed to return.[79]

III

Who came home? It is commonly conceded that, among migrants from countries whose emigration was characteristically of a permanent type, return migration was associated with relative failure, but that the same cannot be said of 'temporary' worker migrations, because return was part of the original intention. But from the evidence we have already discussed it would seem most likely that the quality of the return flow, in the cases of both the 'new' and the newest emigrations from Yugoslavia, was likely to be inferior to that of the outward flow. So, if the home community continued to judge the success of its emigrants in terms of the performance of the returning group, it was likely to receive an unrealistically pessimistic view of how life in emigration affected its emigrants – a view that was almost guaranteed to stimulate strong anti-emigration sentiment.

First, as far fewer returned than went out, and as the home community had difficulty in accepting that permanent settlement abroad was a legitimate desire for a successful emigrant, it was apt to treat failure to return as signifying death or destruction. (Migrant mortality rates were sufficiently high to foster this belief, provided one forgot the low life-expectation of the home community.) In 1912 a deputy in the Serbian *Skupština* (assembly) spoke of the Macedonian *pečalbari* in the following terms: 'Fifty of them depart and about thirty to thirty-five of them come back . . . and fifteen of them remain out there and perish. . . . About those who remained away and perished in the mines, nobody asks questions.'[80] The press too commonly equated non-return with death and ruination abroad – so as to discourage emigration, it is true, but also because the press not only formed, but also reflected, popular belief. Bereavement is the central theme of the cycles of folk poetry which built up round emigration, and 'cursèd America'. Take the following, from Macedonia, in which the prospective emigrant asks his bride what she would like him to buy her with the money he will earn:

> What should you buy me?
> Ah, the first thing, my darling,
> Is a black shawl,
> So that first I may wear black, my love,
> To mourn you.[81]

As if to confirm the unwholesomeness of conditions in emigration, a high percentage of returners came home in poor physical shape.

They included the industrial-injury cases, hastening home to conserve their compensation money, and the sick and enfeebled to whom the homeland still provided a refuge. One-fifth of the passengers on an American immigrant ship returning with a cargo of east European returners were sick. An American writer described this with satisfaction as the 'self-elimination of the weak'.[82] To the home community, such people were seen as having been burned out by their hardships abroad. The average age of the returners was also relatively high, because of the greater return propensity of the older migrant, and because many waited to draw their pensions before going home.

It also seemed as if the sacrifice of youth and health had been in vain, for the average emigrant did not return much better off than he departed, for he had not allowed himself enough time abroad. The most careful contemporary calculation showed that, even under optimal conditions, an emigrant needed to work in the United States for more than the three years which was the normal target period.[83] Many stayed only two, and netted about $82 over their expenses, which was probably less than their opportunity cost at home.[84] And even these could have been in a minority. We have no comparable figures for the Yugoslav experience, but a document from neighbouring Hungary shows that of a group of 1000 emigrants returning from America to Hungary in December 1907, 719 had spent less than two years in America, 368 had spent less than a year, and only 115 had spent more than the three needed to make it worthwhile.[85] American statistics show that 92 per cent of Bulgar, Serb and Montenegrin re-emigrants departed after less than five years of residence.[86] Only a small minority could have returned substantially enriched. F. Kraljic from her discussions with elderly returners broadly confirms this point, and emphasises that their resources were still further eroded by the practice of their families at home of living beyond their means.[87]

Current research in Yugoslavia into the problems of the returning emigrant reveals strong similarities. As Komarica, writing of the *Gastarbeiter* migration, gloomily remarks, 'The historical experience of all migrations teaches us that those who have achieved exceptional success do not return to the homeland, rather the majority of those who have not realised their expectations.'[88] This is confirmed by Baučić, who noted that those who were first to return were the less capable, those who found it difficult to adapt to conditions abroad, those who had been 'worn out' or injured at work, and those who had family problems at home. Among the returners the more able had by no means accepted that their sojourn at home was permanent, and they frequently returned abroad. Most telling of all, 'Fewest are the returners who will not go to work abroad any more because they have achieved the aims for which they took employment abroad.' It was noted, moreover, that those who left Yugoslav firms for jobs abroad were better skilled than those who joined these firms after re-entering the country.[89]

So the newest immigration repeated the experience of its predecessor in respect of its returners. And this was a predictable reflection of the other similarities between the two movements. Repatriates who were still fit for work tended to return home poor and those who came back enriched were usually past working. The myth was created that strong healthy youths went out, but came back as spent and sickly old men,[90] and that, consequently, emigration was in nobody's interest, not even that of the emigrant.

Notes

1 G. Prpic, *The Croatian Immigrants in America* (New York, 1971) pp. 89–90.

2 Based on an estimate in I. Mladineo, *Narodni adresar Hrvata-Slovenaca-Srba* (New York, 1937) p. ix, of slightly over 900,000 'Yugoslavs', to which we add an estimated 95,000 Bulgars, all but 10,000 of whom (see note 5) came from outside Yugoslavia. On the Bulgars see *25-godišen jubileen almanah na v-kv 'Naroden glas' i B'lgarite v Amerika* (Granite City, Ill., 1933) pp. 130–1.

3 According to the same Bulgarian source (p. 132) only 30 per cent of the Bulgars came from Bulgaria proper.

4 O. M. Jeremić, *O problemu emigracije i imigracije* . . . (Belgrade, 1928) p. 14.

5 Jelenko Petrović, *Pečalbari narocito iz okoline Pirota* (Belgrade, 1920) p. 7.

6 I. Čizmić, 'O iseljavanju iz Hrvatske u razdoblju 1880–1914', *Istoriski zbornik*, XXVII–XXVIII (1974–5) 31.

7 Calculated from data in *International Migrations*, vol. I, ed. W. F. Willcox, compiled I. Ferenczi (New York, 1929), United States tables 13 and 19.

8 Arrigo Nikolić, *O našim iseljivanju* (Zadar, 1909) pp. 7–8.

9 N. Bjelovučić, 'Poluostrvo Rat (Pelješac)', *Naselja i poreklo stanovništva*, XI (Belgrade, 1922) 208; B. Purić, *Naši iseljenici* (Belgrade, 1929) p. 73.

10 B. Colakovic, *Yugoslav Migrations to America* (San Francisco, 1973) p. 42.

11 On the south-east Serbian *pečalbari* see M. Palairet, 'The Influence of Commerce on the Changing Structure of Serbia's Peasant Economy, 1860–1912' (unpublished Ph.D. thesis, Edinburgh University, 1976).

12 Duško H. Konstantinov, *Pečalbarstvo* (Bitola, 1964) p. 90.

13 The regional pattern of origin of these emigrants is deduced from information

as to birthplace provided in advertisements inserted by 158 merchants born in Bulgaria in *25-godišen jubileen almanah* . . .

14 I. Gešov, 'Našiti gradinarski družestva', *Periodičesko spisanie*, no. 27 (1893) 339.

15 C. Ginčev, 'Nekolko dumi ot istorijata na našeto gradinarstvo . . .', *Trud* (T'rnovo) I, nos. 18–19 (1887) 1192; N. Georgiev, *B'lgari v južna Amerika* (Sofia, 1965) pp. 24–6 and 29–30.

16 Stjepan Pavičić, *Seobe i naselja u Lici* (Zagreb, 1962) p. 274.

17 See example of Krmpote *općina*, in R. Pavelić, *Bunjevci* (Zagreb, 1973) pp. 190, 193 and 197.

18 C. Kostić, *Seljaci industriski radnici* (Belgrade, 1955).

19 Petar Marković, *Migracije i promene agrarne strukture* (Zagreb, 1974) p. 55.

20 P. Kvakan, 'Novi vidici za iseljeništvo . . .', *Novi iseljenik*, nos 9–11, (1928) p. 15, col. 4.

21 *Iseljeničke vijesti*, IV–V (1923) 61.

22 G. A. Abbott, 'The Bulgarians of Chicago', *Charities and the Commons*, no. 30 (9 Jan 1909) 654 and 657.

23 *Emigration Conditions in Europe*, Reports of the Immigration Commission, IV: 61st Congress, 3rd session, vol. XII, (Washington, DC, 1911) pp. 55 and 363; *Statistički godisnjak kr Srbije* 1903 (Belgrade) p. 323.

24 D. Simonović, *Transfer jugoslovenskih seljaka u radnike* (Belgrade, 1971) p. 107.

25 V. Rožić, 'Prigorje. Narodni život i običaji', *Zbornik za narodni život i običaje južnih Slavena*, XII (1907) 266–7.

26 I. Lj. Lupis, *O iseljivanju našega naroda i o Americi* (Zadar, 1910) p. 4.

27 G. G. Govorchin, *Americans from Yugoslavia* (Gainesville, Fla, 1961) p. 22.

28 'Emigracija', *Občinar* XVIII, no. 14 (1900) 105.

29 A. Tresić-Pavičić, *Preko Atlantika do Pacifika* (Zagreb, 1907) pp. 85–7.

30 Čeda Pavić, *Srbi i Srpske organizacije u Americi* (Chicago, 1911) p. 9.

31 L. S. Kosier, *Srbi Hrvati i Slovenci u Americi* (Belgrade, 1926) p. 197.

32 'Pečalbari', *Carigradski glasnik*, XI, no. 47 (1905) I, col. 2.

33 M. M. Savić, *Naša industrija zanati trgovina i poljoprivreda*, XI (1933) 442–3.

34 Kvakan, loc. cit. (see note 20).

35 Dj. Pejović, *Iseljavanja Crnogoraca u XIX vijeku* (Titograd, 1962) pp. 187, 350, 363–4, 366 and 393.

36 'Naše Amerikanke', *Hrvatski narod*, 1906, no. 15, p. 37.

37 'Pečalbari', loc. cit. (see note 32).

38 Purić, *Naši iseljenici*, p. 76.

39 B. Dj. Deželić, *Naša emigracija u Njemačkoj* (Zagreb, 1931) pp. 7–8.

40 V. Holijevac, *Hrvati izvan domovine* (Zagreb, 1967) p. 60.

41 L. Trnjegorski, *Jugoslovenske manjine u inostranstvu* (Belgrade, 1938) p. 8.

42 I. Baučić, 'Radnici u Francuskoj u popisu stanovništva Jugoslavije 1971 godine', in *Iz Jugoslavije na rad u Francusku*, ed. M. Friganović (Zagreb, 1972) pp. 101–2.

43 M. Macura, *Stanovništvo i radna snaga kao činioci privrednog razvoja Jugoslavije* (Belgrade, 1958) pp. 75–6 and 319–22.

44 M. Barjaktarevič, 'Lokalne migracije u pravcu Titova Užica . . .', *Užički zbornik*, I (1972) 251.

45 Markovic, *Migracije i promene agrarne strukture*, p. 65.

46 N. Šipovac, 'Migracije i zapošljavanje – problema našeg vremena', *Glasnik privredne komore Bosne i Hercegovine*, no. 4 (1966) p. 254.

47 See *inter alia* Ž. Tanić, 'Emigraciona žarišta u Bosni i Hercegovini', *Pregled*, no. 6 (1973) pp. 692–4.

48 K. Kozina, 'Neki aspekti suvremene ekonomske emigracije iz SR Hrvatske', *Naše Teme*, no. 6 (1964) p. 872.

64 THE SEARCH FOR WEALTH AND STABILITY

49 *Službeni list SFRJ*, XIX, no. 42 (23 Oct 1963).

50 Z. Komarica, *Jugoslavija u suvremenim Europskim migracijama* (Zagreb, 1970) p. 12; Kozina, loc. cit. (see note 48) 872–3; R. Knežević, 'Neki problemi Jugoslovenskih radnika zaposlenih u SR Nemačkoj', *Sociologija*, XV, no. 2 (1973) 294.

51 'Stručno usavršanje ugostiteljskih radnika u inozemstvu', *Privredni vjesnik*, X, 951 (15 June 1963) iv.

52 I. Baučić, *The effects of Emigration from Yugoslavia and the Problems of Returning Immigrant Workers* (The Hague, 1972), tabulates (p. 3) estimates of this stock between 1954 and 1971.

53 Dj. Julius, 'Naši u Njemačkoj. Nemojte nas vredjati', *Politika*, (7 Nov. 1971) p. 3; Komarica, *Jugoslavija u suvremenim Europskim migracijama*, p. 103.

54 I. Baučić, *Porijeklo i struktura radnika iz Jugoslavije u SR Njemačkoj* (Zagreb, 1970) p. 64.

55 Šipovac, loc. cit (see note 46) 257.

56 E. G. Drettakis, *Yugoslav Migration to and from West Germany, 1962–1973. An Econometrics Analysis* (Zagreb, 1975).

57 *Statistisches Jahrbuch für die Bundesrepublik Deutschland, 1972* (Bonn) p. 54.

58 *Statistički bilten*, no. 679 (August, 1971).

59 I. Baučiž and Ž. Maravić, *Vraćanje i zapošljavanje vanjskih migranata iz SR Hrvatske* (Zagreb, 1971) p. 96.

60 Komarica, *Jugoslavija u suvremenim Europskim migracijama*, pp. 68 and 100.

61 I. Baučić, 'Migration temporaire ou définitive: le dilemme des migrants et les politiques de migration', *Studi Emigrazione* (Mar 1974) p. 123.

62 P. Zlatar, 'Put bez povratka', *VUS* (5 Dec 1973) p. 15.

63 Baučić, *Effects of Emigration*, pp. 20 and 40.

64 J. Bojčev, *Preodoljavane na različijata meždu grada i seloto v NRB* (Sofia, 1964) pp. 76–84.

65 V. Grečić, *Savremene migracije radne snage u Evropi* (Belgrade, 1975) p. 58; *East Europe*, X, no. 10 (1961) 8; W. R. Böhning, 'Migration of Workers as an Element in Employment Policy', *New Community*, III, nos 1–2 (1974) 19.

66 M. Sabitović, 'Neki aspekti spoljne migracije', *Pregled* (1970) nos 7–8, p. 140.

67 Grečić, *Savremene migracije radne snage*, pp. 108 and 151.

68 Tables in Baučić and Maravić, *Vraćanje i zapošljavanje vanjskih migranata* (pp. 78 and 85) show that 77 per cent had held employment in Yugoslavia but only 57·4 per cent had held employment immediately prior to leaving.

69 S. Cvetić, *Iseljeništvo kao društvena pojava i njegov značaj za našu zemlju* (Belgrade, 1975) esp. p. 31.

70 V. Katunarić, 'Dobna struktura, anomija, i distanca u svjetlu vanjskih migracija iz Jugoslavije', paper presented to the Eighth Scientific Conference of Sociologists of Yugoslavia, Opatija (13–4 Feb 1975 (mimeo.)) pp. 1–11.

71 For example, M. Mujačić, 'Trbuhom za auspuhom,' *Borba* (19 Mar 1972) p. 11, col. 1.

72 Ž. Tanić, 'Sociološko objašnjenje radnih emigracija', *Sociologija*, XV, no. 2 (1973) 167 and 177–8.

73 B. Meholjić, *Fenomen naše savremene ekonomske emigracije* (Belgrade, 1974) p. 124.

74 M. Morokvašić, 'Des migrants "temporaires": les yougoslaves', *Sociologie du travail*, XIV, no. 3 (1972) 260.

75 *Treća konferencija saveza komunista Jugoslavije* (Belgrade, 1972) p. 11.

76 *Yugoslav Survey*, XIV, no. 2 (1973) 39–42; *Službeni list SFRJ*, XXIX, no. 33 (14 June 1973).

77 *Statistisches Jahrbuch für die BRD, 1976* (Bonn) pp. 78–9, and *1977* (Bonn) pp. 79–80.

78 R. Lohrmann, 'European Migration – Recent Developments and Future Prospects', *International Migration*, XIV, no. 3 (1976) 233.

79 Meholjić, *Fenomen*, p. 66; Grečić, *Savremene migracije radne snage*, pp. 58–9.

80 Serbia. Narodna skupština XIII redovni sastanak 30, v. 1912, *Stenografski zapisnici*, p. 11, col. 1.

81 Konstantinov, *Pečalbarstvo*, p. 65.

82 Peter Roberts, *The New Immigration* (New York, 1922; repr. 1970) p. 17.

83 H. Sirovatka, *Kako je u Americi i komu se isplati onamo putovati* (Zagreb, 1907) pp. 18–19.

84 *Srbobran* (New York), VI, no. 243 (1914) p. 1.

85 I. Rácz, 'Parasztok elvándorlása a faluból', in *A parasztság Magyarországon a kapitalizmus korában 1848–1914*, vol. II (Budapest, 1972) p. 475.

86 *Emigration Conditions in Europe*, p. 46.

87 F. C. Kraljic, 'Croatian Migration to and from the United States between 1900 and 1914' (unpublished New York University Ph.D. thesis, 1975) pp. 144–9 and 165–6.

88 Komarica, *Jugoslavija u suvremenim europskim migracijama*, p. 67.

89 I. Baučić, 'Neka suvremena obležja i problemi vanjskih migracija jugoslavenskih radnika', *Sociologija*. XV, no. 2 (1973) 212–13.

90 L. Stojović, 'Kako se ide u pečalbu. Odlaze zdravi snažni mladići a vraćaju se iznureni i bolesni starci', *Politika*, XXXV, no. 10931 (1938) 13.

Part II
Britain

4 Did It Fall or Was It Pushed? The Foleys and the End of the Charcoal Iron Industry in the Eighteenth Century

G. HAMMERSLEY

It is given to few undergraduates, however well matured, even in a past so distant as to be well nigh historical, plausibly and convincingly to revise received historical doctrine; Professor Flinn's career began thus with a perceptive discussion of some of the problems of the British iron industry in the sixteenth century.[1] Since then he has done much to release the historiography of that industry from the stultifying embrace of monocausal explanation,[2] and thus legitimised attempts to examine it once again in the round. Until some of this work had been done, it had remained exceedingly difficult to explain convincingly how the charcoal iron industry in Britain managed to survive much beyond the middle of the seventeenth century. Now that these perspectives have lengthened, it seems to have become almost as difficult to provide a reasonably convincing explanation for its demise. Thus it has long been known that a number of charcoal blast furnaces survived, even in Britain, into the nineteenth century, and a few into the twentieth, so that there was no absolute and final physical reason for the end of the industry.[3] Indeed, less than a generation separates the end of the last charcoal blast furnace in Britain and the setting up of a highly sophisticated operation in Australia, which produced very large amounts of charcoal iron during the Second World War, because charcoal happened to be the only economically available fuel.[4] There is no obvious technical reason which inhibits the application of further technical improvement to charcoal-smelting beyond the stage reached in the early eighteenth century: why then did the industry as a whole disappear so rapidly?

At first sight it remains difficult to reject the obvious and simple answer to the conundrum: coal was cheaper than charcoal and, so long as it could be used to smelt and refine iron satisfactorily, it was bound either to undercut charcoal iron and take over its markets, or to attract investors to a vastly more profitable industry. But the smelting and refining of iron is not simply a matter of producing the right temperature, even when coal has been freed from sulphur and other impurities by coking: charcoal is far more reactive than coal or coke, so that smaller quantities of the dearer fuel could for some time work more cheaply than the use of the cheaper fuel in larger amounts, quite apart from the higher silicon content of coke-smelted iron, which increased the expense of refining it. Therefore there now prevails fairly general agreement that charcoal iron continued to be produced more cheaply than coke iron during the first half of the eighteenth century; the most recent attempt to discuss the rise of the coke iron industry argues strongly in support of this view.[5] But Professor Hyde also concludes that the change from charcoal to coke can be explained sufficiently by 'cost considerations alone', and supports this by data showing a rise in costs at charcoal furnaces and a fall in costs at coke furnaces.[6] The data are used in a cautious and sophisticated manner to show that anyone interested in the iron industry after the 1750s was more likely to turn to coke as fuel, because this ensured a much higher profit – but the explanation offered is once again monocausal. It is based upon a small sample of works, especially for the charcoal iron industry; two of the furnaces included in that sample, moreover, managed to survive their relative disadvantage for 90 and 140 years respectively, so the handicap must not be exaggerated.[7] The difficulty is partly that detailed accounts of the operation of either charcoal or coke ironworks during the eighteenth century are not easily found, while prices of either charcoal or coke clearly differed regionally, as did the cost of labour: in this case the simple and obvious conclusion may therefore fail to tell the whole story. Conceivably a closer examination of a few surviving detailed accounts for the charcoal industry may help to elucidate some of its more general weaknesses, without depending wholly upon unexplained changes in relative prices.

The earlier development of the indirect process of ironmaking in and near the Forest of Dean can be easily summarised. It arrived in Dean itself during the 1590s;[8] by 1612 at least four blast furnaces and four fining forges had been set up, adjacent to the royal forest.[9] Without unseemly haste, the Crown had decided to follow other great landowners and to obtain an income from its woods, and this set off competition between a number of enterprising men for the concession it was offering in the royal forest itself.[10] Within a generation twelve furnaces and at least thirteen substantial forges were at work in Dean and in the royal forest, within the approximate triangle formed by the Severn, Wye and a line from Gloucester to Ross-on-Wye; a further five furnaces and four forges closely adjacent to this area also relied to some extent on its ore, cinders and fuel. The intensity of exploitation of so small an area was almost unprecedented for the time and caused some justifiable misgivings regarding its effects upon the woods of Dean. This explosive expansion ended with the civil wars; works changed hands frequently, partly as a result of Parliamentary politics, and production faltered. The Protectorate, pressed by necessity and untrammelled by traditional fears and procedures, found a way to exploit the resources of the State forest rationally: it appointed a trustworthy and competent local man to set up a new ironworks in the forest, placed him under the Admiralty committee, and permitted him to link the smelting and fining of iron with the production of timber – first for the naval yards and then for the local construction of a man-of-war. Between the end of 1653 and the beginning of 1660 a large and efficient furnace and forge produced a reasonable profit; the arrangement proved that a large area of woodland could be used sensibly and productively for timber and industrial fuel while at the same time improving its yield and condition. The accounts of the ironworks and associated enterprises were conscientiously kept and carefully checked; they can be utilised for the construction of a rough-and-ready balance sheet.[11] After the Restoration, as might be expected, the whole undertaking was rapidly abandoned by the Crown, which suffered in equal measure from unsatisfied creditors and traditional attitudes.

The last remnants of the Crown concession were abandoned in 1674,[12] but numerous works just outside the royal forest continued to draw much of their best ore and cinders as well as some of their fuel from it. For the Dean region this was the age of the Foleys; Thomas Foley, of the second generation in the line of Foley ironmasters, not only took over Tintern and Whitebrook wireworks, which had been an important customer for Dean iron, but also, during the Commonwealth and Protectorate, two furnaces adjacent to the forest.[13] By the 1670s the Foleys had managed to gather in many of the ironworks in the region and in Dean, although here some independent owners continued to operate alongside them.[14] By the 1680s at least seven furnaces and seven forges operated in Dean itself, supplemented by six furnaces and seven forges in its immediate environment; nine of the furnaces and eleven of the forges were associated with the Foleys at some time during the last thirty years of the seventeenth century.[15] The number of works in Dean itself had clearly declined, but the Foleys with their network of partnerships, especially after 1691, probably maintained a more regular level of production than before: they favoured stable and planned operation rather than wildcat expansion.[16] One of the interesting aspects of the Foley predominance was the manner of its achievement: local families who in the first half of the seventeenth century had been active in the industry and had tried to enlarge their hold over it to achieve some form of dominance, now either let their works to the Foleys (as did the Halls of Highmeadow[17]) or showed only marginal interest in them, viewing them as a mere adjunct to estate management (as did the Winters of Lydney[18]). No doubt the trade had become more regular, and as a result profits may have declined from the almost spectacular to the merely satisfactory; the owners of large tracts of woodland could now balance this prospect against the secure and risk-free income from the sale of fuel and ores to a lessee or neighbouring works. This also freed them from the necessity of finding outside supplies whenever their own ran short, and may, in some respects, have represented a better long-term use of their resources; none of them held as much woodland as did the Crown in the Forest of Dean. But the enthusiasm of landowning families for their iron-

works may have declined partly as the result of changes in the
generations: the widowed Lady Winter or the surviving daughter
Maria Benedicta Hall may not have wished to manage ironworks,
as Mrs Boevey of Flaxley clearly did.[19]

The Foleys, as has been known to historians of the iron industry
for some time, left behind sets of accounts which cover, in differing
intensity and with some gaps, the period from the 1660s to about
1750.[20] Their volume and diversity have continued to set some
problems for both historians and archivists; the papers have been
extracted rather than used coherently and items once seen cannot
always be readily traced again. The accounts which have been
most widely used lie between the 1660s and the 1720s; most of
these appear to be mere partnership accounts, with some summaries
of the activities of ironworks, rather than more detailed working
accounts of such works or groups of works. The summaries were
presumably based upon such individual detailed accounts, which,
when they had been completed, were either discarded more easily
than the ledgers or left with the works managers. The main body
of accounts, as Professor Johnson registered long ago, shows a
lacuna between about 1717 and 1725; their changed form after
1725 made them less useful for his purposes.[21] But at least from
the early 1730s the working accounts of the ironworks remaining
from the 'Forest Works' of the former Foley partnerships have survived;
they were presented first to Thomas Foley of Stoke Edith and
then to his son by their principal manager.[22] For the moment,
however, the missing accounts are the more interesting, because
their disappearance can be made to illuminate Thomas Foley's
attitude to his business affairs. In 1717 Richard Knight of Bringe-
wood resigned from a partnership between Knight, Phillip Foley,
Thomas Foley, William Rea, John Wheeler and Obadiah Lane,
which had been renewed as recently as 1707.[23] Towards the end
of 1724 Thomas Foley and William Rea, the managing partner
of the forest works, quarrelled and parted company;[24] in 1728
Mrs Lane, presumably Obadiah's widow, resigned and ended the
partnership.[25] These changes resulted in a series of suits and counter-
suits in the Court of Exchequer, where Knight claimed money
yet due on his share, while Foley sued Rea over some payment
for wood bought in the early 1720s, and Warine Falkner or Falkiner
and others for alleged malpractices and debts while managing
the works after Rea between 1625 and 1628.[26] Copies of the partner-

ship accounts from 1716 to 1725 were part of the evidence used; the originals had been removed from the run of Foley accounts to be copied in a house in Monmouth during September and October 1728, and presumably had not been replaced with the others.[27]

The rights and wrongs of these cases matter little for the present purpose: whatever they were, they do not show up Thomas Foley's acumen as a businessman in a favourable light. Paul Foley, his father, had been a notable politician, and he himself was an auditor of the imprest.[28] Richard Knight was a highly successful ironmaster who would presumably have remained in a successful partnership, and he was not notoriously dishonest.[29] Rea too was an ironmaster of some prominence, against whom nothing seriously to his disadvantage has yet come to light. Falkner, the second accused manager, was given very good verbal references both by Knight, who may have had an axe to grind, and by his successor, Pendrill.[30] Therefore it is at least possible that Foley may have been quarrelsome, opinionated and litigious, or at least ignorant of the practices normal in the running of ironworks; all of these would tend to make him a difficult partner and a vexatious employer. If Foley's suspicions were justified, it would still indicate that he had somehow allowed two successive managers to cheat him for eight years, showing either profound ignorance or complete lack of interest in the sordid details, or both. Anyhow, as a result of these disagreements, the Foleys of Stoke Edith, i.e. Thomas senior and his son, Thomas junior, were left in sole possession of the remaining Forest Works, and it is to these that the later accounts refer.

These accounts are the only set so far encountered to invite direct comparison with the accounts for the State ironworks between the end of 1653 and the beginning of 1660.[31] All were charge and discharge accounts, intended primarily to justify the expenditure of any cash received by the accounting official, but not to clarify the financial implications of every aspect of operations. On the whole they may be more reliable in identifying sources of cash income than in the destination of expenditure, much of which went in very small amounts to numerous individuals. They are not even totally conclusive for the income obtained: they sometimes register the whole agreed price as income, even if some of it is yet outstanding; at other times they show money yet owing without indicating what it may be owed for, or what part of the total due has already been paid. Similarly, produce either used in the works or delivered to order without cash payment is nowhere valued; major payments are sometimes made, especially to local landowners, without any indication of whether they were rents, repayment of money lent, or payments for materials delivered on longer-term contracts. Such lack of detail is taken to its extreme in the last of the three accounts for the State ironworks, which notes money paid 'for the use of the ffurnace and fforest' as almost £1370, which could cover a fair number of sins.[32] True to their kind, the Foley accounts here used register all the manager's cash expenditure in a separate section headed 'creditor'; that section always begins with a set of payments such as 'to Lord Gage's account' of £1370 10s 11d, without any further identification; they also include some more or less identifiable payments, and are grouped and added up separately, before being added into the total expenditure shown.[33] Nor do the Foley accounts even attempt to strike a balance of income against expenditure; in some of them the expenditure shown much exceeded the income from sales.

Some large assumptions have therefore had to be made when trying to analyse these and the State ironworks accounts, quite apart from their moderate honesty. On the whole it would seem improbable that any accountant would have omitted any expenditure he could remember and justify, although he might well add a little to balance the books. For the State ironworks an attempt has been made to break down undifferentiated general headings whenever more detailed indications in one of the other two accounts or the summary analysis of costs at the end of the final account seemed to make this possible.[34] In the Foley accounts the group of payments certified as on 'account' at the head of each set of 'creditor' entries has been taken as referring to settlements of debts outstanding from the previous account, and therefore disregarded in that year's reckoning, as the accounts do not show the payments made by customers to settle their own outstanding balances. Transfers of produce within the works, especially the sending of pig iron to the forges and the use of pig or bar iron for repairs and tools, have not been valued but have simply been treated as costs incurred without direct return. Only the Foley accounts for 1746–8, which are in any case incomplete, fail to show opening and closing stocks; the third and final Dean account also shows closing stocks, and all the closing stocks value produce and materials. Where necessary, values of closing stocks have been used to assess the value of opening stocks, and either average or stock values have been allotted to all produce going out of the works but not valued directly in the accounts. This was done partly to make the striking of a crude balance possible, but also to give some reasonable basis for comparison between the State ironworks accounts and those of the Foley works. The State ironworks not only sold commercially but also sent considerable consignments of castings and wrought iron to the naval yards or to the local shipyard, representing something like a quarter of the total value produced.

All this should make clear that the accounts as here presented (see Table 1) are to some extent an artificial construct, which must not be used for too precisely detailed an interpretation. Such caution should even be extended to the four reasonably reliable Foley accounts between 1732 and 1742: they did not employ their headings with any consistency, so that payments shown under 'freight' in one year may be subsumed into the costs of timber or hearthstones the next; expenditures for wood, cutting, cording, coaling and transport of fuel are meticulously itemised for Elmbridge furnace, but lumped together under 'cutting', 'cording', 'colliers' and 'carriers' for the other works; the quantities of raw materials received and used at each works, although shown, are not valued. Stock valuations were made separately for each works, and often appear quite arbitrary: at three furnaces, cinders were in 1734 valued at 5s, 6s and 8s 5d per dozen, although they did not normally buy different qualities or experience uniformly different transport costs for their ore and cinders.

Despite all such misgivings, the accounts permit at least some rough comparisons. In general they convey an impression of surprising similarity and stability: the five Foley accounts seem to indicate variations about norms rather than an identifiable trend, over nearly twenty years; without much difficulty that impression could be stretched to take in the State ironworks ninety years earlier. The norm for finers and hammermen, for instance, had clearly remained at about £1 per ton of bar iron, varied mainly by the mixture of products, which contained special forgings for the State ironworks and some osmund iron for the Foley forges. Founders' pay varied between approximately 3s 9d and 4s 3d per ton depending largely on the amount of special castings required

TABLE 1 Income and expenditure at some Dean ironworks: State
Ironworks[35] and Foley Ironworks[36]

(a) *State Ironworks, 1653–60*

	Total output (1 furnace, 1 forge)		Output per annum	
	ton	cwt	ton	cwt
Pig	4,450	10	672	15
Bar	722	14	109	5

	Total			Per annum			Per ton	
	£	s	d	£	s	d	s	d
Expenditure								
Managers	1,200	0	0	181	8	0	–	
Founders	933	0	0	141	0	0	4	2¼
Finers and hammermen	860	6	8[39]	130	1	0	23	9¾
Clerical workers[37]	300	0	0[40]	45	7	0	–	
Sundries and general labour	3,090	19	6[41]	465	18	0	–	
Repairs, replacements, etc.	288	8	7½[42]	43	9	0	–	
Transport, general	–			–			–	
Wood, bought, cut and corded	8,065	15	6[43]	1,219	5	0	–	
Coaling, buying, transport	5,096	9	7	770	8	0	–	
(Fuel for smelting							40	8)
(fining							58	9)
Cinders and ore	1,998	5	3	302	1	0	8	11¾
Rents	–			–			–	
Total paid	21,833	5	1½	3,298	17	0		
Income (sales)								
Pig and castings	18,565	3	3	2,806	7	0	138	5
Bar, osmund and forgings	11,140	19	6	1,684	2	0	351	8½
Charcoal	924	15	0	139	16	0	–	
Wood, bark, etc. (deliveries)[38]	295	13	2	44	14	0	–	
Pig, etc.	8,412	0	0[44]	1,271	12	0	–	
Bar, etc.	898	13	0	135	17	0	–	
Total produce	40,237	3	11	6,082	8	0		

Continued

TABLE 1(a) *(Continued)*

	Total £	s	d		Per annum £	s	d	Per ton s	d
Net closing stock	3,996	3	0						
Adjusted costs	17,837	2	0						
Profit, on cost	22,400	0	0	= 126%[45]					

Materials per ton

Pig: ore, etc.	3·08 doz. bushels
fuel	2·25 loads
Bar: fuel	3·35 loads
pig	1·31 tons
From ore to bar:	
ore	4·04 doz. bushels
fuel	6·2 loads

(b) *Foley Ironworks, 1732–4*

	1732–3 (2 furnaces, 4 forges[46]) ton	cwt	1733–4 (2 furnaces, 4 forges[46]) ton	cwt
Pig	886	14	1,031	4
Bar	493	10	433	7

	Total £	s	d	Per ton s	d	Total £	s	d	Per ton s	d
Expenditure										
Managers	414	5	10	–		383	12	10	–	
Founders	169	15	0	3	10	192	16	3	3	8¾
Finers and hammermen	493	1	0	19	11¾	479	12	11½	22	1½
Clerical workers[37]	111	0	2½	–		93	1	0	–	
Sundries and general labour	229	6	7½	–		208	5	7	–	
Repairs, replacements, etc.	484	13	8	–		652	10	0½[47]	–	
Transport, general	197	7	1	–		110	9	6	–	

Table 1(b)   *(Continued)*

	1732–3 Total £	s	d	Per ton s	d	1733–4 Total £	s	d	Per ton s	d
Wood, bought, cut and corded	3,016	6	5½	–		1,391	13	4¾	–	
Coaling, buying, transport	1,700	2	2	–		2,006	6	4¼	–	
Fuel for smelting				from 60	2				from 38	11
				to 77	10				to 46	1
fining				from 81	7				from 51	5
				to 86	8				to 54	5
Cinders and ore	904	0	9	13	5	649	9	5	12	7¼
Rents	590	17	0			379	0	0[48]		
Total paid	8,310	15	9½			6,546	17	4		
Income (sales)										
Pig and castings	2,291	15	0	133	8	1,698	5	7	135	0
Bar, osmund and forgings	6,773	8	8	346	9	8,029	8	4	342	2
Charcoal	100	14	11½	–		12	6	0	–	
Wood, bark, etc. (deliveries)[38]	15	11	0	–		–			–	
Pig, etc.	35	1	8¼	–		8	9	3	–	
Bar, etc.	25	10	2¼	–		12	6	11	–	
Total produce	9,242	1	6			9,760	16	1		
Net closing stock	495	9	0			593	3	0		
Adjusted costs	7,815	7	0			5,953	14	0		
Profit, on cost	1,426	15	0	= 18%		3,807	2	0	= 64%	

Materials per ton

	1732–3	1733–4
Pig: ore etc.	2·5 doz. bushels	2·5 doz. bushels
fuel	1·92–2·46 loads	1·83–2·17 loads
Bar: fuel	2·58–2·75 loads	2·42–2·58 loads
pig	1·35–1·4 tons	1·25–1·4 tons
From ore to bar:		
ore	3·38–3·5 doz. bushels	3·13–3·5 doz. bushels
fuel	5·17–6·19 loads	4·71–5·62 loads

(c) *Foley Ironworks, 1738–48*

	1738–9 (2 furnaces,[49] 3 forges[46])		1741–2 (2 furnaces, 1 forge[51])		1746–8 (2 furnaces, 1 forge[51])	
	Ton / cwt		Ton / cwt		Ton / cwt	
Pig	974 / 16		1,043 / 1		1,166 / 7	
Bar	205 / 19		196 / 13		152 / 2	
	Total £ s d	**Per ton** s d	**Total** £ s d	**Per ton** s d	**Total** £ s d	**Per ton** s d
Expenditure						
Managers	260 15 3	—	208 15 0[52]	—	460 0 0[53]	—
Founders	184 14 8	3 9¼	197 17 4	3 9½	140 4 6[54]	—
Finers and hammermen	241 6 5	23 5¼	182 6 9	18 6½	77 9 8[54]	—
Clerical workers	78 0 9	—	72 18 2	—	63 0 7	—
Sundries and general labour	522 11 4¾[50]	—	147 14 0	—	228 13 3¼	—
Repairs, replacements, etc.	290 2 10	—	281 10 5	—	827 11 2½[55]	—
Transport, general	277 17 3	—	255 12 5	—	194 8 11	—
Wood, bought, cut and corded	933 17 1½	—	1,260 12 1½	—	1,938 14 6[56]	—
Coaling, buying, transport	1,276 13 7½	*from* 32 0	1,179 17 10½	*from* 32 7)	2,198 5 0	—
(Fuel for smelting		*to* 41 5		39 11) *to*		—
(fining		54 2		43 3)		—
Cinders and ore	538 8 7	11 0½	320 9 5	11 8¾	719 13 0	—
Rents	27 15 8	—	43 16 8	—	28 10 10	—
Total paid	4,632 3 6¾		4,151 10 2		6,876 11 5¾	

Income (sales)	1738-9 £ s. d.	1738-9 tons	1741-2 £ s. d.	1741-2 tons	1746-8 £ s. d.	1746-8 tons
Pig and castings	4,892 11 6	121 7	3,057 16 4	121 6	5,083 6 10	121 3
Bar, osmund and forgings	3,045 6 6	325 4	3,120 2 4	321 7	2,207 4 6	302 11
Charcoal	—		—		95 15 0	
Wood, bark, etc. (*deliveries*)	—		—		10 16 5¼	
Pig, etc.	9 8 10		—		2 5 7	
Bar, etc.	17 7 7		5 15 0		6 15 0	
Total produce	7,964 14 5		6,183 13 8		7,406 3 4¼	
Net closing stock	954 17 0		215 14 0		550 4 0 [57]	
Adjusted costs	5,587 1 0		3,935 16 0		6,326 7 0	
Profit, on cost	2,377 13 0 = 43%		2,247 18 0 = 57%		1,079 16 0 = 17% [58]	

Materials per ton	1738-9	1741-2	1746-8
Pig: ore, etc.	2·58–3·25 doz. bushels	2·42–3·21 doz. bushels	2– doz. bushels
fuel	1·79–2·33 loads	1·94–2·37 loads	2– loads
Bar: fuel	3·04 loads	2·58 loads	—
pig	1·33 tons	1·34 tons	1·39 tons
From ore to bar:			
ore	3·42–4·31 doz. bushels	3·24–4·29 doz. bushels	
fuel	5·41–6·13 loads	5·15–5·26 loads	

and on the amounts paid to them for odd jobs around the furnace. The manager's salary had remained at about £200 a year for a similar group of works, although the Protectorate manager also had to supervise the forest for the amount which Thomas Pendrill, the Foley manager, received in 1741-2. The extraction rate of ore had hardly changed; if there was rather better fuel economy, that may have been partly the result of the deliberately indiscriminate use of all fuel wood by the State ironworks, and just possibly of the use of some mineral coal in the chafery at the Foley works.[59] Even more remarkable is the stability in the cost of wood and fuel; this differs significantly from the average fuel costs incurred by the works. The State ironworks relied wholly on wood taken from the former royal forest, so that its fuel costs consisted entirely of the expense of felling, cording, coaling and carrying, which were exceptionally high, partly because the manager employed dear labour but also because they included the expenses connected with the cutting and cleaning of all timber. Similarly, the Foley works used considerable quantities of wood from the Foley estates, which often supplied more than half the wood for Elmbridge furnace for the price of merely cutting and cording it. As the accounts for the other works lump together payments for fuel without indicating quantities, some of their wood may have come from the same source or from some of the favourable long-term contracts concluded with the actual owners of their ironworks (such as the Halls, and the Gages, who followed them), which were negotiated with the lease. It would be difficult to estimate the proper market value of these woods, and do violence to the contemporary view of the matter if this were taken as part of the costs of making iron. But the stocks of wood held by the State ironworks were valued at 5s per short cord in 1660;[60] wood bought in for Elmbridge furnace between 1732 and 1748 cost, on average, between 4s 6d and 5s 3d cut and corded, only in one year reaching 5s 9d. The cost of a load of charcoal at Elmbridge furnace was 32s in 1733-4 and 29s in 1732-3; for the other three accounts it was uniformly 26s a load.[61] This certainly bears out Professor Hyde's contention that charcoal prices remained low before the 1750s;[62] it is, however, difficult to attempt exact comparisons with his or Professor Johnson's data,[63] because it is not certain that these were based on a similar calculation of costs actually incurred.

Some of the costs did increase, most notably both cost and

price of ore and cinders.[64] The State had paid about 3s 6d a dozen sacks for the mixture it employed in the 1650s; by 1691 it was reliably thought to cost 5s 2d,[65] and Lydney furnace paid 6s 1d per dozen in 1699.[66] By the 1730s the price of ore could vary from 3s 6d to occasionally 10s a dozen, of cinders from 5s to 9s. That would explain why the cost of the mixture had risen by 20 to 30 per cent during the ninety years, despite an overall reduction in the amount used. Some of the increase could simply reflect a widening of the market for Dean ores, which had been relatively cheap: at Pontypool in 1703–5 the ore and cinders for a ton of pig iron cost £1.[67] The increase was not disastrous but may have been slightly ominous: an historian steeped in the local history of Dean has suggested that 'easily won supplies of local ores were running low'.[68] In fact mining in Dean during the eighteenth century tended to concentrate increasingly upon coal, and energetic mining for deeper iron ores did not revive until the mid-nineteenth century.[69]

The wages of unskilled and semi-skilled labour cannot easily be determined. The accounts rarely, if ever, give either the number of men or the number of days for which they were being paid; the work was identified by job or site. Woodcutting and the rather more responsible job of cording were relatively unskilled and thus sometimes performed by seasonal labour or by men who changed between this and other occupations. Charcoal-burning was a little more specialised, but a 'collier' could, without loss of status or differentials, work for a number of customers or change from one to the other rather more easily than the relatively highly paid founders and finers. A load of charcoal was, one may assume, a reasonably constant measure, normally a cartload of a dozen sacks. The amount of wood which would produce a load of charcoal depended on the quality and seasoning of the wood, as well as the skill of the collier, but, very crudely, it was also fairly constant. This makes it possible to get at least some general impression of the movement of such wages, although it would be rash to try and convert them into a daily rate (see Table 2).

The indication would seem to be that unskilled wages were the most volatile, and that, on the whole, the growth in them exceeded that of skilled and unskilled wages in the building trade, which had doubled between the 1620s and the 1730s.[70] Colliers' pay rose too, but evidently far more slowly and reluctantly, lagging

TABLE 2   Payments for woodcutting, cording and charcoal-burning for ironworks, 1620s to 1740s

Works	Date	Cutting, etc.		Coaling		Source
		s	d	s	d	
Carey forge	c. 1628	3	7	2	6	BL, Add. MS. 11052
Goodrich forge	c. 1628	3	0	2	6	Bodleian, Selden supra 113
Carey forge	1630	2	6	2	4	BL, Add. MS. 11052
Redbrook furnace	1659	7	6	4	0	Glos. RO, Gage MS. 1557
Parkend furnace	1662	7	0	3	6	BL Harleian 6839, fo. 334d
Dean (proposal)	1691	9	6	3	6	Morton (see below, note 65), p. 38
Pontypool furnace	1704	6	0	3	0	Mon. RO, 'Hanbury Memo.', p. 5
Llancillo forge	1723	5	8	3	6	PRO, C105/24, pt 1
	1725	5	8	3	6	Ibid.
Elmbridge furnace	1733	6	4	3	8¾	Here. RO, Foley Papers, Fvi/DGf
	1734	7	3	3	8¾	Ibid.
	1739	5	11	3	9¼	Ibid.
	1742	5	6	3	8¾	Ibid.
	1746–8	7	0	4	0	Ibid.

Note. Explanation of principal abbreviations on p. xi.

well behind the rise in building wages. Between the 1720s and 1740s growth seems to falter: the rates fluctuate, more vigorously for the unskilled, but the changes do not seem to indicate a pronounced trend. On the whole, these fragmentary and unrefined data do seem to bear out the suspicion of some historians of the iron industry that its skilled wages remained extraordinarily rigid; indeed, they almost hint at an inverse relationship between degrees of skill and rates of wage increases. Of course, it did not mean that woodcutters earned more than founders and finers, whose cash income was increased by the provision of housing and the consciousness of status, as well as other minor rewards in kind. In any event, none of these changes, separately or together, were rapid or striking enough to place the iron industry under serious pressure.

To all appearances, it would have been difficult to conceive of any particular change, short of a natural disaster or a sudden collapse of the market for iron, which could have menaced the industry's profits. The most expensive forge and furnace, built

from scratch with all their ponds, sluices and water-conduits, cost
£1500 in all.[71] With annual interest at 5 per cent and an estimated
lifetime of ten years, £250 a year should have covered it; £500
would have reduced the rate of profit in the worst year for the
Foley works to a mere 8 per cent on cost or rather more than
£700. No charcoal ironmaster ever calculated like that: building
costs were treated as repairs and replacements, totally written off
when incurred.

On the other hand, if the accounts themselves demand much
detailed extrapolation and guesswork to complete them, the profits
must not be interpreted too literally: they may be no better than
an approximation, with a possible range of error of from plus
to minus 10 per cent. Indeed, the State ironworks accounts present
an almost insoluble problem: in the first three years they cast
701 tons of shot, which was the purpose for which they had been
originally intended. The naval yards complained bitterly about
its inadequacies, but kept it and set to work to clean it up.[72]
Clearly, it would have been as reasonable to write it off altogether
as to value it, as has here been done, at over £8000. Again,
if the wood used for the State ironworks is valued as it was in
the final stocks, the rate of profit shrinks to a more normal 18
to 20 per cent on costs; but the enterprise was really not just
an ironworks but an integrated forestry enterprise, supplying timber
for the yards and the warships and seedlings for the nursery, which
were transplanted at the right time. Therefore the reduced rate
of profit gives no better picture: the accounts do not clearly separate
the costs of making iron from those of all the other occupations.
As far as the contemporary landowner or investor was concerned,
he did not employ this particular method of indicating profit,
but he would probably have recognised it as corresponding to
his own view of the true position. That implies that it would
have needed a quite staggering increase in fuel costs, for instance,
to make charcoal iron production truly unprofitable.

The prospects for the industry were certainly not menacing
enough to dissuade any enterprising landowner from maintaining
his charcoal ironworks; indeed, four Dean charcoal furnaces and
a number of forges survived, under professional ironmasters, into
the early nineteenth century.[73] Moreover, the Foley accounts for
the 1730s and 1740s may present a slightly misleading picture.
His lawsuits, as has been pointed out, suggest that Thomas senior

may not have been an outstanding businessman: perhaps that was too much to expect in the fourth generation.[74] His treatment of his works, once he had obtained sole control of them, suggests that he lacked drive and ambition in that direction. The old partnership had held and fairly regularly used Blakeney, Bishopswood, Guns Mill and Redbrook furnaces in Dean, with Elmbridge/Newent and St Weonard's just outside it; it also operated three Lydbrook forges, Monmouth forge and Llancillo,[75] as well as the storehouse at Bewdley, which promoted sales in the Midlands.[76] In 1732 the Foleys still retained Elmbridge, Redbrook, Bishopswood, Guns Mill and St Weonard's furnaces, Monmouth forge, three Lydbrook forges and the Bewdley store, but used neither Guns Mill nor St Weonard's or Bishopswood. In fact Guns Mill still had a stock of fifty-seven tons of pig iron, which was sold off in 1732–3 and so indicates that the furnace may have worked until quite recently, but St Weonard's and Blakeney's inventories give an impression of long-term dereliction and, when Bishopswood was repaired in 1734, it needed more than £170, which suggests that it had almost collapsed. Moreover, for at least three years it had carried a stock of more than 5800 dozen sacks of cinders, enough for five to six years and valued at more than £1400. Presumably Bishopswood was being repaired because the lease of Redbrook furnace and of two Lydbrook forges was due to expire in 1737;[77] thenceforth it operated alongside Elmbridge to make all the pig iron for Foley. But at some time between 1734 and 1738 Foley had also let go of Monmouth forge, which had until then produced about half his bar iron; by 1741 he was left with only Lydbrook Lower Forge,[78] yet there is no indication of any attempt to build a new forge until 1746–8.[79] St Weonard's furnace had been abandoned before 1738; in 1742 Blakeney, Guns Mill and Bewdley storehouse were formally written off, having been left derelict for some time. Indeed, the shape of the account for 1746–8 indicates that Thomas junior was even less interested in the ironworks than his father had been: the works, other than Elmbridge, which lay on a Foley estate, had been left virtually without supervision for two years, and the manager was trying to reconstitute some sort of account from the notebooks of founders and other chargehands. Bishopswood furnace itself may have been abandoned soon after 1751;[80] the half century marks the end of the Foley concern with Dean iron.

Thomas junior's son married into the nobility and eventually became Lord Foley, after the death of his cousin who had held the title.[81] If Thomas senior and junior kept up the works, they seem to have done so without enthusiasm, certainly without any intention of making the best of them. To some extent that may explain the static impression given by the Foley accounts overall; for them it had become a routine business providing a comfortable addition to their income, even in a poor year. But this cannot altogether explain the apparent continuity with Dean works of ninety years before; less so, when the rate of improvement in the industry before the 1660s is taken into account. In the first 150 years of its existence in Britain, the indirect process had achieved major improvements in output, diversification, standardisation and efficiency. That was the point at which the great partnerships took over; their control of the market, their strength *vis-à-vis* the wood-owners, and their partial elimination of competition may have helped to slow down the impulse towards innovation, which would have done proportionately much less to improve the return attainable than the efficiency of their organisation. It is of course possible that the range of innovations in charcoal-smelting available at that level of technology had been largely exhausted by the third quarter of the seventeenth century; the new pattern of organisation may have weakened any impulse towards new methods and new ideas still further. The impression given by the accounts here displayed is, by and large, static rather than dynamic; perhaps the Foleys were not the only owners who preferred dignity and estates to the menial occupation of making iron. There were of course others, even in Dean, who still succeeded for a while in making charcoal iron; this may be a sign that the charcoal iron industry, despite some sluggishness, retained as yet sound-enough prospects.

Meanwhile the coke iron industry was almost forced into improvement and innovation. Fine iron castings were profitable, but not all iron coming from a blast furnace makes equally good castings and, if it is to run at optimum efficiency, a furnace is bound to produce more iron than can easily be cast. Therefore the coke industry had every incentive to try and equal the lower costs of charcoal smelting and refining; coke pig did not become consistently cheaper than charcoal pig until after about 1770, nor coke bar cheaper than charcoal bar until about 1800.[82] It is by no means clear that all charcoal prices everywhere rose after 1750, or that they were likely to remain at this higher level when faced with a reduction in the market for it;[83] it is abundantly clear that a static branch of the iron industry was faced by a dynamic competitor that undersold it. There is no fundamental reason which made it impossible for the charcoal industry to seek its own inovations or even to adopt or adapt some of the new methods introduced by the coke industry. It may have been difficult, though, to overcome the inertia of the last hundred years; the coke industry challenged ingenuity and offered to reward it, while the charcoal industry may have sunk under its own inanition: effortless profits of 18 per cent or more may not encourage risk and enterprise. In the end, the coke industry was bound to be able to out-produce the charcoal industry, because its fuel was more concentrated and available in larger quantities, but that need not have stopped the charcoal industry from continuing to maintain itself at an entirely reasonable level. Its disappearance, if a little less rapid than sometimes assumed, was perhaps as much the fault of its organisation and its inertia: it rather fell than was pushed.

Notes

1 M. W. Flinn, 'The Iron Industry in Sixteenth Century England', *Edgar Allen News*, 1951.

2 M. W. Flinn: 'The Growth of the English Iron Industry, 1660–1760', *EHR*, end ser., xi (1958) 144–53; 'Timber and the Advance of Technology: A Reconsideration', *Annals of Science*, xv (1959) 109–20; *Men of Iron: The Crowleys in the Early Iron Industry* (Edinburgh, 1962); 'Consommation du bois et développement sidérurgique en Angleterre', *Actes du colloque sur la forêt*, ed. C. Fohlen (Paris: Les Belles Lettres, 1967) 107–22.

3 H. R. Schubert, *History of the British Iron and Steel Industry* (London, 1957) appendix v, pp. 354–92; J. M. Lindsay, 'Charcoal Iron Smelting and its Fuel Supply: The Example of Lorn Furnace, Argyllshire, 1753–1876', *Journal of Historical Geography*, 1 (1975) 283–98.

4 A. Constantine, 'Charcoal Blast Furnaces Operations: Wundowie, Western Australia', United Nations, Interregional Symposium on the Application of Modern Technical Practices in the Iron and Steel Industry in Developing Countries, Nov 1963 (mimeo.).

5 C. K. Hyde, *Technological Change and the British Iron Industry, 1700–1870* (Princeton, NJ, 1977) pp. 23ff.

6 Ibid., pp. 56–60.

7 Bunawe lasted until 1876, Backbarrow until 1920; cf. note 3 above.

8 PRO, E134/44 Eliz. I/Trin. 3, 39 Eliz. I/Hil. 23, and 4 Chas. I/East. 40, suppl. 902/22; BL, Harleian MS. 4850, fo 47d; Longleat, Devereux MS. 1648, lease of 2 Jan, 12 James I; Devereux Papers, III, fo, 172.

9 PRO, E112/82/310 and MR 879; BL, Lansdowne MS. 166, fos 350, 352, 356, 362, 366 and 368; Bodleian MS. Gough Glos. 1, fos 61d, 62; Glos. RO, Winter MSS., D421/E1 and T22.

10 BL, Lansdowne MS. 166, fos 350ff, 372, 374 and 388; PRO, SP38/10, 16 May 1611; SP14/63/76; C66/1904, 14 June 1611. The remainder of the summary of the history of the Dean industry is based upon pp. 138–240 of G. Hammersley, 'The History of the Iron Industry in the Forest of Dean Region, 1562–1660' (unpublished Ph.D. thesis, London University, 1971).

11 PRO, SP18/130/102 for 1653–6; SP18/157B for 1656–7; E178/6080, ms 25–50d, for 1657–60.

12 *Calendar of Treasury Books, 1672–5*, vol. IV, pp. 227–8, 489.

13 BL, MS. Loan 16, 'Minute Book of the Society of the Mineral and Battery Works', II: 1620–1713, fos 94–5; PRO, SP18/130/102; SP23/245/76, fo. 141; E134/20 Chas II/East. 37; Here. RO, Typescript calendar of the Oxenhall Deeds, nos 6, 7, 9, 10 and 11; Foley Papers, Box 'Ironworks/Miscellaneous/Unsorted', receipts of 23 July 1657 and of 2 Sep 1657. I am greatly obliged to A. T. Foley Esq., Stoke Edith Estate Office, Stoke Edith, Herefordshire, and to the Hereford branch of the County of Hereford and Worcester Record Office for permission to consult and use the Foley Papers.

14 Glos. RO, Foley Papers, Fvi/DBc/2 and 3, EBf/(5322), DAc/1, 5 and 6; B. L. C. Johnson, 'The Foley Partnerships: The Iron Industry at the End of the Charcoal Era', *EHR*, 2nd ser., IV (1952) 324. The Winter ironworks at Lydney and, for most of the time, the Flaxley ironworks remained independent.

15 As note 14, plus C. E. Hart, *The Free Miners* (Gloucester, 1953) p. 103; Schubert, *History of the British Iron and Steel Industry*, pp. 385–6 and 390–1; *7th Report*, Lords, p. 94; Bodleian MS. Top. Glouc. c. 3., fo. 137; Glos. RO, Winter MSS., D421/T22 and E9, and D2184, fo. 6; HRO, Foley Papers, Fvi/DAc/2 and 3; Suffolk RO, Gonning MSS., 331/7/16 and acc. 331, 8 and 21 Sep 1649.

16 Johnson, *EHR*, 2nd ser., IV, 338–9.

17 Glos. RO, Gage MSS., lease of 10 Aug 1702; Here. RO, Foley Papers, Fvi/DBc/2 and 3.

18 Glos. RO, Winter MSS., D421/E9.

19 C. E. Hart, *The Industrial History of Dean* (Newton Abbot, 1971) pp. 61–113.

20 B. L. C. Johnson, 'The Charcoal Iron Trade in the Midlands, 1690–1720' (unpublished MA Geography thesis, University of Birmingham, 1950), and several articles by him, in which he first used a large proportion of the Foley material systematically.

21 B. L. C. Johnson, 'New Light on the Iron Industry of the Forest of Dean', *Transactions of the Bristol and Gloucester Archaeological Society*, LXXII (1953) 141.

22 They are all signed by Thomas Pendrill, who described himself as about forty years old and of Newland in 1731. Therefore he may have supervised Redbrook furnace directly at first, while relying on undermanagers for the other works. (PRO, E134/4 Geo. II/East. 11).

23 PRO, E134/5 Geo. II/Hil. 11, m. 6, deposition of Edward Kendall; HRO, Foley Papers, Fvi/DFc, agreement of 20 June 1706. By 1728 a number of the original partners had died, but their shares had generally passed on to their heirs.

24 PRO, E134/3 Geo. II/Hil. 8, m. 5, and 5 Geo. II/Hil. 11, ms 6 and 7.

25 PRO, E134/4 Geo. II/East. 11, m. 6, depositions of Ambrose Gallymore and of David Daniell.

26 In addition to the depositions by commission, PRO E134, referred to in notes 23 to 25 above, the cases are spread over E134/1 Geo. II/East. 8/3 Geo.

II/Trin. 4 and Mich. 26, 4 Geo II/Mich. 21 and Hil. 13 and 16/5 Geo. II/Trin.
7, Hil. 8, Mich. 25 and East. 19.

27 PRO, E134/5 Geo. II/Hil. 11, deposition of Edward Kendall/4 Geo. II/Hil.
13, m. 2, deposition of James Thomas.

28 Kidderminster Public Library and Museum, MS. 11228, 'Abstract of the
Title of Thomas Lord Foley to the Manor ... called Great Witley ...', contains
a convenient 'pedigree' of the Foleys. PRO, E134/5 Geo. II/Hil. 8, m. 4, gives
Thomas's post; his father had been an important member of Harley's political
following.

29 R. A. Lewis, 'Two partnerships of the Knights' (unpublished MA thesis,
Birmingham University, 1949).

30 PRO, E134/4 Geo. II/East. 11, ms 6 and 7, and *passim*.

31 As note 11 above.

32 PRO, E178/6080, pt 1, m. 31d.

33 Here. RO, Foley Papers, Fvi/DGf. The five Foley accounts here utilised
had not been allotted clear individual reference numbers when last inspected; in
the text they will therefore simply be identified by their dates.

34 PRO, E178/6080, pt 1, ms 50–50d.

35 PRO, SP18/130/102; SP18/157B; E178/6080, pt 1, ms 25–50d. These are
three separate but connected accounts, the first two taken by Exchequer auditors,
the last by a specially appointed local commission. They cover the period 13
Sep 1653 to 26 Apr 1660 in three unequal portions, and with some differences
in compilation. The summary account for the whole period more or less agrees
with the balances and state found by the auditors; the second column represents
only an arithmetical average for one year, for ease of comparison.

36 As note 33 above. The first four accounts run from Michaelmas to Michaelmas;
the account for 1746–8 is an amalgam of two separate accounts, one covering,
somewhat haphazardly, Bishopswood furnace and Lydbrook forge from 29 Sep
1746 to 5 Nov 1748, the other in a different but fairly regular fashion Elmbridge
from 29 Sep 1746 to 29 Sep 1748. Many of the items in these accounts look
more dubious than usual; they have therefore simply been analysed jointly, like
the other combined accounts, but no attempt has been made to reduce them
to an annual average.

37 This includes ordinary clerks (who did not manage a works), stocktakers
and similar employees.

38 This includes all products registered as going out of the works to some
stated recipient, but without any indication of payment made or expected for
it. The values here shown against such 'deliveries' have been estimated with the
help of averages of payments registered for the same kinds of products in the
same accounts.

39 Partly estimated, as the account for 1656–7 does not indicate payments
for finers and hammermen.

40 Partly estimated, as the appropriate figures are only shown in the account
for the first three years.

41 Excessively large, as it includes undifferentiated payments for repairs, maintenance, general transport and perhaps some wages.

42 Appears too low; the balance presumably included under 'sundries'.

43 Only the costs of cutting and cording are shown in the accounts; these
were high, for reasons explained in the text.

44 This is an arbitrary figure, as indicated in the text.

45 This seems the simplest and perhaps therefore the most appropriate measure
for figures which are so uncertain. Only the State accounts show building costs,
so these have been excluded from the accounts. The profits here shown are based

on more realistic evidence than calculations based on contemporary summaries, which tend to oversimplify, and may reflect working efficiency better than the return on investments made in the industry.

46 Three of these were the Upper, Middle and Lower Forges in Lydbrook, which are distinguished in the accounts but operated as one enterprise.

47 This includes at least £171 10s 0½d spent from the 'general' (i.e. Redbrook) account on the restoration of Bishopswood furnace.

48 Rents shown in the account only amount to £79. But the lease of Lydbrook forges and Redbrook furnace stipulated a rent of £300 a year, which included favourable prices for stated quantities of wood and cinders. The money may have been paid under the general heading of 'Lord Gage's account', which has not been included in this summary (except for the £300 added to the 'Rents'). See PRO, C108/415, indent of 21 Dec 1716.

49 Bishopswood had now replaced Redbrook.

50 Includes £180 for the building of a house for an employee, £97 arrears, £63 for purchase of Cumberland pig iron, and an interest payment of £58.

51 This was presumably the forge which was advertised for sale by the Vaughan estate in 1808: HRO, E59/SP/40, printed advertisement for 'forge ... at LIDBROOK ... within a few yards of the Navigable River Wye'.

52 This only included the pay of the managing clerk at Elmbridge for a little over a quarter of the year: presumably there had not been one for the rest of the year.

53 No costs of any management shown in either of the accounts; the estimate is meant to pay for a manager and one managing clerk for two years.

54 Both these figures are clearly incomplete: it seems improbable that the founder's pay should have slumped to 2s 5d per ton; the Lydbrook account showed no payment for the hammerman.

55 Includes about £250 spent on the 'New Forge'.

56 At least £34 of this may not refer to the purchase of wood; the proper classification of many of the items which went into this total was largely a matter of guesswork.

57 Purely the value of pig and bar iron made but not disposed of: this account has no inventory of stocks.

58 The details are so dubious, quite apart from the absence of a closing stock, that this is an almost meaningless figure.

59 Unspecified amounts of mineral coal were bought in each of the Foley accounting periods; there is some indication that much of it was for the use of senior employees.

60 PRO, E178/6080, pt I, m. 37.

61 G. Hammersley, 'The Charcoal Iron Industry and its Fuel, 1540–1750', EHR, 2nd ser., XXVI (1973) 609, contains a table with similar data. It is not certain that they are strictly comparable with figures derived from the present set of accounts, as those in the table taken from other published work may have been based on a different method of calculation.

62 Hyde, Technological Change, p. 33.

63 Johnson, 'The Charcoal Iron Trade', appendix VI.

64 In Dean, 'cinders' at one time meant almost solely the old bloomery cinders, which contained much iron, besides acting as a flux in smelting. By the 1730s the Foley works were also using 'forge cinders', presumably solely as a flux. Originally bloomery cinders, which were easier to get, had been cheaper than ore; now they were usually dearer. In the first two Foley accounts the mixture was three parts cinders to one part ore; in 1739 and 1742 that became three to two, and for Elmbridge in 1746–8 it was almost one to one. In the State ironworks the

proportion may have been about nine to six.

65 G. R. Morton, 'The Reconstruction of an Industry', *Journal of the Lichfield and South Staffs Archaeological and Historical Society*, VII (1966) 37–8.

66 Glos. RO, Winter Papers, D421/E9.

67 Mon. RO, 'Hanbury Memorandum Book', p. 5.

68 Hart, *Industrial History of Dean*, pp. 63 and 226.

69 Ibid., pp. 228–30; Hart, *Free Miners*, p. 238.

70 E. H. Phelps Brown and Sheila V. Hopkins, 'Seven Centuries of Building Wages', in *Essays in Economic History*, ed. E. M. Carus-Wilson, vol. II (London, 1962) pp. 177–8.

71 PRO, SP18/130/102.

72 PRO, SP18/111/71, lists the complaints. The value used is £12 per ton, rather below the market price.

73 Hart, *Industrial History of Dean*, pp. 70–2, 80 and 94–5.

74 Kidderminster Public Library, MS. 11228, m. 1.

75 PRO, E134/4 Geo. II/East. 11, m. 6, deposition of John Jones; HRO, Foley Papers, Fvi/DGf/1725–32, account for 1728–9. Some historians mention forges or a forge at Newent: these do not appear in the accounts.

76 In 1732–3 Bewdley sales of bar and osmund accounted for more than 17 per cent of total income, in 1733–4 for 24 per cent. In 1738–9 the storehouse was not used, and its total equipment was valued in the inventory at £7 7s.

77 PRO, C108/415, indent concluding a lease for twenty-one years from 21 Dec 1716.

78 Cf. note 51 above.

79 Cf. note 55 above.

80 Hart, *Industrial History of Dean*, p. 94.

81 Kidderminster Public Library, MS. 11228, m. 1.

82 Hyde, *Technological Change*, pp. 28, and 104.

83 Ibid., pp. 58–9.

5 The Middle Class and the Property Cycle during the Industrial Revolution

R. J. MORRIS

The many excellent company and business histories of the Industrial Revolution period need to be complemented by studies of the middle-class family and household as an economic unit. A major part of consumption decisions and an important part of those decisions involving savings and the allocation of resources to different forms of investment were taken in the context of family and household rather than with reference to the firm or unit of production.

For the successful middle-class family during the Industrial Revolution there was a property cycle as characteristic as the poverty cycle of the wage-earning family.[1] At each stage in this cycle, property had important social uses, and made a distinctive contribution to different and specific types of capital formation. The main stages in the property cycle of the successful middle-class male were the following.

1. Childhood – dependence on parents.
2. Training (normally fourteen to twenty-one years of age) – dependence on parents for financial support during professional training or apprenticeship, perhaps with merchant or shopkeeper.

This dependence often included cash to buy into a partnership. Many successful professional and commercial careers were based upon the accumulated savings of a shopkeeper or the wealth of a landed estate.[2] Occasionally this support came from other relatives or even an employer.[3] Once the business had been established, son might follow father in the manner of the Jowitt family, discussed below, and of many others.[4]

3. Adult – earned income and net payer of interest. In this phase earned income exceeded consumption and the family house was often rented or under mortgage. Many personal and business loans were outstanding. These debts were commonly incurred with other family members, as parents or cousins, or to the executors of a family estate in which money was held in trust for the widow and daughters. Although such debts were accounted with meticulous care, they were a more stable form of finance than money borrowed from outside the family, such as trade credit and mortgages obtained through solicitors. The excess income was used to pay off these debts and to accumulate trading capital. This phase usually began with marriage or the setting up of an independent household.

4. Adult – earned income and net receiver of interest. Once debts were paid and the family house under owner-occupation, capital was accumulated not only as trading capital but increasingly in the form of houses or landed property, mortgage debts, government stock or joint-stock shares. This period often began when property was inherited from parents or other relations. The change usually took place when a man was in his late thirties or early forties. Income was still dominated by earned income from trade, manufactures or professional activity.

5. Adult – unearned income. Capital accumulation slowed down and income sources became dominated by unearned income from rents, dividends and interest on loans and mortgages. Profits and fees declined in importance as the man concerned withdrew from business. This phase was not retirement in the twentieth-century sense, as the break with business was often partial and took place over several years. This change usually took place in the early to mid-fifties.[5]

6. Life after death. An individual's property was rarely dispersed immediately after his death but was handed over to the executors or trustees of the estate. In their hands it was used to maintain

the living standards of widow and daughters. After this had been achieved the property was divided amongst all living children. In most estates such a system of equitable inheritance ensured units of capital finance which were rarely enough to provide an adequate rentier income, but often large enough to provide capital for industrial, commercial or professional enterprise, or to create the means of opening phase 4 of the property cycle for the next generation.

It must be emphasised that this scheme represented the optimum path for the development of the middle-class family as an economic unit. The evidence presented here came from the papers of three extremely successful men and there were only hints of the problems of failure. In following this path a man and his family had to survive a wide variety of demographic, economic, social and moral hazards, ranging from bankruptcy to early death.

I

Robert Jowitt was a wealthy Quaker woolstapler. Although he came last in point of time of the three examples examined in this paper, his fortunes in the property cycle will be presented first because of the unusual completeness of the information contained in his papers. His business had been established by his father, John Jowitt junior, who had begun as a clothier's son in Churwell, a village near Batley, in the woollen district of the West Riding of Yorkshire. John moved to Leeds and passed through several partnerships before joining with Robert, his only son, in 1806, when the boy came of age.[6] Robert married Rachel Crewdson of Kendal in 1812. She brought with her a substantial marriage portion (£3000) which was soon followed by a legacy from her mother (£3606 in 1814–15). The marriage portion remained in trust to provide Robert with a stable though minor part of his income until his wife's death in 1856. The inheritance, which became Robert's own property under existing married women's property law, was placed in the firm.[7] His father died late in 1814, leaving personal property valued for probate at under £30,000, a substantial house off Woodhouse Lane to the north-west of Leeds town centre, and 'all my messuage, warehouse and other buildings and tenements in Albion Street Leeds'.[8] Robert had a sixth interest in all this. His share enabled him to purchase Carlton House from his father's estate for £3000 and released him from the £3000 debt to his father which he had incurred when he had entered the partnership in 1806. This sum was put into 'hotch-potch' when the division of the estate was made. Although his

TABLE 3   The debts of the Jowitt firm to the executors of John Jowitt, 1816–42 (£)

Year	Amount due	Robert Jowitt's capital
1816	17,281	9,509
1817	14,156	12,779
1818	14,235	16,396
1819	12,612	15,727
1820	12,244	13,561
1821	12,173	13,506
1822	12,475	14,601
1823	12,353	14,839
1824	13,639	15,490
1825	13,539	19,288
1826	12,388	10,795
1827	10,883	10,653
1828	10,925	11,423
1829	8,726	10,453
1830	6,510	12,919
1831	5,998	16,080
1832	6,118	16,559
1833	5,029	19,348
1834	5,218	20,396
1835	1,093	20,548
1836	224	18,939
1837	380	14,638
1838	844	15,541
1839	69	18,853
1840	436	16,353
1841	1,833	14,694
1842	1,189	11,143

Sources. John Jowitt and Son private ledger A, 1806–29, BAJ 10; Robert Jowitt and Sons private ledger B, 1830–44, BAJ 17, fos. 40–9 (for location, see note 6).

Note. The firm continued to hold small amounts for the executors after 1842, but these were in the nature of cash balances and not substantial invest-ments as those before 1835.

father's death enabled Robert to make a substantial change in his level of consumption, it did not end his period as a net payer of interest. Through the firm he inherited substantial obligations to the executors of the late John Jowitt (see Table 3). The old man's capital remained in the firm until the mid-1830s. The substantial interest payments were part of the trust income which maintained an annuity for Susanna Jowitt, the widow, until her death in 1819, and for John Jowitt's daughters for the remainder of their lives. These arrangements enabled John Jowitt both to deal equitably with his six children and to leave his capital as an undivided working unit. Robert was trustee under the will and thus kept control of the capital provided he fulfilled the obligations of the trust.[9]

Robert Jowitt's ledgers and account books enable his earning and spending pattern to be reconstructed for the whole of his adult life (1806–62; see Table 4). The main characteristic of his income was its violent fluctuation. The changes between 1823 and 1826 involved a rise of 150 per cent, a fall of 390 per cent and another fall of 35 per cent. These fluctuations were reduced in the 1840s, when the dividends and interest from railway shares and loans began to provide a more stable form of income than commercial profits. This stability is even greater when the two extreme years of 1848 and 1854 are omitted.[10] The high income of these two years is in both cases owing to exceptional circumstances: a legacy of £6000 following the death of Robert's son in 1848 and the transfer of Rachel Jowitt's trust capital to her husband's own account shortly before her death. Robert's average income was £2291 and the evidence of a slight upward trend was produced almost entirely by the high incomes of 1848 and 1854, and not by any changes in his regular sources of income. Robert may indeed have aimed for a rentier income similar to his expected normal earned income. Such an aim would have affected his investment decisions, especially the timing of his withdrawal from active commercial life, which took place between 1842 and 1844.

Robert's consumption spending again fluctuated, though less violently than his income. Figure 1 traces two indicators of his consumption spending. The differences between his consumption (cash plus interest payments – see notes to Table 4) and his household spending (same sources as Table 4) may be explained in

TABLE 4   Robert Jowitt: income, consumption and savings, 1806–62 (£)

Year(s)	Income	Consumption	Savings	Firm's loss attributed to RJ's account
1806–08	577	130	448	–
1808–10	1676	209	1467	–
1810–12	399	582	−184	169
1812–13	696	628	68	–
1813–14	1744	702	2014	–
1814–15	5390	785	4805	–
1815–16	968	604	364	1139
1816–17	4086	833	3253	–
1817–18	4451	850	3601	–
1818–19	2838	664	2174	2844
1819–20	1050	700	350	2518
1820–1	814	653	161	215
1821–2	1775	680	1095	–
1822–3	918	668	250	12
1823–4	1762	588	1174	–
1824–5	4394	852	3542	–
1825–6	1130	1127	3	8436
1826–7	736	673	63	200
1827–8	1344	625	719	–
1828–9	1059	783	276	–
1829–30	3006	692	2314	–
1830–1	4325	1207	3118	–
1831–2	970	972	−2	47
1832–3	4522	1002	3520	–
1833–4	2080	988	1092	–
1834–5	1686	955	731	–
1835–6	2969	947	2022	–
1836–7	1164	867	297	4161
1837–8	2526	857	1669	–
1838–9	2275	1221	1054	–
1839–40	1067	1386	−319	603
1840–1	2134	1116	1018	–
1841–2	2578	2293	285	–
1842–3	1776	1101	675	–
1843–4	3043	1022	2021	–
1844–5	1803	1113	690	n. a.
1845–6	2095	1391	704	,,
1846–7	2235	1832	403	,,
1847–8	2091	1368	723	,,
1848–9	8245	1183	7062	,,
1849–50	2272	943	1329	,,

TABLE 4 *(Continued)*

Year(s)	Income	Consumption	Savings	Firm's loss attributed to RJ's account
1850–1	1546	915	631	n. a.
1851–2	1528	1102	426	,,
1852–3	3576	1084	2492	,,
1853–4	2130	1007	1123	,,
1854–5	6955	1198	5757	,,
1855–6	2075	1130	945	,,
1856–7	3973	1094	2879	,,
1857–8	2021	970	1051	,,
1858–9	1707	955	752	,,
1859–60	1673	726	947	,,
1860–1	1649	747	902	,,
1861–2	1482	753	729	,,
1862–3	731	326	405	,,

Sources. John Jowitt and Son private ledger A, 1806–29, BAJ 10; Robert Jowitt and Sons private ledger B, 1830–44, BAJ 17; Robert Jowitt and Sons private ledger C, 1839–62, BAJ 18 (for location, see note 6).

Notes. Income is calculated as total cash receipts minus capital transfers. The incomes for the early two-year accounting periods are given as annual figures for ease of comparison. In the early years several odd cash transactions were included in the books. These have been omitted here as they were transfers within the family, Robert Jowitt settling bills in Leeds for relatives in Liverpool and Kendal and being then repaid. These sums have been deducted from income and consumption. The years affected are 1808–14 and 1818–22. Consumption includes all cash transactions not attributed to specific investment. The interest charges on Robert's running account with the firm (usually small) are also included as consumption. Savings are calculated as income minus consumption and then checked by calculating gross savings (all purchases of income-earning assets) minus capital transfers (all sales of income-earning assets). The years when the firm made a loss have been noted. Losses resulted in a reduction of capital assets. They have been included in gross savings and were in the main covered by withdrawals from capital held in the firm. The direct impact on income thus appears in the reductions owing to the lack of any profit.

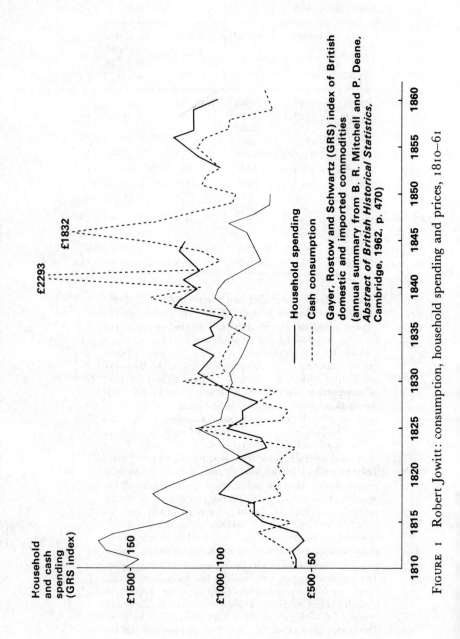

FIGURE 1   Robert Jowitt: consumption, household spending and prices, 1810–61

several ways. After 1815, he added an imputed rent of £120 to his household costs, which, as he owned his dwelling house, did not appear in cash accounts. In addition to the interest payments, other items of non-household spending occasionally appeared in his cash consumption. The exceptional totals of 1841 and 1846 coincide with the marriages of two of his daughters. There was little relationship between the fluctuations in either indicator and fluctuations in income.[11]

There were three influences on Robert's consumption spending. First, if his adult life is divided into five periods, 1810–15, 1815–29, 1830–7, 1838–56 and 1857 until his death, then within each of these periods spending fluctuated fairly narrowly around a norm which must have been fixed by the current needs and ambitions of the household. The break points were clearly marked by events in the life cycle of Robert's family and his own accumulation of property. In 1810 he married. In 1815 his father died and he bought Carlton House. In 1829 he became a net receiver of interest rather than a net payer. This was one of the few changes directly related to the fortunes of the firm, for it coincided with the prosperity of the late 1820s and the recovery from the bad years 1818 to 1826, when losses were made in six years out of nine. The break in the mid-1830s came when he had cleared all his debts and begun to accumulate rentier capital. The final change came with the death of his wife. Some of the fluctuations within these norms were related to changes in prices, which form the second influence. The household once having fixed upon a normal standard of living was able to maintain this standard by increasing spending in the face of rising prices. This happened in 1818–19, 1825, 1838–39, 1846–7 and in the mid-1850s. The third influence was the incidence of sporadic and occasional demands specific to the needs of the Jowitt household, such as the replacement of the family carriage in the mid-1820s and the two marriages in the 1840s. The basis of the stability and security of the standard of living of the middle-class household was clear. The normal surplus of income over consumption, and, when this failed, as it did in 1810–12, 1831–2 and 1839–40, the massive reserves of capital assets, meant that that surplus and those reserves could be drawn upon to maintain standards, or even increase them, as happened after Robert's marriage when his consumption rose in the face of the losses of 1812. Thus family and household were protected against fluctuations in both income and prices.

Robert's savings were a residual after the needs of a constant level of consumption had been satisfied and thus the level of saving each year was closely related to the level of income.[12] The proportion of income saved increased sharply with the level of income.[13] Although the savings schedule changed little in relation to the life cycle, the influence of the life cycle was apparent in the changing nature of the assets which Robert acquired (see Table 5). The nature of his gross asset acquisition changed between 1835 and 1840.

TABLE 5   Robert Jowitt: acquisition of assets, 1810–60

Period	% to business	% to rentier assets	Of which % to railways
1810–15	98	2	–
1815–20	70	30	–
1820–5	92	8	–
1825–30	68	32	–
1830–5	92	8	–
1835–40	39	61	51
1840–5	9	91	74
1845–50	6	94	92
1850–5	25	75	71
1855–60	25	75	61

Sources. As for Table 4.

The years 1806 to 1835 were dominated by a massive accumulation of capital in the firm. Robert's capital in the firm rose from £3000 in 1806 to £20,548 in 1835. Occasional allocations of capital were made to other forms of investment, a £60 loan to the Lancastrian School in 1812–13, a small personal loan in 1823–34, house purchase in 1815–16 and the purchase of public-utility securities from the firm in 1829. Capital transfers were made only to cover losses, as in 1825–6. After 1835, the size of capital transfers rose dramatically, as did the direction of asset acquisition, which was directed to railway shares and a small interest in the local gas company. Brief attention was paid to the firm in 1837–9 to rebuild capital after the losses of 1837, but thereafter investment in the firm was accounted for by odd cash balances and the repayment of loans. Table 6 shows the changing sources of income

TABLE 6   Robert Jowitt: sources of income 1806–62,
annual averages (£)

Period	Profit and interest from the firm	All forms of rentier income
1810–15	978	17
1815–20	1810	41
1820–5	1741	51
1825–30	1270	60
1830–5	2386	139
1835–40	1544	298
1840–5	1282	660
1845–50	389	1309
1850–5	87	1450
1855–60	50	1972

Sources and notes. As for Table 4.

as Robert withdrew both his capital and entreprenurial attentions
from business and entered phase 5 of the property cycle.

The change began in the mid-1830s, when he took out two
life-insurance policies of £1000 each for himself and his wife with
the Friends Provident Society. He already had shares in three
local public utilities, the Leeds Gas Light Company, Leeds South
Market and Leeds Water Works, and shares in the Leeds and
Yorkshire Assurance Company. These had been purchased by the
firm in the 1820s and transferred to Robert's private account in
1829. His next move was a disastrous venture into the Humber
Union Steam Company, in which he lost £781 (1835–40), and
into the Victoria Bridge in Leeds, in which he had lost £300
by 1840. Even for the knowledgeable Quaker merchant, reliable
sources of rentier income were scarce.[14]

Success came with his ventures into the railway-capital market,
first into loan finance and then into the purchase of equity and
debenture stock. Railway shares were accepted by the family as
sound investment as early as 1832, when the trustees under Rachel
Jowitt's marriage settlement put £3000 into the Liverpool and
Manchester Railway after the end of the Smyth mortgage. Robert
waited until the capital reserves of his own firm had risen to
a satisfactory level and he had been freed of the firm's obligations
to his father's executors. Then he was drawn in on his own account.
In 1836 he loaned £3000 at 4½ per cent to the Stockton and

Darlington Railway after he had been approached by the Pease family. In the same month he began investing in the North Midland Railway, when he placed £131 with J. H. Ridsdale, one of the leading Leeds sharebrokers, for deposit and premium on ten shares. Successive calls drew in more funds over the next four years, although no new purchases were made until 1840, when he extended his shareholding in the North Midland and the following year bought shares in the York and North Midland, Hudson's Company and the Newcastle and Darlington Junction. The next batch of investment came in 1844–5, when he bought widely in the railway stock of companies operating in the Midlands and North of England. With several of the early purchases, he sold about half his holding in early 1845 as the share-price boom mounted and used profits of some 50 to 80 per cent to pay further calls and make further deposits. Although the main aim was to acquire a secure rentier income, this activity could not in practice be separated from speculative gains, and indeed was supported by such gains in the months of rising stock prices. With the exception of the Buckinghamshire line (Oxford–Bletchley) he did not move from the North and Midlands until 1848, when he began to deal through Foster and Braithwaite, a major firm of London stockbrokers, and purchased Chester preference stock and shares in the Eastern Union and North British Railways.[15] In 1853–4, he moved further afield with massive purchases of United States railway stock. His behaviour justified historians' claims that the railway stock-market boom of 1844–5 drew provincial capital to a wider geographical spread of investment, thus breaking old habits of looking only to local investment opportunities.[16] Railways dominated his asset-holding by 1850. Only his growing holding in the local gas company survived from his earlier interest in the securities of public utilities.[17]

His investment strategy was revealed directly and by implication in a letter he wrote to his cousin in 1844:

I think when thou wast over, I mentioned that I had withdrawn from business – I am therefore rather seeking desirable investment for my money, rather than wanting to borrow, as my sons don't wish for spare capital in their business – such being the case I regret to say it will not be convenient for me to receive the £400 thou speaks of –

I would not venture to recommend an investment in Railway

shares to my cousins as I did to my daughters when similarly circumstanced but I may say that I think it would be an easy matter to invest money so as to pay rather more than 4% at present, with a strong probability that the dividends will not be less for some years to come.[18]

Robert took little major interest in one major alternative investment, houses and landed property. In letting his sister's old house, which came to him after her death, he admitted that its rental value had fallen 20 per cent 'in the last few years' and showed a certain irritation with the details of property management.[19] At times the management of a portfolio of railway stock proved equally tiresome. 'It will be well if some of us don't find that these concerns have too large a *share* of our attention', he told his brother-in-law in 1844.[20] Robert's correspondence became a turmoil of requests for scrip, remittance of calls and requests for information from sharebrokers and company secretaries. He demanded a report of the last general meeting of the London and Birmingham Railway 'to test the accuracy of the payment' of the last dividend. He upbraided his sharebroker for sending him shares upon which all due calls had not been paid, 'until that is done I cannot consider that thy duty as a broker can be terminated'. In the heat of the mania, he admitted that he had mislaid his scrip certificates for the West Yorkshire Railway.[21]

Robert's railway investment was part of a natural process of withdrawing capital from the business to purchase rentier assets. What the railway boom did was to affect the detailed timing of that withdrawal and make it more rapid and complete than such changes had been in earlier decades. There is little evidence that this did any damage to the firm, although in 1847 Robert had to delay the payment of some calls because 'at this moment [I am] finding it almost impossible to get cash'.[22] In the next three years his capital account with his sons' firm was in deficit, although by an amount which represented only a small part of the firm's total assets. Robert's investments formed part of the flood of rentier capital seeking stable income which Reed has identified as a part of the second phase of financing the railway projects of the 1830s and 1840s.[23] Robert showed that such capital might indulge in a little speculative gain on its way to phase 5 of the property cycle.

II

The papers of John Atkinson, solicitor of Leeds, and of John Jowitt junior (Robert's father) are not as comprehensive as those of Robert Jowitt, but they are enough to show an accumulation of rentier income-earning assets at a similar stage in the lives of all three men. The attractions and opportunities of the railway investment booms of the late 1830s and the 1840s were not essential to the switch of assets and income sources made by Robert Jowitt.

John Atkinson was the son of a tallow-chandler whose rented shop stood in Briggate, the main business and shopping street in Leeds. In 1788 John qualified to act as an attorney. In 1796 he became a sub-distributor of stamps, along with his partner Thomas Bolland, which required a bond of £500.[24] He probably married in the same decade. During his training and the building up of his place in the partnership, he relied on his father's financial resources. When his father died in 1806, probate tax was paid at 'under £1500' valuation of personal property. Of the personal loans which were due to Thomas Atkinson, £500 was owed by John Atkinson himself.[25] Thus, the successful professional career began with the support of the accumulated wealth of a tradesman generation.[26]

Between 1788 and 1815 John gained income from a wide variety of legal business, including property transactions, bankruptcies and executorships. No evidence of his total earnings has survived.[27]

By 1815 he had begun to build a substantial income from property in land. A rent book of 1810 suggests that the process began some years before that, possibly at the death of his father.[28] The pace and direction of this accumulation are indicated by the rising rental and number of properties (see Table 7). The major acquisitions took place between 1818 (when he was fifty-one years old) and 1822. Like his father he also had an income from personal loans, but this never gained the same importance as income from property. The property involved included a farm at Goole, and several farms and closes of land at Pudsey, Bramley and other villages to the south of Leeds.[29] There was nothing in the central area, but in 1822 he bought an estate at Little Woodhouse (which included the house in which he lived until the end of his life) in the growing middle-class suburbs to the north-west of the town.[30]

Between 1818 and 1821, his income from rent and interest grew

TABLE 7   John Atkinson: rental and finance, 1815–32.

Year	Rent due (£)	Number of tenants	Interest from loans (£)	Cash due to Mary and Ann Dibb at the start of each year (£)
1815	–	–	–	450
1816	–	–	–	850
1817	–	–	–	2000
1818	670	15	125	2300
1819	915	17	128	2770
1820	871	16	127	3570
1821	917	16	126	3800
1822	1116	20	141	4650
1823	1075	20	160	5250
1824	1081	21	158	5000
1825	969	23	147	5000
1826	1074	23	168	5000
1827	1097	23	153	5000
1828	1101	23	153	4100
1829	1088	22	163	–
1830	971	24	156	–
1831	895	23	148	–
1832	848	23	132	–

Sources. John Atkinson's rental, 1818–33, DB 5/58; John Atkinson in account with Mary and Ann Dibb, 1815–28, DB 5/57 (for location, see note 24).

rapidly. After 1821, the increase in the number of tenants would suggest that he was still buying land, but the general decline in urban rents from 1825 onwards meant that such purchases did not result in an increase in his income from rents. After 1830, this source of income declined as the farm rent declined and one holding remained empty. This slump in the property market hindered his strategy of gaining a stable income of around £1200 from his investments and deterred any further accumulation. His principal source of finance was a running debt with Mary and Ann Dibb.[31] They were relatives, possibly daughters, of his old partner. He may have used trust monies to provide them with income and himself with capital. His debt to them rose at the same pace as his accumulation of land. In 1826, when interest rates rose to 5 per cent and Atkinson was fifty-nine years old, he began to run down the debt. There was no way of knowing whether he used current income or drew money from the firm for this purpose, although liquidating a debt of £3743 in 1828 suggests either a capital transfer or further debt.

Somewhere around the age of fifty, John Atkinson, like Robert Jowitt, began to accumulate an increasing amount of capital in the form of rentier income-earning assets. He chose landed property because his own professional experience gave him a specialised knowledge of such investment, just as Jowitt's network of Quaker contacts would have helped inform him in his railway investment. Atkinson's need for such assets coincided with the decline in returns from Government stock after 1819, and the boom in the urban-property market in the early 1820s.[32]

John Jowitt junior, Robert's father, was like him a woolstapler. He started business in or before 1775. His father was a clothier in Churwell who died in 1784, at which time his son owed him £883 12s 11d and had recently received a gift of £1000.[33] Again, father was the major source of initial capital. The account books indicated a growing woolstapler's trade, purchasing wool in London and Norwich and selling to the clothiers of the villages to the south and west of Leeds.

In the 1790s, John Jowitt began to place money on loan and mortgage. The main sums involved are listed in Table 8. There was a small rent income from an estate in Churwell and some smaller debts in the villages to the south. One of these, to the Horsfalls of Gildersome, paid only 7s in the pound when those brothers went bankrupt in 1808. Smaller amounts of money, in addition to the usual trade credit, were lent through the firm. In addition to £5000 to John Lister Kaye, there was £1400 in lesser sums, including £200 to the Leeds Water Works.

On the death of his brother Joseph, the partnership with Joseph and Samuel Birchall, his youngest brother-in-law, was broken up. He spent a short period on his own before going into partnership with his son. After 1802 the business expanded westwards into the worsted and heavy-woollen areas, selling in Golcar, Holmfirth, Honley, Saddleworth and Huddersfield as John followed the expansion of the textile industry in those areas during a period of slower growth in the Leeds area. Despite the creation of a rentier income in the 1790s, John Jowitt junior never entirely withdrew from trade before his death in 1814.[34]

His choice of investment was again influenced by his personal

TABLE 8 John Jowitt junior: loans and mortgages, 1796–1814

Name of debtor	Dates, sums involved and comments
Nevins and Gatliff	1796, £1000 1801, £350 1802, £326 (This seems to have grown as a trade debt. It was transferred to the executors of John Jowitt junior in 1814 and helped support his widow and daughters. See also Pim Nevins.)
Leeds and Liverpool Canal	1796–1802, £2000
Sir Henry Carr Ibbetson	1799–1805, £1400
Walter Fawkes of Farnley Hall	1799–1814, £1500 (This debt also was transferred to the executors.)
Pim Nevins	1801, £700 1806, £2000 more was raised (The Nevins family were related to the Jowitts by marriage to John's sister Elizabeth. In part this loan provided finance for the building of Larchfield Mill.)
Sam Elam	1804, £1500 1808, £1000 outstanding.

Source. John Jowitt junior, ledger 1775–1815, BAJ 38, 39.

contacts and knowledge and by the economic opportunities of the period at which he reached the relevant stage in his life cycle. Thus, he contributed loan finance to the canal boom; capital to merchanting and manufacturing in wool textiles, through links forged by family and Quaker contacts; and, finally, mortgage finance to the agricultural sector, in a period when rising food prices added to the value of agricultural land.[35] There was no way of knowing if these funds went to agricultural development in the final high-cost round of enclosure or to sustain the consumption patterns of the Ibbetson and Fawkes households. The contact was probably made by lawyers acting as mortgage brokers.

The timing of the transfers of capital from the firm to loan and mortgage finance was clearly related to the high profits of the mid-1790s, but the relevance of age to this decision was demonstrated by the different behaviour patterns of John and of the younger partner Samuel Birchall. After the high profits of 1793–5, of which John took £3515 and Birchall £1758, the older man withdrew £8001 to finance loans and mortgages whilst the younger partner withdrew only £1136 and allowed the rest to accumulate as capital in the firm.[36]

III

These three examples all fit the pattern of the middle-class property cycle outlined in the introduction. This cycle is one possible explanation of the manner in which consumption and investment decisions were taken. The switch, somewhere around the age of forty, from investment in business capital to investment in assets producing a rentier income, and the slow withdrawal from business sometime after the age of fifty were features common to all three examples. The typicality of these three examples in this respect may be tested against the imperfect but readily available data of the printed census returns which relate occupation to age structure (see Table 9).

Both the solicitors and merchants were dominated by men in their thirties and forties, reflecting the long and costly period of training. The proportion of solicitors declined sharply in the mid-fifties. The decline was greater than can be accounted for by the normal demographic fate of that age group. The merchants survived longer, reflecting the partial withdrawal from business which was possible for those who went into partnership with their sons. One drawback of using the printed census returns is their failure to take account of multiple occupational titles, a practice which would obscure the gradual change of income source suggested by the three examples. House proprietors have been chosen as an example of those with a rentier income, as this category was more likely to be dominated by the urban middle class than those groups labelled landowners or fundholders. The share of this group in the population rose sharply in their late forties and fifties as the successful middle class moved from other occupations.

IV

This paper has concentrated on one aspect of the property cycle. Somewhere around the age of forty, the successful middle-class man began to accumulate assets, not in trade or business but

TABLE 9   Age structure of solicitors, merchants and house proprietors, Great Britain 1851

| | Each age group as % of those over 15 | | | | | | | | | | | | | | | Total (no.) |
	15–19	20–4	25–9	30–4	35–9	40–4	45–9	50–4	55–9	60–4	65–9	70–4	75–9	80–4	85+	
Solicitor, attorney, writer to signet	–	6·1	11·7	13·7	14·1	13·5	12·7	11·4	6·8	4·5	2·4	1·6	1·0	0·4	0·1	13,256
Merchant	4·5	6·6	10·9	12·5	11·7	11·0	9·6	9·5	6·8	6·8	4·1	3·1	1·7	1·0	0·2	10,103
House proprietor	0·3	1·5	2·7	3·9	5·5	7·0	9·3	11·3	11·2	13·3	11·9	10·3	6·9	3·5	1·3	12,184
Total male population of Great Britain 15 years of age and above	15·8	14·3	12·5	11·0	9·4	8·5	7·0	6·2	4·5	4·1	2·7	2·1	1·2	0·6	0·3	6,484,234

Source. Census of Great Britain, 1851.

in a form which produced an unearned or rentier income. In doing so he often accepted lower rates of return than those expected in trade or business, but he gained an income which fluctuated less and which required less effort and attention to maintain. Thus, this switch of asset acquisition fulfilled the social purpose of preparing an income for old age. This social purpose explained the willingness and indeed the eager need of the middle class to acquire assets of this kind in land, mortgages, bonds and shares. This need explained the willingness of investors to move capital from the relatively high-profit areas of commerce, industry and the professions to assets attracting these lower returns. This provided not only loan finance for industry and commerce but also capital through shares and mortgages for public utilities, urban house-building and the transport system. The property cycle was the mechanism which created the willingness to provide such capital. Willingness was not the same as ability and this must be explained by the market opportunities and cost structures of the Industrial Revolution. Although the nature of this switch of assets and the broad timing of the change for each individual can be explained by the life cycle, the details of the timing of the change were related to prosperity in business. Thus Robert Jowitt's property cycle was delayed by the losses of the early 1820s, and change was made possible by the profits of the 1830s. The timing and nature of the change were also determined by the availability of suitable assets. Each man's choice of assets reflects not only his personal knowledge and contacts but also the economic attractiveness of each form of asset in different decades.

Although the property cycle has been outlined in terms of the conditions of 1780–1860, this cycle was not specific to that period. Most readers will recognise a version of this cycle in their own lives, for in the last fifty years an increasing portion of the British population has become locked into a property cycle dominated by the pension fund, life-insurance companies and building societies.[37] The development of these institutional intermediaries and the mandatory saving which feeds many of them have spread the risk of investment, taken away from the individual most of the responsibility for managing his own property cycle, and masked the process of acquiring and receiving rentier income, as such an income now comes to the bulk of the population in the form of pension rights and the imputed rent of an owner-occupied house rather than as interest and dividends. In the 'pre-industrial' period, recent studies of inheritance customs in sixteenth- and seventeenth-century Europe have shown that old age was provided for by the handing over (investing) of the farm to selected children in return for care in old age.[38] The mechanisms differed but the social need was the same, tempered only by harsher demographic conditions, which reduced the number of people too old to work and reduced the length of time they survived. The Industrial Revolution not only increased the need by improving demographic chances of survival, but also improved the ability to purchase such assets by the wider range of commercial, industrial and professional opportunities during the earlier stages of the life cycle, and by providing an increasing number of assets which could satisfy such needs. This symbiosis of social and economic need was part of the mechanism which provided capital for the economic infrastructure of housing, public utilities and improved transport during the Industrial Revolution.

Notes

1. B. S. Rowntree, *Poverty: A Study of Town Life* (London, 1902) p. 137; John Foster, *Class Struggle and the Industrial Revolution* (London, 1974) pp. 96–9, 255–8.

2 R. G. Wilson, *Gentleman Merchants: The Merchant Community in Leeds, 1700–1830* (Manchester, 1971) pp. 9–34, 241–8; T. Wemyss Reid, *A Memoir of John Deakin Heaton, MD* (London, 1883); W. G. Rimmer, *Marshalls of Leeds, Flax Spinners, 1788–1886* (Cambridge, 1960) pp. 1–14; R. A. Church, *Kendricks in Hardware; A Family Business, 1791–1966* (Newton Abbott, 1966) pp. 19–46.

3 S. Pollard, *The Genesis of Modern Management* (London, 1965) pp. 150–6; J. P. Addis, *The Crawshay Dynasty* (Cardiff, 1957) pp. 5–15.

4 M. W. Flinn, *Men of Iron: The Crowleys in the Early Iron Industry* (Edinburgh, 1962) pp. 3–95; Rimmer, *Marshalls of Leeds*, pp. 162–228.

5 When Paine advocated welfare provisions for his democratic state, he suggested a partial pension at age fifty, when a man 'begins to earn less and is less capable of enduring wind and weather', and a full pension at sixty, when 'his labour ought to be over, at least from direct necessity' – Thomas Paine, *The Rights of Man* (1791), Everyman edn (London, 1906) p. 249. He thus reflected the practice amongst the middle class who had adequate financial resources.

6 Letters to John Jowitt, clothier at Churchwell near Leeds, 1775–6 (despite the occupational attribution, the transactions described in the letters are those of a woolstapler), Business Archives Jowitt (BAJ) 30, Brotherton Library, Leeds University. The BAJ papers are fully described in P. Hudson, *The West Riding Wool Textile Industry: A Catalogue of Business Records* (Pasold Research Fund, 1975), but note that her numbering differs from that of the Brotherton Library. For other details see John Jowitt junior ledgers 1775–1815, BAJ 38, fo. 84 and BAJ 10, fos 1–12, stock account; and Wilfred Allott, 'Leeds Quaker Meeting', *Publications of the Thoresby Society*, L (1965) esp. 50.

7 Robert Jowitt, private ledger, 1803–45, BAJ 2 fos 3–4.

8 Will of John Jowitt late of Leeds, woolstapler, Court of Ainstie, Sep 1815, Borthwick Institute of Historical Research, York.

9 This was the eternal problem of all individuals and communities when devising the rules of inheritance. See Jack Goody, Joan Thirsk and E. P. Thompson, *Family and Inheritance: Rural Society in Western Europe, 1200–1800* (Cambridge, 1976) p. 4.

10 Mean income 1806–42 was £2085 with a standard deviation of £1349, whilst that for 1843–62, excluding the two extreme years of 1848 and 1854, was £2090 with a standard deviation of £773.

11 Mean income 1806–62 was £2291 with a standard deviation of £1563 and coefficient of variation ($100s/\bar{x}$) 68·2, whilst mean cash consumption spending 1806–62 was £922, standard deviation £353 and coefficient of variation 38·3. If a linear relationship is sought between cash consumption and income (Y) then $r = 0·3$ with $s = 0·01$. The result would be even poorer if the two large incomes (1848 and 1854) had not occurred in the high consumption period.

12 If a linear relationship is sought for S and Y, then $r = 0·97$.

13 For the relationship between savings ratio and income, $r = 0·65$. The relationship is linear only in the middle ranges of income, £1000 to £4000.

14 Robert Jowitt and Sons, private ledger B, BAJ 17; John Jowitt and Sons, private ledger C, BAJ 41.

15 Robert Jowitt, private ledger, 1803–45, BAJ 2; Robert Jowitt and Sons private ledger B, 1829–45, BAJ 17; Robert Jowitt and Sons, private ledger C, 1845–62, BAJ 18; M. C. Reed, *Investment in Railways in Britain, 1820–1844* (Oxford, 1975) p. 87; J. R. Killick and W. A. Thomas, 'The Provincial Stock Exchanges, 1830–1870', *EHR*, 2nd ser., XXIII (1970) 96–111.

16 Reed, *Investment in Railways*, pp. 193–223.

17 His behaviour reflected the availability of such assets within Great Britain, as shown by Table 10.

TABLE 10   Total capital investment in Great Britain, gas and railways, 1826–46

Year	Gas (£m) (historic cost)	Railways (£m) (total share loan and debenture capital)
1826	3·150	0·401
1838	7·600	26·788
1846	11·800	120·951

Sources. M. E. Falkus, 'The British Gas Industry before 1850', *EHR*, 2nd ser., XX (1967) 494–508; G. R. Hawke and M. C. Reed, 'Railway Capital in the United Kingdom in the Nineteenth Century', *ibid.*, XXII (1969) 269–86.

18 To John Jowitt Nevins, 26 Dec 1844, from Robert Jowitt letter copy book, Mar 1844 to Apr 1846, BAJ 32. All letters cited in notes 19–21 are from the same source.

19 To Joshua Hepworth, Park Lodge, 25 Apr 1840.

20 To Dillworth Crewdson, 5 Dec 1844.

21 To Henry Booth, Liverpool, 18 Mar 1846; to William Simpson, 21 July 1846; to R. Otley, Halifax, 18 Oct 1845.

22 To John Close, York, 27 Oct 1847, from Robert Jowitt letter copy book, 17 Sep 1846 to 17 Mar 1852, BAJ 33.

23 Reed, *Investment in Railways*, pp. 125–6, 131, 152 and 203–4.

24 DB 5/84, professional papers of John Atkinson. All references prefaced DB are to a collection of solicitors' papers in Leeds City Archives. My thanks to Mr Michael Collinson for showing me these.

25 DB 7/71, executors' papers for the estate of Thomas Atkinson, including the receipts for legacy duty and the probate copy of the will.

26 Reid, *A Memoir of John Deakin Heaton MD*, describes the manner in which the heavy opportunity cost and direct costs of the early stages in the career of a leading Leeds physician of the mid nineteenth century were financed by the wealth of his bookseller father.

27 DB 5/85, note book of accounts, 1888-9.

28 DB 5/54, rent account book, 1810-15.

29 DB 5/58, John Atkinson's rental, 1818-32; DB 5/68, property-tax receipts.

30 DB 5/3, conveyance of property in Little Woodhouse, Leeds, to John Atkinson, 29 Jan 1822.

31 DB 5/57, John Atkinson in account with Mary and Ann Dibb, 1815-28.

32 A. D. Gayer, W. W. Rostow and A. J. Schwartz, *The Growth and Fluctuations of the British Economy, 1790-1850* (Oxford, 1953) pp. 147-67 and 171-85; J. Parry-Lewis, *Building Cycles and Britain's Economic Growth* (London, 1965); A. K. Cairncross and B. Weber, 'Fluctuations in Building in Great Britain, 1785-1849', *EHR*, 2nd ser. IX (1956) 283-97; M. W. Beresford, *Time and Place* (Leeds, 1961); R. J. Morris, 'The Friars and Paradise: An Essay in the Building History of Oxford', *Oxoniensia*, LXVI (1971) 72-98; B. L. Anderson, 'The Attorney and the Early Capital Market in Lancashire', in *Capital Formation in the Industrial Revolution*, ed. F. Crouzet (London, 1972) pp. 223-55.

33 Will of John Jowitt of Churwell in the parish of Batley, clothier, 8 Jan 1782, Court of Ainstie, Sep 1784.

34 John Jowitt junior, ledger 1775-1815, BAJ 38 and 39.

35 J. R. Ward, *The Finance of Canal Building in Eighteenth-Century England* (Oxford, 1974); D. T. Jenkins, *The West Riding Wool Textile Industry, 1770-1835* (Pasold Research Fund, 1975); B. A. Holderness, 'Capital Formation in Agriculture', in *Aspects of Capital Investment in Great Britain, 1750-1850*, ed. J. P. P. Higgins and S. Pollard (London, 1971).

36 John Jowitt junior, ledger 1775-1815, BAJ 39.

37 Royal Commission on the Distribution of Income and Wealth, *Report no. 1. Initial Report* (London: HMSO, 1975) pp. 72-96 and 110-20.

38 J. Goody, *et al.*, *Family and Inheritance, passim*; M. Spufforth, *Contrasting Communities: English Villagers in the Sixteenth and Seventeenth Centuries* (Cambridge, 1974) pp. 80, 104-6.

6 Research and Development in British Industry from the End of the Nineteenth Century to the 1960s

S. B. SAUL

I

There is little doubt that at the end of the nineteenth century Britain was falling behind in the science-based industries developing new products and new technologies. In the traditional steam sector she had her final triumph with Parsons's steam turbine, though the high-speed generator he devised to go with it was in many ways as remarkable as the turbine itself. Ferranti had persuaded the London Electric Supply Corporation to build at Deptford a power station using generators of over ten times the capacity of anything successfully tried before that time and transmitting at the unheard of pressure of 10,000 volts. Nearly everything had to be designed from scratch, including the cables. It was a marvellous technological feat, but it failed because its costs were too high and demand for electricity grew more slowly than had been estimated. In that sense it was a very British piece of advanced technology, not unlike the nuclear-power stations of our own day. But the land of Faraday made only a minimal contribution to the further development of electricity before 1914.

It was, however, in the chemical industry that the contrast between Britain and her competitors seemed most alarming. Beginning with the failure to move wholeheartedly behind the Solvay ammonia process – a failure which in the short run at least could be justified on economic grounds – it stretched to a complete inability to match the brilliant German and Swiss achievements in organic chemicals. The new forms of power, such as diesels and petrol engines, also saw Britain lagging; for example, she imported a substantial proportion of her automobile engines and all her aircraft engines from France prior to 1914, and all the early experiments with motor ships originated elsewhere. Some have argued that this was simply a matter of rational specialisation, and that, but for the peculiar problems created by the war, it would be considered a reasonable and successful exercise of the principle of comparative advantage. In other words, the users wanted cheap dyes more than they wanted home-made dyes and they were right. But many contemporaries were more far-sighted; they knew that advantages did not just exist but had to be created by technological progress. It was important for Britain to adjust her industrial structure, to bring her trade patterns more in line with those of world trade as a whole and to move from the slower to the faster growth sectors.

The reasons behind this lag in advanced-technology industries have been much discussed. The weaknesses seemed to lie not so much in the field of pure research as in the unwillingness of British industry to show interest in the world of science. Possibly the fault lay with the managers of industry – self-made, practical men who scorned theory and research on principle, or men whose right to manage derived from nepotism, not from merit. There was widespread concern over the low level of scientific and, especially, technological education, which was felt to be deficient all down the ranks of industry. Some argued that the problem was not so much technological indifference on the part of industrialists as disinterest among the financial community. In some industries, electricity above all, the market offered little incentive to innovation. Argument over these matters continues, but undoubtedly Britain was lagging basically because the skills, methods and knowledge which had served so well in the past were largely irrelevant to the new world of advanced technology.

Yet the picture was not wholly black: change was coming about under both internal and external influences, so that, when the crisis of 1914 came along, the response was rapid and effective. If the chemical industry showed up the weaknesses in sharpest relief, it also provided the most distinct signs of a new attitude. Of all the individuals who played a more positive role, none was more important than Henry Roscoe, Professor of Chemistry at Owen's College, Manchester, who did more than any other to make that institution the only real competitor in Britain to the German university as a source of chemical education. When Hamilton Y. Castner, an American, came to Britain in 1887 to seek financial backing for his sodium process for the manufacture of aluminium, it was Roscoe who helped him obtain the money. That process was soon outmoded, but Roscoe and the same group of financiers went on to help develop Castner's electrolytic sodium process, which became the most modern way of manufacturing pure caustic soda and chlorine.[1]

It is interesting to note, too, that, when the new Hall and Héroult aluminium processes killed off the Castner method, they were quickly taken up in Britain. The British Aluminium Company, using cheap hydroelectric power, built its first plant on the shores of Loch Ness in 1894 and a bigger development at Kinlochleven in 1903. Its share of world output rose from 8 per cent (600 tons) in 1900 to 11 per cent (5000 tons) in 1910. Further growth was limited by the availability of power, so they moved energetically to buy falls in Norway and by 1914 had at least part ownership of three plants there.[2] The real pioneer of the new approach to chemistry, however, and a supporter of Roscoe, was Ludwig Mond, who in 1873 with J. T. Brunner began to manufacture sodium carbonate in England by the Solvay method. Mond was the scientific and technological genius of the firm and brought to it a real German flavour, laying the foundations of a successful, expanding and profitable business. His first chemists were Swiss, German or Hungarian, and when one of them, a foreigner not related to the owner, was made a member of the board of directors, it marked the company out as something very different in Britain.

Marconi, another foreign innovator, came to Britain for money and with the hope of putting his equipment in British ships. By early 1915 there were a total of 706 coast stations and 4846 ship wireless installations in the world and of these 225 and 1894 respectively had been built by Marconi in Britain. The company's research was led by Dr J. A. Fleming, professor of electrical engineering at University College, London.[3] In 1904 he invented the thermionic valve, the diode, though in the next year an American, Lee de Forest, brought out the triode by inserting the vital third electrode. Neither of them realised at the time the importance of what he had done, though the main stream of valve development was subsequently to come from the United States.

The import of technology was clearly extremely important in bringing an awareness of new ideas, but at least one major development in the advanced-technology field was very much a home product. In 1883 Sir Joseph Swan had patented his process for dissolving nitro-cellulose in acetic acid and extruding the resulting collodion under pressure through a series of holes, fibre emerging as fine threads. It was a process of major importance for the electric-lamp industry and also for artificial fibres, though it was not immediately followed up for that purpose. By the turn of the century many groups in Europe and the United States were working away at the chemical and engineering problems of producing viscose. Then in 1904 Samuel Courtauld bought the viscose rights of a small English firm. Soon he resolved the problem of developing a reliable process, capable of producing a yarn of consistent quality cheaper than the existing Chardonnet yarns and yet technically capable of wider use. It was management skills, engineering know-how, greater financial resources and the backing of their existing textile business that saw Courtauld through, not any very brilliant research. It gave the company a world lead, and in 1910 it established manufacturing across the Atlantic, through its American Viscose Company.[4]

As for other advanced industries, one might mention Dunlop and the pneumatic tyre. In automobiles there was F. W. Lanchester's astonishing series of technological advances: mechanically operated inlet valves, torsionally rigid chassis, compound epicyclic gear, propellor-shaft drive, preselector controls, forced lubrication, manufacture by interchangeable methods. All set him out as a giant among inventors, but he had no skill either as a manufacturer or salesman. What point was there in manufacturing to scale in an industry in its infancy, with technology changing at such a rapid rate? Lanchester failed to read the message of his own inventions. In the armaments industries, so important in Britain, demands on engineering skills and on metallurgy had early spin-off consequences. By contemporary standards, firms such as Vickers and Armstrongs put an unusual amount of their profits into research. The pressure for better gun technology, for armour plate and for lighter ammunition brought important benefits for shipbuilding, motor cars and general engineering. It was in the course of testing the suitability of high chromium steel for gun barrels that Harry Brearley in 1912 came across stainless steel – though, to be sure, he was not alone in his discovery.

As a further indication of change, though technical education itself was slow to develop, around 1900 several full new universities on more modern lines were opened: Manchester, Sheffield, Birmingham, Leeds, Liverpool and Bristol. At Birmingham, Joseph Chamberlain defined the purposes of the new university: 'We desire to systematize and develop the special training which is required by men in business.'[5] A department of brewing was set up, for example, and so was a faculty of commerce, though from the pictures on the walls most of the early students seem to have come from Japan. Industrialists began to endow these institutions generously. In 1907 the Imperial College of Science and Technology was established in London. J. B. S. Haldane, who was one of the great driving forces behind the newly emerging structure of higher education, may have exaggerated when he called it the 'Charlottenburg of London', but this amalgamation of three existing colleges was a major scientific event, and before the war, significantly enough, its main industrial link was with the dyestuffs industry.[6]

II

War in 1914 intensified these trends – eventually at least, for one of the early follies was an indiscriminate recruitment of scientists into the armed forces. In 1916 the Department of Scientific and Industrial Research (DSIR) was formed, to administer funds provided by Parliament for that purpose. Three lines of policy were followed. Grants were made to encourage the formation of research associations by industry. The first of these was set up in 1918 for the photographic industry and by 1923 there were twenty-four of them, though the number declined in the depression of the 1930s and the expenditure was never large – only £552,000 in 1939. Research was also encouraged in universities and finally a number of research stations were established, the total eventually rising to fifteen.[7]

The most significant industrial development for the future of advanced technology in Britain was undoubtedly the rapid growth of aircraft production and the entry of firms such as Rolls Royce and Napier into the manufacture of aero engines. By 1918 the British industry was the largest and technologically the most advanced in the world. There was intense pressure to eliminate the need to import the products of science-based industries from Germany. University departments helped make up the lag in the production of drugs, especially the laboratories at St Andrews, where dulcitol, inulin and novocaine were all produced, the last in particular eventually at higher-quality levels than in Germany.[8] Similarly, King's and Imperial Colleges, London, and Sheffield University tackled the problem of eradicating Britain's lag in the production of optical glass. Chance Brothers had closed their research laboratory in 1905, with neither Government help nor assured orders from the Army and Navy available. By 1917 the firm had a staff of 125 research workers and were marketing seventy-two types of optical glass, many previously only available from Germany. After the war, however, military demand collapsed, German competition was renewed and soon Chance's research staff was down to three. Recovery had to await Government aid to glass research and the impact of rearmament during the 1930s.[9]

Changes in the chemical industry were more dramatic. Not only was there a shortage of dyestuffs, but, in addition, it became apparent that the bulk of German explosives were being produced in factories that had previously made dyes. Temporarily dyes could be imported through Switzerland, but development of home production seemed the only logical answer. Progress was not encouraging at first, but in 1918 the British Dyestuffs Corporation was formed on the basis of Government loans and with import restrictions in force of quite unprecedented peacetime severity. Money and resolution were combined with excellent effect. A research department was set up under Professor W. H. Perkin, son of the inventor of mauve, and in 1920 a hundred chemists were being employed there. By 1928 over 90 per cent of British consumption was being met at home and during that decade seventy-eight new British vat colours were developed, some certainly new in the world. The Ionamine dyes, introduced in 1922, for example, solved the difficulty of producing a dye for acetate rayon, and the Duranol dyes, made by one of the few British firms outside British Dyestuffs, were yet more important in providing a wide range of colours.

One writer has suggested that, of seven major developments in the chemistry of dyes between the wars, five were of British origin.[10] The merger within the industry to form Imperial Chemical Industries (ICI) in 1926 brought much needed financial strength. The dyestuffs sector of the industry grew at an astonishing rate even during the depression, raising sales from £2·2 million in 1930 to £4·3 million in 1936, and Britain's share of world output rose from 3 to 12 per cent between 1913 and 1937.[11]

So one deficiency was remedied. Meanwhile Brunner Mond had been looking at the Haber Bosch ammonia-synthesis process. During the war the Ministry of Munitions had spent over £1 million on plant for nitrogen fixation without making very significant progress. Brunner Mond agreed to take over the operation if they were allowed to visit the German BASF works at Oppau, then under Allied control, to obtain all the information they could about how the process worked. However, they met with passive resistance from the German workers and did not learn as much as had been hoped. The Government set aside the BASF patents in Britain, but the breakthrough into production only came when two Alsatian engineers offered to sell all the drawings, tests and other data relating to a more advanced Haber Bosch works then under construction in Germany.[12] It was a dubious offer legally and even more so morally, but Brunner Mond decided to pay. Burglary and espionage had played their part, but Brunner Mond, now with a first-class laboratory at Winnington in Cheshire fully matching any on the Continent, after four years of slow progress began to add much of excellence of their own to the Haber process. The firm had a wide-enough profit margin, a sympathetic board and, in F. A. Freeth, a first-class director of research. Freeth believed that the chemical industry depended too much on university research and to bridge the gap gathered around him senior research staff who would undertake both background research and act as knowledgeable consultants to those engaged in developing industrial plant.[13] It was at Winnington, for example, that polythene was discovered in 1933 – rather fortuitously, perhaps, because the research team was working on a different project at the time. The minute amount of solid polythene, formed in the apparatus after experiments with ethylene, was identified, and, although two more years were to pass before a small sample of eight grams was deliberately made, it was decided to go ahead and develop the material. The first commercial production began in 1939 for use with submarine cables and then high-frequency cables for airborne and ground radar. Another major development was the transparent sheeting Perspex, which owed a lot of its initial success to demand from the aircraft industry; and to the end of the 1950s these products were easily the most profitable of all ICI's discoveries. Research expenditure in ICI rose markedly after the merger, but, even so, before 1939 it never significantly exceeded £1 million a year. By contrast, in 1927 and again in 1938, IG Farben was spending £7·5 million annually.[14] Another outstanding laboratory was that of the electrical group Metro-Vickers, where research was carried out into accoustics, high-voltage work and atomic physics.[15] Further, the General Electric Company (GEC) was employing 200 research staff in its new Wembley laboratories by 1927. In electrical engineering as in chemistry the emphasis passed from university to industry. The great advances before 1914 had come from university men such as Wheatstone, Kelvin, Clerk Maxwell and Lodge, but now Metro-Vickers, Siemens, GEC and English Electric were changing all that.

On the other hand, in man-made fibres the situation was less promising, as Courtaulds had little interest in basic research, and, from a practical point of view, were happy to buy the rights of others. They had broken through before 1914, when Continental works bristling with chemists had failed, so why change? They had pioneered some developments of their own (their hot-stretch process gave the yarn higher tensile strength – important for tyre cords), but the dilemma was there. It was typical of the type of problem often before British industry. Practical men might lead the way, but what then? Could they maintain their position by simply buying knowledge? The most successful, such as Pilkingtons in the glass industry, mixed both very effectively, but real success was never forthcoming over a long period without a considerable degree of individual initiative in research. Fortunately Courtaulds were to take the path to science-based expansion in good time, but the 1930s were years of low technical dynamism – though their rival, British Celanese seems to have been more active.

The immense and costly mass attack on fundamental problems by Du Pont which led to the discovery of nylon had no parallel in Britain, but terylene emerged there as the result of some very intelligent and inexpensive research, making use of the data published on the nylon experiments. The roots of the British technological revival were indeed deeper than is sometimes suggested. J. R. Whinfield, the discoverer of terylene, had been a pupil of two chemists, C. F. Cross and E. J. Bevan, who in the 1880s had had a practice as consulting chemists in London and had built up a worldwide reputation in cellulose chemistry and technology.[16] Whinfield joined the Calico Printers Association, which had a research budget of a mere £20,000 a year. There his investigations into some of the raw materials used in the industry, especially starch, chemically related to cellulose, led him on to work on artificial fibres and eventually to terylene. It was an invention deliberately sought and found, and thus contrasts with polythene, which was the result of careful and shrewd observation of an accident of technology. The necessary development expenditure, which proved to be around £4 million, was quite beyond the means of the Calico Printers and a licence was sold to ICI, who then made quite slow progress with it during those overloaded years of the late 1940s.

Between the wars Britain hardly maintained the pre-eminence in radio that had earlier been established by Marconi. On the other hand, although research for television was very active in the United States, it was Electrical and Musical Industries (EMI) in Britain that enabled the BBC to start the world's first service in 1936. The earlier Baird mechanical system had in fact been on trial since 1929, but it was inferior in picture quality and in reliability and Baird's own lack of faith and lack of knowledge of electronics lost him the lead. This was in any case an area for firms with considerable laboratory resources and finance, for it was not at all clear how quickly success could be won. The EMI achievement was remarkable in that work began three years later than at Radio Corporation of America (RCA), and yet the British began regular broadcasting three years earlier than their rivals. For once Britain won partly because of the actual level of resources employed. EMI had thirty scientists and 120 assistants at work in its laboratories in 1935, and, although RCA between 1930 and 1939 spent $2·75 million on R & D for television, EMI spent only a little less over the shorter period 1932 to 1939.[17]

The aircraft industry had mixed fortunes. It faced huge problems of readjustment from the boom of wartime to the very limited civil and military markets existing after 1918. Unfortunately, in

general the industry was dominated by men who had enjoyed
the successes of the war but had little vision of the future, and
technological advance was much influenced by the then highly
conservative Government research establishments. Consequently
Britain contributed little to the main developments in aircraft design
between the wars. There were, however, some areas of progress,
mostly in the military sector. The crucial invention in the development of flaps – the slotted wing – was made at Handley Page
during the 1920s with the help of the young immigrant German
scientist–aviator, G. V. Lachmann. The most original work was
done by Barnes Wallis on geodetic construction – a highly efficient
basketwork-like metal structure, though it proved too expensive for
civil use. The combination of R. J. Mitchell's designs of metal-
braced monoplanes for Supermarine and Rolls Royce water-cooled
engines won the Schneider Trophy races for seaplanes in 1927, 1929
and 1931 and the experience gained there was to lead to the development of the Spitfire with the Merlin engine in the late 1930s. The
Merlin engine was a brilliant technological success and was later
to be used for the highly successful American P51 Mustang. In
a general sense Rolls Royce was moving away from the old British
craft traditions. Its emphasis on hand work and neglect of new
technological ideas had led to a crisis in the car division in the
1930s. Symptomatic of the old methods was the fact that the
Eagle engines of the First World War were not made interchangeable and had to go back to the factory for repair. The firm was
to be rescued by brilliant work in the aero-engine field, but above
all – and significantly so – by the arrival of the dynamic Hives
as managing director, with an eye as firmly on making money
as upon technological feats. Then came the Anglo-German struggle
for the jet engine. Dr Griffith at the Royal Aircraft Establishment
worked on the problem in the 1920s, but from 1929 to 1936
research was discontinued, largely because of lack of funds during
the depression. Whittle, too, made only slow progress, even with
the modest financial backing (from 1935) of Power Jets Ltd. Not
until the war did the Government take a real interest. In Germany
the work of Hans von Ohain was developed much more actively
by Heinkel and Junkers, possessed of far greater resources than
Power Jets, and by 1939 the Germans were well ahead.[18] The
old British pattern of brilliant science but poor industrial resources
was all too apparent.

The experience of the inter-war years showed a real continuity with the pre-war developments through a growing concern for technology on the part of a wide range of British industries. Numerous firms had begun to build small research laboratories from the 1890s onwards and many more followed during and after the war: for some it was a good way of spending the otherwise 'excess' profits of wartime – but no matter, the outcome was valuable. Some, such as the chemical firms, wanted to be in the van of progress: some such as Colman's, the mustard-makers, wanted to diversify: some simply wanted a speciality in their usual line of business. Tootal Broadhurst Lee, a modest-sized textiles firm, set up a research establishment in 1918 with a group of scientists deliberately chosen, unusually enough, for their lack of special knowledge of textiles. They were positively directed to look for ways of reducing the tendency of cotton fabrics to crease. In 1932 they announced that their invention was ready for commercial application. A survey by the Federation of British Industry found 422 firms spending a total of £1,736,000 on R & D in 1930 and 566 spending £5,422,000 in 1938, a quite striking rate of growth. If we add for 1938 the DSIR grants to the research associations, along with their privately funded expenditures, then 0·15 per cent of national income was going to industrial R & D as compared with 0·5 per cent in the United States.[19] It was still small but the wind of change was obviously gathering strength. Nevertheless, the research efforts of some major industries remained derisory: from 1920 to 1926 the research association of the motor industry spent £26,000 and no individual company spent more. That industry's contribution to advanced technology was minimal and the steel industry was little better. The machine-tool industry remained, too, a negligible force in invention and innovation and consequently unable to give to mechanical engineering as a whole the taste for new ideas that so focal an area of advanced technology provided in the United States and Germany, for example. Industry in general still seemed unable to make itself attractive to university graduates, though, strangely enough, an astonishing amount of university effort went into training mining engineers, even if there was precious little benefit to show for it. The number taking pure science courses rose from 6300 in 1920–1 to 7400 in 1928–9, but the number in applied science fell from 7000 to 4100.[20] Nevertheless, Britain was now more aware of its commercial and strategic dangers, and some industries at least were far better placed than they had been to face competition. After all, it is worth noting that the share of Britain's industrial output coming from the most research-intensive industries by the Organisation for Economic Co-operation and Development (OECD) classification was 32 per cent in 1935 as compared with 28 per cent in the United States.[21] Something had been achieved.

III

The Second World War was dominated by technology to a remarkable degree – in aircraft, electronics, synthetics, materials, drugs and many other areas. In all of this Britain played a large part and, as we have seen, came to the war well prepared to do so. The build-up of science in her universities and in Government research establishments, the steady growth of advanced-technology industries with research capabilities of their own and men in charge receptive to new ideas now paid off. The traditional weaknesses in production and marketing were set aside by the overwhelming needs of the war effort. Of course, the greater resources and market of the United States and her smaller relative commitment to the actual prosecution of the war put that country even more firmly in the role of prime initiator of new technologies so far as the West was concerned. After the war the impotence of Germany, in particular, for some years gave Britain a competitive edge, and, although her relative role inevitably declined thereafter, she remained a major force in the development of advanced technology, ranking only below the United States and the Soviet Union.

In 1945 R & D expenditure was still only of the order of £30 million, as compared with about £6 million in 1938, but there then followed a period of very rapid growth, bringing the total to £187 million in 1955, of which 63 per cent was spent on defence and under one-third funded by private industry. By 1961 the total was approaching £400 million. It then grew slightly more slowly to reach £680 million in 1969, of which only 19 per cent was attributable to defence and two-thirds privately financed.[22] In 1962 the United Kingdom spent 2·2 per cent of her GNP on R & D, as compared with 3·1 per cent for the United States, 1·5 per cent for both France and the Netherlands, 1·3 per cent for West Germany and 1 per cent for Belgium. However, since R & D is very labour-intensive, it has long been recognised that research activities are more expensive in the United States, because of that country's high labour costs. To get some idea of 'real' research, therefore, research exchange rates are sometimes used to reflect more accurately the cost patterns of the United States relative to the others. These make the British ratio of R & D to GNP 50 per cent greater than that of the United States, the French ratio 24 per cent greater, and, by contrast, the West German 35 per cent smaller – all figures for 1962.[23] Table 11 gives the distribution of this effort; it excludes research in government research stations. The important but not overwhelming role of aerospace in Britain and the United States is apparent, as is the West Germans' heavy commitment to chemicals. The bulk of the research in the aircraft industry was government-financed in all countries, but in general some 60 per cent of industrial R & D in the United States was government-financed, as compared with 50 per cent in the United Kingdom.

TABLE 11   Percentage distribution of industrial R & D, 1962

	United States	United Kingdom	France	West Germany
Aircraft	36·3	35·4	27·7	
Machinery	8·2	7·3	6·4	19·2
Vehicles	7·4	3·0	2·6	
Electrical machinery and instruments	25·5	24·0	25·7	33·8
Chemicals	12·6	11·6	16·8	32·9
Metals	2·6	4·1	3·2	6·6

Source. C. Freeman and A. Young, *The R & D Effort in Western Europe, North America and the Soviet Union* (Paris, 1965) p. 73.

Expenditure by the DSIR rose from £682,180 in 1938–9 to about £2 million in 1946–7 and £3·4 million in 1957–8, and assistance was given to sixty private research associations.[24] Under the Development of Inventions Act 1948, the National Research Development Corporation (NRDC) was set up to develop inventions arising from public research bodies (excluding atomic energy) and to help private inventors and industry to develop their ideas to the commercial stage. The NRDC's first major contribution was to give orders for the early digital computers, but its most spectacular involvement was in the development of the hovercraft. It began to back Christopher Cockerell's invention in 1958, setting up a subsidiary, Hovercraft Development Ltd, for the purpose. Altogether some £15 million of public money was invested to 1974, but, though undoubtedly the work encouraged private firms such as Westlands to take up the idea, HDL had a very poor financial record, possibly because living on royalty income is less lucrative than the profits from successful production.[25] The NRDC became increasingly involved in joint ventures with industry, and in May 1971 186 of 404 current projects were joint ventures. 25,500 inventions had been submitted and 5360 accepted, though of these only a handful earned any revenue. New antibiotics, electric motors, a potato-planter, dental cement, selective weedkillers and carbon fibres were the most successful in this respect. From 1949 to 1972 expenditure was £57 million and income £30 million, though revenue continued to accrue in later years on the basis of existing licences.

Partly as a result of all this effort, Britain was able to continue to shift the distribution of her manufacturing output towards the most highly research-intensive areas, making the proportion 49·6 per cent in 1964, as compared with 48 per cent for the United States, 44·8 per cent for West Germany, 44 per cent for France and 33 per cent for Belgium.[26] No longer could concentration on the traditional slow-growth industries be considered a relevant reason for Britain's industrial weaknesses.

More strikingly, however, in 1964 her payments for technological royalties, licences, patents, manufacturing rights and so on were £45 million, as compared with an income of £42 million. This contrasted sharply with West Germany, where in 1963 payments at DM 541 million compared with income of only DM 199 million. In France the ratio was similar and in Italy in 1964 receipts were $39 million and payments $159 million. All countries had a large royalty deficit with the United States, though between 1964 and 1970 the ratio of British payments to the United States and her receipts from that country fell from four to one to three to one.[27] Britain's surplus ratio with the European Economic Community also improved. So, whereas the continental European countries were overwhelmingly importers of technology, Britain sent out as much as she took in. Whether she was wise to do this is another matter.

TABLE 12   Indicators of post-war advanced-technology achievements

	(1) Sources of 110 major innovations since 1945	Ranking of (1), corrected for country size	(2) Patent receipts ($m)	Ranking of (2), corrected for country size	(3) Share in the exports of research- intensive goods by these countries	Ranking of (3), corrected for country size
Belgium	1	5	7·9	6	3·5	9
Canada	–	10	6·2	8	3·4	9
France	2	9	46·3	5	7·7	6
Italy	3	7	9·9	9	5·9	8
Japan	4	8	5·9	10	5·3	8
Netherlands	1	6	26·0	2	5·3	4
Sweden	4	2	7·1	4	2·8	5
United Kingdom	18	3	76·1	3	14·2	3
United States	74	1	348·7	1	30·8	1
West Germany	14	4	49·4	7	22·1	2

Source. *Technological Innovation and the Economy*, ed. M. Goldsmith (London, 1970) p. 95.

Table 12 gives a good indication of the size of the British post-war effort. In columns 1 and 2, which refer above all to pure innovation, she was second to the United States in absolute terms and yields only one place when correction is made for country size. She yields place only to West Germany and the United States where exports of advanced technology goods are involved (column 3). This last measure has to be qualified in two important respects, however. Research-intensive goods have no monopoly of fast growth in world trade and there is some evidence that by this second standard of performance Britain was less successful. In 1968 the share of her exports in the three fastest–growing groups in world trade as a whole was 59·4 per cent, slightly below the world average and well below the shares of the United States, Switzerland and West Germany.[28]

IV

Looking to particular industries, in certain major areas of electronics, for example, British achievements were distinctly limited:

the US market advantage was overwhelmingly significant there. Home firms made most of the early computers in Britain and these were used largely for scientific purposes, but, as elsewhere in Europe, International Business Machines (IBM) quickly came to dominate the field as commercial data-processing spread. In 1966, output of computers was lower in Britain than that in France and West Germany, even though her R & D expenditure was almost half as big again.[29] In 1957 the British firm Plessey developed the world's first integrated circuit, under contract from the Royal Radar Establishment, whose scientists had first formulated the idea five years before. However, they were unable to develop it further at the pace achieved by Texas Instruments and Fairchild in the United States. Partly this arose from lack of money, partly because the first major use was for missiles, which Britain was then abandoning.[30] She had the technology but not the market, and the impetus was lost. Britain was, however, more successful in certain specialised areas. Elliott Automation, significantly already makers of thermostats and regulators, were very much to the fore in producing industrial electronic control equipment, for example. But the greatest success derived from the original work on radar, in which Britain had taken a significant lead during the war. Decca and Marconi played a dominant role in the development of marine and airborne radar and navigation and display systems. Three-quarters of all ships at sea by the 1960s had British radar and most of the world's civil airports outside the American continent used British navigational equipment. There was also the unique development of blind landing equipment, first used by British European Airways in the Trident. Much of the civil work in radar was a fall-out from defence work, though experience showed that direct use of military equipment for civil needs was usually unsuccessful. The best firms doing military work also had large civil R & D teams; knowledge came from the spill-over, but development had to take a specialised path.

The British chemical industry made a major effort in synthetics after the war and, without really matching the work of American and German firms, became a potent force in world markets. By 1960, for example, her share of world exports of all synthetics, at 12 per cent, was half as big again as in 1938.[31] ICI had raised its expenditure on R & D from £783,000 in 1938 to just over £6 million by 1952. Though the expansion was spread across all activities, much the largest increases were made in dyestuffs and pharmaceuticals, in agricultural chemicals and in plastics.[32] ICI experienced the usual problems involved in linking technical advances to its general organisational structure and economical policies. It was difficult, for example, to disentangle pharmaceuticals from the Dyestuffs Division during the 1940s and early 1950s, when pharmaceuticals throughout the world were undergoing a revolution, and as a result the ICI effort was very half-hearted. The therapeutic revolution began in the late 1930s, with the discovery in France of the qualities of sulphanilamide. By 1950 the explosion of products and of demand was well under way and output of the pharmaceutical industry in Britain rose from £21 million in 1937 to £280 million in 1965, even though 60 per cent of her sales were in the hands of foreign-owned firms, whose R & D effort was generally well below that in their home bases. In 1973 only one-third of the industry's R & D in Britain was carried out by these subsidiaries, whose parent firms viewed Britain as an export base rather than as a research centre. The wholly British Beecham group, whose laboratories were entirely a post-war venture, in 1957 made a major advance in the development of semi-synthetic successors to penicillins. Beecham had no manufacturing experience for this kind of product and consequently made an exchange agreement with the US firm Bristol Myers, obtaining production know-how in return for certain manufacturing rights. Between 1957 and 1966 the group spent £10 million on development, and by 1968–9 world sales of ampicillin, the most important of the series, stood at £70 million annually and it was then the leading broad-spectrum antibiotic on the market. Sales of all new penicillins produced by or under licence from Beecham equalled 20 per cent of all antibiotic sales. The royalty income of the group in 1968–9 was £3·7 million mostly from antibiotics.[33] In 1971 Britain held about a fifth of world exports, slightly more than the United States and as against a quarter for West Germany and 17½ per cent for Switzerland. The ratio of exports was most favourable to Britain too, though there was a substantial net payment of royalties and profits. The figures in Table 13 show the relative size of the British research effort, and, considering the somewhat negative role of the foreign-owned subsidiaries, and the need for British firms to make good early deficiencies, the results were certainly impressive.

TABLE 13   R & D in pharmaceuticals, 1950–67

	R & D ($m)	R & D (% of sales)	Major inventions
United States	365	7·5	67
West Germany	44	7·0	15
Japan	42	6·0	1
United Kingdom	33	8·5	10
France	28	6·5	11

Source. C. T. Taylor and Z. A. Silberston, *The Economic Impact of the Patent System* (Cambridge, 1973) p. 262.

The most striking innovation of all came in the glass industry, through Pilkington's float-glass process for producing plate glass. The basic idea was to produce a continuous ribbon of glass from the furnace and to float it on a surface of molten metal. The surface of the glass was unspoiled and consequently the expensive process of surface grinding of the glass was eliminated. It was a remarkable innovation – the idea of one man, Alistair Pilkington – involving fundamental changes in production methods. From 1952 to 1958 £4 million was spent on it, but between 1962 and 1969 licence receipts came to £17·5 million and in 1971–2 royalties were running at £9 million per annum and the process had been licensed to twenty-one manufacturers in twelve countries.[34]

In some fields a great deal of help came from American subsidiaries. Their role had grown sharply between the wars, and in 1967 there were 1600 US subsidiaries and Anglo-American financed firms in Britain, employing 6 per cent of the labour force. Furthermore, 82 per cent of the net assets of these firms were in research-intensive industries, as compared with 42 per cent of the assets of all UK firms. Of this total of 82 per cent, chemicals accounted for 35 per cent, mechanical engineering for 19 per cent and motor vehicles for 18 per cent.[35] There were those who argued that such firms tended simply to take over the benefits of British technology and to stifle the research effort in Britain. On the other hand, it could be said that the British research effort was too widely dispersed in relation to her resources of skilled scientists and engineers, and in such a context US firms were being helpful in not doing further research. A major point being made in this essay is not that the British research effort after 1945 was weak, but that British firms, for the most part, did not possess the resources or the flair to exploit what had been discovered. In this sense US firms were bringing what was most lacking. In fact, however, there is some evidence that US subsidiaries generally did more R & D than their British counterparts, as Table 14 shows, though it will be seen that there is no great difference in the chemical industry, the largest single area of US interest.

TABLE 14   R & D compared with net output, 1961

	US subsidiaries in UK	All UK firms
Chemicals	4·8	4·5
Office machinery	16·3	2·3
Instruments	3·4	6·0
Vehicles	6·2	1·4
Machine tools	6·4	2·3
Other non-electrical engineering	8·6	2·3
Electrical engineering	4·8	5·6

Source. B. R. Williams, *Technology, Investment and Growth* (London, 1967) p. 21.

There have been areas where the outcome of British research has disappointed, and none more so than atomic energy. Britain exploded her first atomic bomb in 1952. Civil nuclear development had been entrusted to the Ministry of Supply and then in 1954 to the Atomic Energy Authority (AEA), which subsequently undertook much more of the manufacturing work for nuclear-power stations than the US Atomic Energy Commission. In 1956 the world's first nuclear-power station was opened at Calder Hall in Cumberland and between 1955 and 1963 four Magnox gas reactors were commissioned. In 1957 a prototype advanced gas-cooled reactor (AGR) was started at Dounreay in Scotland and was in full power in 1963. Two years later the first commercial plant was ordered. Progress thereafter was agonisingly slow, however, and during the 1960s American water reactors swept up all overseas orders. After a series of cautious moves from small to large experimental reactors, then on to larger prototypes, the US commercial companies had accepted heavy initial expenditures for the sake of an effective future programme.

It is now generally agreed that it was unwise to move so quickly with the Magnox and the AGR from a small prototype to a

full-scale programme of nuclear-power stations, leaving both technical and engineering problems inadequately worked out, and that
the decision to concentrate on this type of reactor was mistaken,
because it had inherent characteristics likely to lead to high costs
and slow development. The reasons are difficult to determine:
one may well have been a desire for speed in the hope of maintaining
Britain's technological lead, a problem encountered in other high-
technology areas. Antagonism between the AEA and private industry and the inability to control effectively the massive civil
engineering works required have also played a part. The result
has been a meagre and expensive contribution to Britain's power
supplies and no success in exports at all in return for a very
heavy investment.[36]

The greatest effort, however, went into the aircraft industry,
and here both the successes and failures of Britain's large post-war
R & D programme have been clearly apparent. In 1942 the Government had asked a committee under Lord Brabazon to recommend
the types of civil aircraft to be developed after the war. The
more ambitious turned out to be absurd and costly failures, but
the Viscount, the world's first turbo-prop airliner, with Rolls Royce
Dart engines, was a great success. Turbo-props were a unique
contribution of the British industry, and though the later, large
turbo-prop airliners, the Vanguard and Britannia, suffered from
jet competition – the rigid structure of fares made it impossible
to make competitive use of their excellent economics – several successful smaller aircraft were built and Dart engines were employed
also in a number of foreign aircraft, most notably the Fokker
Friendship.

The failure of the world's first jet airliner, the Comet, as a
result of metal fatigue, was inevitably a major commercial set
back to the industry. The incident illustrates well a major problem
Britain has faced in many advanced-technology goods. The US
advantage in the home market was so great that the British
(and the French) could compete only by offering something new
or of very rare quality. In so far as Britain was ahead in engine
technology, that was where the lead might come. It was won
with the turbo-prop. The Comet was a more adventurous step
and failed. Sud Aviation, using the same Avon jet engine, penetrated
the medium-range field through the brilliantly original concept
of the Caravelle, with its rear-mounted engines, though its sales

were restricted by its failure to penetrate the US market. The supersonic Concorde involved infinitely greater strides. Incredibly enough, all the technical prognostications came very close to fruition – the US supersonic aeroplane, the SST, went awry so obviously so early that the decision to cancel was inevitable. The problem was that, with so much of the aircraft's load devoted to fuel, errors of under 0·5 per cent in the forecasts could cumulatively have devastating consequences for the economics of the aircraft, quite apart from questions of noise and rising fuel prices. So another bold venture resulted in commercial disaster. The Fairy Rotodyne form of helicopter also tried – with far less justification – to move from one extreme to another. The whole concept depended on a largely theoretical rotor blade of stainless steel with a life of up to 3000 hours, and nothing like this was ever achieved. By and large the great leaps did not succeed, but a truly cautious aircraft such as the Vanguard failed badly too. The problem was to find the right niche in time: the Viscount did this; so did the BAC 111, which sold to three US airlines; and so did the executive jet DH125 and the Canberra fighter bomber, actually manufactured in the United States as the Martin B57.

In a technological sense the British industry in no way fell behind its competitors. The Lightning was, for example, the first aircraft with a 60 per cent wing sweep.[37] In engines Britain was to the fore in the early jets, in turbo-props and in vertical-lift engines; the Conway was the first fan jet and radical new design concepts appeared in the RB211. Another special element of the British industry was its strong equipment base, something quite lacking in the rest of Europe. Equipment was placed in many foreign as well as British aircraft but the most important returns came to those firms also serving wider needs. Electronic control and navigation systems of all kinds were, as we have seen, one major example, and it is significant that in West Germany, where the defence effort was much slighter, the industrial electronics sector was slow to develop, despite the existence of a large general electrical industry. Prior to 1939 the hydraulics industry in Britain was confined to very low pressures, and yet by the post-war period the demands of the aircraft industry had so transformed the technology that high pressures could now be combined economically with reliability. In coalmining the new knowledge was used to develop hydraulic props and from this came a situation whereby cutting, transport and roof control could all be remotely controlled. In a different field came hydrostatic transmission, whereby the relatively inefficient clutch, gearbox and mechanical transmission with its stepped ratios were replaced by a system giving complete stepless control from one lever with no clutches or gearboxes – mostly for use in heavy vehicles. Disc brakes were used for aircraft just after the war and in the 1950s Dunlop began to experiment with them on racing cars: in 1956 disc brakes were first used in production cars for Jaguar. The spin-off from the Rolls Royce aero engines in the form of industrial and marine gas turbines was very considerable. To April 1974 over 1300 engines worth £164 million had been sold. The spin-off from aerospace R & D, intelligently developed for civil use, was an important aspect of post-war advanced technology in Britain, especially as such industries were less developed elsewhere in Europe.

V

One of the most serious factors bedevilling the relationship between the advanced-technology industries in Britain and the general health of the economy has been the excessively nationalistic view of this question pressed with great force by engineers and scientists who believe that 'the more research the better' is the only approach. Selectivity, or lack of it, has in fact been a major post-war weakness. In the post-war years Britain has not been a net importer of licences in the way that West Germany and France have been, but it is not clear that the latter have been misguided. There are, of course, difficulties in relying on licences. The licensor always has the greater depth of experience and lies at least one jump ahead. Often he requires further knowledge to be passed back to him and clearly there is a threshold of R & D that is necessary in order to keep in touch and to retain the possibility of unique advances of one's own. The problem is one of balance. In the nineteenth century countries with small populations, such as Sweden, Switzerland and the Netherlands, realised that they had the resources only to concentrate on limited fields of activity. The costs of modern R & D must now inevitably force intermediate-size countries to do the same.

There are those who have argued that expenditure on R & D has been wrongly directed towards the so-called 'high-technology industries' and that it should have been spread more widely over industry in general. The evidence for this is not very strong. There is no indication of any relationship between growth of output and productivity on the one hand and R & D expenditure on the other, either in Japanese industry, whose experience is most commonly contrasted with that of Britain, or indeed in British industry itself.[38]

A recent study comparing the growth of total productivity in British industry in 1963–8 and the ratio of R & D to net output failed to show any close direct link between the two. There were some examples of correlation. Man-made fibres headed the list, with total productivity growing by 56 per cent and an R & D ratio of 10·6 per cent. Plastics had a similar ratio and a growth of 36 per cent. Productivity growth for pharmaceuticals was 27 per cent and the ratio 7 per cent. At the other end came iron and steel, with a growth rate of 2 per cent, and shipbuilding, where productivity declined by 7 per cent, and both with R & D ratios of only 1·4 per cent.[39] Nevertheless, it was concluded that, taking all industries into account, the link was only an indirect one, through the relationship of both R & D and productivity to the rate of growth. R & D is simply an input like any other and a high level of activity is more appropriate to some industries than to others: of itself it does not ensure high productivity, which will come only by bringing the technology effectively to production and then to the market. It is a matter for concern that so few qualified scientists and engineers are to be found in production and marketing; possibly the dispersion of effort leaves too few available. In 1962 the proportion of such men in R & D was 25 per cent in Britain, as compared with 17 per cent in France and 15 per cent in Japan and West Germany.[40]

The point remains, however, that investment in R & D for the development both of new processes and of new products offers an opportunity to British industry but no guarantee that industry will successfully carry out production and marketing. What one can surely argue is that in the competitive world that Britain now faces, with no great advantages in mass-production industries, facing competition from third-world countries with very low wage costs in many sectors, but having herself lower labour costs in science-based and developmental industries than have most other advanced countries, and with a background of high-technology development that we have seen expanding markedly over this century, the obvious course is for British industry to continue to develop its research-intensive industries as its niches for future participation in world trade. It is to be hoped, however, that this will be done with greater commercial acumen and success than in the past.

Notes

1 See generally D. W. F. Hardie, *Hamilton Young Castner* (Widnes: ICI, 1952).

2 L. Ferrand, *Histoire de la science et des téchniques de l'aluminium et ses dévelopements industriels*, vol. I (Paris, 1960) p. 274.

3 See W. J. Baker, *A History of the Marconi Company* (London, 1970) esp. ch. 11. Scarcely less important was Fleming's continued training of engineers.

4 D. C. Coleman, *Courtaulds*, vol. II (Oxford, 1969) p. 63.

5 Quoted in M. Sanderson, *The Universities and British Industry* (London, 1972) p. 82.

6 See H. E. Heath and A. L. Hetherington, *Industrial Research and Development in the UK* (London, 1945) p. 249.

7 OECD, *Research Associations in the UK* (Paris, 1967) p. 41.

8 Sanderson, *Universities*, p. 223.

9 See generally R. and K. MacLeod, 'Government and the Optical Industry in Britain, 1914–1918' in *War and Economic Development*, ed. J. M. Winter (Cambridge, 1975) p. 170.

10 H. W. Richardson, 'The Development of the British Dyestuffs Industry before 1939', *Scottish Journal of Political Economy*, IX (1962) 118–22.

11 W. J. Reader, *ICI: A History*, vol. II (London, 1975).

12 Ibid., vol. I (London, 1970) p. 364.

13 J. A. Allen, *Studies in Innovation in the Steel and Chemical Industries* (Manchester, 1967) pp. 37–42.

14 Reader, *ICI*, vol. II, pp. 34 and 87.

15 M. Sanderson, 'Research and the Firm in British Industry, 1919–39', *Science Studies*, II (1972) 110–113.

16 Allen, *Studies in Innovation*, p. 56.

17 C. T. Taylor and Z. A. Silberston, *The Economic Impact of the Patent System* (Cambridge, 1973) p. 308.

18 See R. L. Perry, *Innovation and Military Requirements*, Rand Corporation memo. RM 5182 PR (Aug 1967).

19 Sanderson, in *Science Studies*, II, 119–22. Another source puts *total* investment in R & D in 1938 at 0·28 per cent of national income. See *The Role of the Government in Research and Development*, Hill Samuel Occasional Paper no. 4 (London, 1969) p. 10.

20 L. F. Haber, *The Chemical Industry, 1900–1930* (Oxford, 1971) p. 364.

21 C. Freeman, 'R & D. A Comparison between British and American Industry', *National Institute Economic Review*, May 1962, p. 30.

22 'Resources Devoted to R & D by Manufacturing Industry', *Economic Trends*, Mar 1974, p. xxxiii.

23 R. Caves, *Britain's Economic Prospects* (London, 1968) p. 449.

24 G. L. Payne, *Britain's Scientific and Technological Manpower* (Stanford, Cal., 1960) p. 345 ff.

25 See generally P. G. Johnson, *The Economics of Invention and Research* (London, 1975) pp. 144 and 153.

26 Caves, *Britain's Economic Prospects*, p. 47.

27 Central Statistical Office, *R & D Expenditure* (London, 1973) pp. 122–5.

28 H. Panić and A. H. Rajan, *Product Changes in Industrial Countries' Trade, 1955–61* (London: National Economic Development Office, 1971) pp. 10 and 41.

29 OECD, *Gaps in Technology, Computers* (Paris, 1967) pp. 17 and 57.

30 OECD, *Gaps in Technology, Electronic Components* (Paris, 1967) p. 59.

31 G. C. Hufbauer, *Synthetic Materials and the Theory of International Trade* (London, 1966) p. 42.

32 Reader, *ICI*, vol. II, p. 449.

33 Taylor and Silberston, *Economic Impact*, pp. 258–9.

34 Ibid., p. 365 and T. C. Barker, *Pilkington Brothers and the Glass Industry* (London, 1960) pp. 193–210.

35 J. H. Dunning and Max Steuer, 'The Effects of US Direct Investment on British Technology', *Moorgate and Wall Street*, Autumn 1969.

36 See generally D. Burn, *Nuclear Power and the Energy Crisis* (London, 1978).

37 Perry, *Innovation and Military Requirements*, p. 47.

38 See S. B. Saul, 'There's More to Growth than R & D', *New Scientist*, (23 Sep 1976) pp. 633–5.

39 Taylor and Silberston, *Economic Impact*, p. 71. Subsequent research has suggested a greater correlation with growth if R & D is treated as capital expenditure.

40 B. R. Williams, *Technology, Investment and Growth* (London, 1967) p. 5.

7 Ungentlemanly Conduct: The Control of Soccer-crowd Behaviour in England, 1888-1914[1]

WRAY VAMPLEW

Soccer, in its modern form, stems from the formation of the Football Association (FA) in 1863.[2] The gradual but general acceptance of the rules issued by that body enabled teams to play each other without a debate as to which side's rules should apply. For about two decades soccer was dominated by Old Boys' teams, who emphasised the way in which the game was played rather than the result of the match, and whose matches did not draw large crowds. Even the FA Cup Final, the premier event of the soccer season, attracted an average of fewer than 3500 spectators in the 1870s.[3] In the North and Midlands, however, soccer became adopted by the working classes and winning became all-important. This desire to win led to professionalism, at first veiled, but eventually legalised by the FA in 1885. At this time most matches were 'friendlies' and teams frequently turned up late or not at all. On other occasions, 'through Cup-tie interference, clubs [were] compelled to take on teams who [did] not attract the public'.[4] When clubs were paying their players such a situation could not be countenanced. The demand for certain, regular and meaningful fixtures resulted in the formation of the Football League in 1888. Initially with twelve clubs, the League was expanded to fourteen in 1891, and to sixteen in 1892, the year in which a second division of twelve clubs was begun.[5] Soccer had taken off as a spectator sport. By the mid-1890s 'it [was] no rare thing in the North and Midlands for twenty to thirty thousand people to pay money to witness a League match or important cup-tie'.[6] Club receipts reflect this interest: in successive quinquennia from 1889–90, Everton's seasonal gate receipts averaged £6880, £8749, £8916 and £14,642,[7] and those of Aston Villa rose from an average of £261 per season in the three years from 1878–9, to £1481 in the period 1884–5 to 1886–7, and to £3925 in 1890–1 to 1892–3.[8]

II

Along with the growing popularity of soccer came the problem of crowd misbehaviour. A study of contemporary comments on the game has led one historian to conclude that 'riots, unruly behaviour, violence, assault and vandalism appear to have been a well-established, but not necessary dominant pattern of crowd behaviour at football matches at least from the 1870s'.[9] A reading of the minute books of the FA and the Football League Management Committee confirms this view for the 1880s and 1890s.

Many clubs, even those with enclosed grounds, did not separate the spectators from the playing area by anything more than a painted touchline. Thus, when excitement got the better of the crowd, or simply when too many people were allowed in to watch the match, spectators were apt to encroach onto the pitch. There were several instances, particularly in the 1890s, when crowd invasions forced games to be abandoned. Even worse was actual crowd disorder involving assaults on persons and property.

Recent work by social psychologists has argued that such outbursts can be classified according to the major motivation of the spectators involved. Mann and Pearce, for example, have differentiated five categories of sports-crowd riots, known as the FORCE typology – a handy mnemonic for *f*rustration, *o*utlawry, *r*emonstrance, *c*onfrontation and *e*xpressive disorders.[10] Of these five types of disturbance all but 'remonstrance' (political protest) can be found at soccer grounds in the nineteenth and early twentieth centuries, though the majority of incidents appear to have been of the frustration or confrontation varieties.

Frustration disorder occurs when spectators' expectations of access to the game and the way it will be played or adjudicated are thwarted. A prime example of this was at Blackburn on Christmas Day 1890, when over 3000 spectators turned up in anticipation of an exciting first-team struggle between the home side and their local rivals, Darwen. Blackburn, however, had a hard match due on Boxing Day at Wolverhampton and fielded what was virtually their second team. Darwen responded by taking their players from the field and replacing them with their reserve eleven. The crowd was not amused. Hundreds swarmed onto the pitch to uproot the goalposts, while others attacked the grandstand, smashing windows and tearing up the carpets in the section occupied by the Blackburn directors.[11] The abandonment of matches which the fans believed should have continued also sparked off frustration riots, as at Everton in 1895, when the referee declared the pitch unplayable after only thirty minutes of the game. A mob threw stones through every window they could find, woodwork was smashed for use as weapons, and threats were made to burn down the stands. Eventually two contingents of police answered the call for assistance, drew their batons, attacked the rioters and cleared the ground.[12] Perceived injustice can also become a source of frustration, as when fans believe that an incompetent or biased official has cost their team victory. In the early years of the Football League, referees frequently had to run the gauntlet of disgruntled spectators: a brief random survey of complaints to the League or FA in 1895 reveals referees assaulted at Wolverhampton and Woolwich Arsenal, hit by mud at Sheffield, and insulted at Derby.

Confrontation disorder breaks out when spectators from rival religious, geographic, ethnic, or national groups come into conflict. Given the appropriate circumstances, smouldering resentment can easily spark into open hostility. Local 'derby' games where regional supremacy is at stake are an ideal setting for confrontation riots. In 1880, a time at which Darwen and the neighbouring Blackburn Rovers were fierce rivals, an incident involving Marshall of the home side and Suter of Blackburn inflamed the 10,000 spectators. Their views as to who was at fault divided according to their allegiance, and the subsequent riot forced the abandonment of the match.[13]

In *expressive disorder* the intense emotional arousal which accompanies victory or defeat, particularly if it is exciting or unexpected, triggers uninhibited behaviour in which members of the crowd become completely abandoned. Cup matches with sudden-death exits from the competition are the likeliest sources of expressive disturbances. Following non-League Norwich City's game with first-division Chelsea in 1913, the East Anglian supporters went on the rampage outside the ground, throwing missiles and damaging property.[14]

Finally there is *outlawry disorder*. This occurs when groups of violence-prone spectators use sports events to act out their anti-social activities by attacking officials, fighting with rival fans and destroying property. Such crowd violence is seen as the work of a delinquent or criminal element. Although it is difficult to pinpoint historical examples, particularly as this type of rioter would no doubt join in other kinds of disturbance, a description of soccer fans in 1899 may be illustrative of outlawry disorder:

> there were many thousands at Shrewsbury on Easter Monday, and the concomitants of betting, drinking, and bad language were fearful to contemplate, while the shouting and horseplay on the highways were a terror to peaceful residents passing homewards.[15]

Another revealing remark was the comment that 'it all depends upon the measure of civilisation in your locality whether there is or is not a good deal of fighting after the match'.[16]

The above categorisation concentrates upon the apparent motivation of the unruly spectators, but it is likely that deep-rooted structural strains and social tensions underlay many of the disturbances and provided a set of conditions conducive to disorder. Many sociologists would argue that any explanantion of collective violence, including disorder at sports events, requires an analysis of such strains and tensions existing in society at the time.[17]

Whether one accepts Walvin's theory that the bulk of soccer fans came from among those members of the industrial working class who first gained Saturday half-holidays, the workers in 'textiles, metals, engineering, mining, shipping and port industries' or Hutchinson's view, based on an examination of photographs and accident reports, that soccer was followed by the upper levels of manual workers, skilled tradesmen and foremen, and the lower levels of white-collar workers, clerks and minor administrators, it is clear that soccer, at a spectator level, was a game for the working classes.[18] Why else would most grounds be located in working-class areas? These men often became not just fans but fanatics because of the deprivation and alienation they faced in wider society.[19] Deprived of power and esteem at work, they found a surrogate identity as partisan team-supporters, basking in the reflected glory of a winning team or regarding defeat as an intolerable deprivation to an already deprived group. To many men sport performed a compensatory function, providing relief from the monotony of work and also allowing them openly to challenge authority by barracking the referee. Although such supporters themselves could rarely triumph over the real social and economic institutions with which they were surrounded, their team at least could defeat its opponents. Thus the personal psychological frustrations and tensions of the working men were released by group identification. The intense role of sport in such persons' lives meant that their reactions to sports events became highly emotional: thus anything which threatened their enjoyment of their sport could easily lead to a frustration riot, and the euphoria of winning or the despair of defeat easily spilled over into expressive disorder.

Conflict between rival fans also stemmed from the emotional attachment of supporters to their team. Their identification might be based on several factors, among them geographical attachment, or a common bond of religion, ethnic or national background. Such identification was often strengthened by the local team providing a source of popular culture in the community. The supporters of that team became an identifiable subculture with their team songs and distinctive garb; the team became their reference group, conferring vicariously a sense of pride and esteem. Where supporters developed a strong sense of collective identity, their 'us' *versus* 'them' conflict situations could erupt into disorder, with matches becoming symbolic struggles for supremacy between Protestant and Catholic, between one area of the city and another, between England and Scotland. Team, group, and personal status was at stake.

III

Football's ruling authorities[20] made it clear that they expected clubs to keep their supporters in order. Two statements, selected from many available in the respective minute books, illustrate this. In October 1895 the Football League Management Committee 'held all clubs responsible for any assault on visiting teams or referees' and in March 1911 the FA reiterated its warning that 'misconduct by spectators will not be tolerated. It is the duty of the clubs to stop it.'[21]

In 1892 the Football League produced a poster which was approved by the FA and which all affiliated clubs were instructed to display prominently. It read:

> Spectators and players are requested to assist in keeping order at all matches on this ground, and to prevent any demonstration of feeling against the referee, the visiting team, or any player. The consequence attending any misconduct of this kind may result in the closing of the ground for purposes of football. Such a course would not only entail great monetary loss, but would bring considerable disgrace to the Club.[22]

This was no idle threat. If misbehaviour did occur, then cautions, fines and closures soon followed, though, as will be seen, relationships between the authorities and the clubs were not totally punitive. As well as meting out punishments, the League and the FA also proffered advice, made suggestions and occasionally gave direct orders as to what precautions clubs could take to minimise crowd disorder.

The FA and the Football League were in a powerful position to force clubs to take action. In 1881 the FA had taken powers to expel 'any associated club which shall be deemed to have done anything derogatory to the game' and three years later a ban was placed on matches between such disqualified clubs and clubs that remained within the FA's fold.[23] At its inception in 1888 the Football League declared 'that any offending clubs or players shall be dealt with by the League in any manner that they may think fit'.[24] Thus any clubs that were unwilling to accept the League's authority could forfeit a place in the most financially rewarding and highest status-giving league tournament in English soccer, and clubs that were unwilling to recognise the paramount authority of the FA could find it difficult to obtain fixtures at all.[25]

By 1914, thanks partly to this prompting and persuasion by

the soccer authorities, five major policies had been devised to assist in the control of crowd behaviour. These were efforts to control misconduct in the sport, improved organisation of matches, the segregation of spectators from the pitch and from each other, attempts to ban gambling on soccer, and the use of control agents.

The major triggers to crowd disorder lay in what happened on the field of play: violent fouls and bad decisions could easily provoke a disturbance. As early as 1880, following disgraceful scenes at a Darwen *versus* Blackburn game, the FA had given the referee power to order off players and had taken the responsibility to impose suspensions on such offenders. By the early 1890s any player who had been sent off could expect to be a spectator for at least a month.[26] Although sending-off and suspension possibly could have deterred players from deliberately playing in a violent manner, their total deterrence is questionable, as soccer is a body-contact sport with much room for heat-of-the-moment violence.

A great deal, of course, depended on the referees. Initially the Football League refused to entertain any complaints about a referee's competence: indeed, apologies were often demanded from those rash enough to question the official's judgement. When the Darwen executive made 'an outrageous and totally unfounded' accusation that the referee in their team's match with Bolton was under the influence of drink, they were ordered to make a full and public retraction in several newspapers. The League Management Committee also refused to recognise Mr A. F. Reeves as secretary of Stoke until he made ample apology and withdrew his 'serious imputations' against a referee.[27] Later, however, possibly because fewer members of the Management Committee were themselves referees but more likely because of the growing financial importance of match results, the League authorities became less dogmatic on the issue of the referee's omniscience. In 1897, following complaints from several clubs about particular officials, 'note was taken to avoid as far as possible their appointments in matches of complaining clubs'.[28] By 1900, although the referee's views were still accepted on specific decisions, such as penalties, goals, the state of the ground and the accuracy of the timing, when his general competence or efficiency was questioned, particularly by more than one club, observers were sent to report on his matches. This new policy resulted in incompetent referees being suspended, removed from the list, or being given a hint to retire, as in the case of an official who 'while in West Yorkshire and Lancashire for the purpose of acting as a referee in certain matches during Christmas Tide did not keep himself in the condition that the FA and the Football League would have the right to expect from persons who are appointed to such responsible positions'.[29] Nevertheless, it should be stressed that these officials were in the minority. Generally the Management Committee continued to support the referee: in the season 1912–13, for example, of some fifty-four complaints only one resulted in a referee being suspended. By this time referees underwent a stiff selection procedure and had to work their way up from being linesmen and referees in lower-grade soccer.

By the original rules of the League, referees had to be neutral. They also had to be seen to be neutral, so other decisions, usually taken after specific complaints, warned clubs not to allow referees to have luncheon with either players or club executives; not to write to congratulate referees who had secured a place on the list; and not to pay a referee more than his just fee and railway expenses. For their part, referees were told of the undesirability of speaking to players during the game and of supplying critiques to the clubs of matches in which they had officiated, and they were banned from writing for the press or betting on football matches.[30]

Undoubtedly it was better to have competent and unbiased referees, but no official is perfect and any one of the many decisions which he has to make during a game may be sufficient to spark off disorder. In any case little could be done without the partiality of the football fans. When the League Management Committee circularised referees to request them to cut down violence in the game, they told the referees to distinguish between 'robust' and 'rough' play.[31] Such distinctions are far easier for the partisan team-supporters with their distorted perceptions than for the match official.[32]

Frustration disorder could easily break out if spectators felt that a team was not giving of its best. Obviously, if the team was out of form the remedy lay within the club, but if the cause was premeditated corruption or misconduct then the football authorities had a role to play. Whenever there were suspicious circumstances, as revealed in referees' reports or even in anonymous letters, it appears that the incident was investigated by either the League or the FA. Generally the allegations were not substantiated: for example, Leicester Fosse's 12–0 thrashing by Nottingham Forest was attributed to the 'remarkably good form' of the Forest players and the fact that the bulk of the Fosse team had attended a wedding two days before and had kept up the celebration the night preceding the match.[33] However, when misconduct was believed to have taken place, action was swift and severe. Billy Meredith of Manchester City, for instance, was banned for three years for offering a bribe to an Aston Villa opponent.[34] Retribution was no respector of persons, as is best illustrated in the infamous incident of 1910 when Colonel T. Gibson Poole, Chairman of Middlesborough, offered £30 to Charles Thompson, the Sunderland captain, to arrange to lose the Teeside derby so as to boost Poole's chances at a Parliamentary election the following week. Thompson, however, informed his own chairman, who in turn reported the matter to the FA. Both Poole and A. D. Walker, the secretary and manager of Middlesborough, who had acted as intermediary, were expelled from the FA and hence from most organised football.[35]

Whether the scandals which came to light were the tip of an iceberg is a matter for conjecture, but it is likely that they were not. Even a stern critic of professional football acknowledged that the game seemed 'irreproachably straight'.[36] Admittedly this was in the 1890s, but a search of the later literature reveals no general belief that soccer was a corrupt sport. It would thus appear that the threat of banishment acted as a deterrent, particularly as the onus was on the accused to prove himself innocent.[37]

Improved organisation could also reduce the stimuli to frustration disorder. A major issue was that of matches starting late, sometimes so late that darkness forced the game to be abandoned. For more than a decade League teams were at liberty to fix their own kick-off times and occasionally this led to a miscalculation as clubs sought to give the paying spectator time to get to the ground after finishing work. The main offenders, however, were usually visiting teams or officials who failed to arrive on time. In 1892 the Football League warned that teams and officials not turning up in time were 'open to a charge of objectionable conduct' and thereafter offenders were usually fined and, in the early years, compensation was paid by late teams for any loss of gate receipts.[38] If a late start forced the match eventually to be abandoned, a replay was usually ordered, with the offending club or official paying some financial penalty. Initially, however, only the unexpired time was replayed, which led to some ludicrous situations, as when Stoke, 4–2 down to Wolves, had to journey to Wolverhampton to play only three minutes.[39] Later the Management Committee began to use its discretion either to let the score stand as it was at the time of the abandonment or to insist that the whole game be replayed.

Another organisational problem which could anger the crowd was the fielding of weak teams, either because first-team players were being rested prior to an important game or because teams turned up short-handed. That teams should be at full strength was one of the original rules of the Football League and clubs that broke this rule were fined, sometimes as much as £250, which was the equivalent of a 10,000 gate. When it was a matter of not having enough players, initially it was the player who failed to arrive who was fined, but by 1904 the emphasis shifted to disciplining the clubs for not having sufficient reserves available. As with kick-off times, these policies seem to have been generally successful and by 1914 abuses of the rule were rare.

One aspect of crowd segregation was the construction of different viewing areas by the use of fences, walls and stands and the allocation of spectators among these areas by differential pricing. Although it was laid down that the minimum admission charge to a League game was to be 6d for men and 3d for ladies and boys, clubs were free to charge extra for entrance to the stands. Most clubs initially settled on an extra 6d, but, with the later investment in improved facilities prices were increased; when Manchester United, for example, opened its Old Trafford stadium in 1910, it cost 1s, 1s 6d and 2s for various sections of the covered stand and 5s for a reserved seat in the centre stand.[40] Physical segregation and differential pricing were primarily economic policies designed to increase returns by supplying different spectator markets, but they did have the indirect effect of making it easier to contain disorder to the areas in which it broke out, thus rendering it less offensive to those elsewhere and perhaps also enabling it to be put down more readily. Unfortunately, it is possible that in certain circumstances segregation actually encouraged disorder. Crowd density, a significant influence on spectator behaviour, may have intensified disorder in certain areas; moreover, if segregation led to the grouping together of similarly motivated spectators from the same class, then, as communication is facilitated where persons have pre-existing group ties, the dynamics of crowd disorder could spread faster.[41] The best segregation policy, so far as the clubs were concerned, was the exclusion of undesirable spectators, a matter insisted upon by the FA in the case of known troublemakers and aided by the adoption of the turnstile.

Both the FA and the Football League were keen that fans be kept off the pitch, partly to prevent matches from having to be abandoned because of encroachment, but also to lessen the chances of assault on players and officials. When overspill did occur, clubs were generally fined, replays ordered (often with a proportion of the gate money going to the visitors) and the clubs told not to let it happen again. How to ensure this was left to the club executives. As regards the prevention of assault, the basic policy was to request rather than insist that clubs take action. In 1895, following an attack on the referee at Woolwich Arsenal, the League 'suggested' that 'clubs rail in their grounds and take every precaution to prevent spectators crossing the playing field at the conclusion of their matches', and, three years later, clubs were told that they should 'try to make the best possible arrangements to prevent crowding on the ground after the play is ceased and also to make arrangements for the visiting team to have as good an exit as possible'.[42] However, at stadia where assaults did occur, railings and fences were demanded on penalty of ground closure.

There was no doubt in the minds of the football authorities that a strong link existed between betting and crowd disorder. Nevertheless, as the law stood in the late nineteenth century, it was not clear that clubs had any legal right to forbid betting at their matches.[43] Gambling appeared to be legal at all sports events at which gate money had been charged: indeed, it was felt that the police could not eject bookmakers from the ground even if the club executives requested them to do so. Fortunately for the clubs, however, new interpretations of the law towards the turn of the century made it difficult for bookmakers to set up business inside the sports grounds and the FA determined to enforce these interpretations. In 1892 clubs were 'required to take all reasonable measures to prevent gambling by spectators', and in 1897, following several court decisions, bills were posted on all grounds pointing out the illegality of gambling on the terraces.[44] Warnings and the co-operation of the police led to a reduction

in the degree of observed betting at soccer matches.[45] In the immediate pre-war years, however, came the development of coupon
betting, in which bets were lodged by post prior to the matches.
Although both the FA and the Football League made strong con-
demnatory statements about coupon betting, there was little that
they could do about it.[46] Thus, as spectators could well have
had a bet on the match which they were watching, there was
always a possibility of dissatisfied gamblers causing trouble.

Preventing betting at the matches, keeping the crowd segregated,
ejecting troublesome spectators, and stopping field invasions or
encroachment required the use of control agents – namely, gatemen
and stewards supplied by the club and police hired from the local
force. The role of the stewards and police was primarily to enforce
compliance with regulations and to act as a deterrent to trouble-
makers, but should a disturbance occur they could be employed
to contain and put down the disorder, as they most certainly
did at Blackburn in 1900 and at Stockport in 1912.[47] The FA
and the Football League encouraged, and occasionally ordered,
clubs to prosecute spectators who were guilty of causing disturbances
and they expected clubs to provide sufficient police protection
to keep the crowd in order.[48]

IV

The football authorities and the clubs could do nothing to rectify
the social structural strains which may have been at the root
of crowd disorder. Instead they looked to a collection of measures,
some designed to remove the triggers to disorder, others to contain
any outbursts which did erupt. Contemporary observation suggests
that generally these were successful. Hutchinson's study of soccer
crowds notices growing references to 'the respectable nature of
the spectators, their enthusiastic but controlled behaviour', and
finds that by the early twentieth century mention of field invasions
was infrequent.[49] There is some statistical support for this view.
Table 15 shows that there was a significant drop in the number
of clubs being cautioned or having their grounds closed for spectator
misconduct.

Although the measures were not always undertaken with crowd
control as their primary objective, their efficacy had consequences
for spectator behaviour. Improvements in the organisation and

TABLE 15   Football clubs punished for crowd misbehaviour, 1895–1912

	Closures	Cautions
1895	4	8
1896	10	13
1897	6	2
1910	–	3
1911	3	1
1912	1	1

Source. FA minute books.

conduct of soccer matches reduced the stimuli to frustration and confrontation disorders; the fencing-off of pitches, the segregation of various sectors of the crowd, and the exclusion of specific spectators lessened the dangers of confrontation and outlawry disturbance; and the stricter controls on betting and the deterrent effects of control agents reduced the likelihood of all kinds of disorder. When trouble did occur, both the segregation of the crowd and, especially, the presence of the police acted to weaken the contagion dynamics of disorder and to contain the disturbance.

Much credit for the reduction in crowd disorder must go to the FA and the Football League Management Committee, not only for specific measures which they themselves undertook, but also for their insistence that a club control its own supporters and their willingness to impose penalties on clubs should the fans get out of hand. Additionally it can be suggested that, as time progressed, the economic costs of crowd disorder also encouraged the League clubs, and possibly others, to take action to curb spectator misconduct. In response to growing spectator demand, many clubs invested heavily in their grounds. Manchester United, for example, expended nearly £36,000 on its new stands at Old Trafford in 1909, Blackburn Rovers spent £33,000 on Ewood Park between 1905 and 1915, and Everton laid out £41,000 at Goodison in the three years to 1909.[50] Thus there was a significant amount of property at risk in the early twentieth century and clubs naturally wished to protect this investment from damage by rioting fans. In addition, of course, the increased gates[51] meant that the closure of a ground inflicted heavier financial penalties on the clubs concerned.

Crowd disorder at soccer matches did not disappear. It was impossible to remove all the triggers to disturbance: few controls could be exerted on coupon betting, heat-of-the-moment violence by players, or the bias of the partisan supporter. Even crowd segregation could have adverse effects. In any case the social structural strains, which were an important antecedent to disorder, still remained. Indeed, since the working man was becoming more aware of his relative economic and social deprivation, it might have been anticipated that soccer-crowd disorder would worsen.[52] Possibly, in the absence, from the 1890s, of such a sustained campaign of action and reform from the football authorities and the clubs, this would indeed have been the case; as it was, the behaviour of the soccer crowd improved just as strikes became more numerous and violent, suffragettes took to direct action and the gunrunners of Ulster prepared to stand and fight. Evidently not all the indicators of public order on the eve of the First World War point in the same direction.

Notes

1 I am grateful to the Football Association and the Football League for permission to consult their minute books, held at, respectively, Lancaster Gate, London, and Lytham St Annes. Where generalisations are made based on these records no specific references will be given: otherwise the abbreviations FA and FL will be us d to indicate the source. Thanks also go to the Flinders University of South Australia for assistance towards the research costs of this paper, which is part of an on-going project on the economic and social history of sport in Britain.

2 For a good study of the development of Association Football, see P. M. Young, *A History of British Football* (London, 1969). See also G. Green, *The History of the Football Association* (London, 1953).

3 Calculated from data in Green, *History of the FA*, p. 592.

4 Letter of William McGregor, 2 Mar 1888, outlining his idea for the formation of a league by the leading English clubs. Quoted in C. E. Sutcliffe, J. A. Brierley and F. Howarth, *The Story of the Football League, 1888–1938* (Preston, 1938) p. 2.

5 Although this paper concentrates on League football, the major crowd-puller, there were several thousand other teams playing in England and drawing varying degrees of support. In 1909 the FA estimated that around 1 million people watched soccer every Saturday, of which about a quarter were at Football League games. (Green, *History of the FA*, p. 253.)

6 M. Shearman, *Football* (London, 1895) p. 166.

7 Calculated from data in T. Keates, *History of the Everton Football Club, 1878/79–1928/29* (Liverpool, 1929) p. 126.

8 Calculated from data in D. D. Molyneux, 'The Development of Physical Recreation in the Birmingham District from 1871 to 1892' (unpublished MA thesis, University of Birmingham, 1957) p. 282.

9 J. Hutchinson, 'Some Aspects of Football Crowds before 1914', Society for the Study of Labour History conference on 'The Working Class and Leisure', (University of Sussex, 1975), paper 13 (mimeo.) p. 11.

10 L. Mann and P. Pearce, 'Social Psychology of the Sports Spectator', in *Psychology and Sport*, ed. D. Glencross (Sydney, 1978).

11 C. Francis, *History of the Blackburn Rovers Football Club, 1875–1925* (Blackburn, 1925) pp. 150–1.

12 Keates, *History of Everton FC*, p. 147.

13 Francis, *History of Blackburn Rovers*, p. 27.

14 FA Emergency Committee, Feb 1913.

15 Quoted in J. Walvin, *The People's Game* (London, 1975) p. 76.

16 C. Edwardes, 'The New Football Mania', *Nineteenth Century*, XXXII (1892) 622.

17 N. Smelser, *Theory of Collective Behaviour* (New York, 1962); M. D. Smith, 'Sport and Collective Violence', in *Sport and Social Order: Contributions to the Sociology of Sport*, ed. D. W. Ball and J. W. Loy (Reading, Mass., 1975).

18 Walvin, *The People's Game*, p. 53; Hutchinson, 'Some Aspects of Football Crowds', pp. 7–9.

19 For the views of modern sociologists, see J. Clarke, 'Football and Working Class Fans: Tradition and Change', in R. Ingham *et al*, *Football Hooliganism* (London 1978); and S. Edgell and D. Jany, 'Football: A Sociological Eulogy', in *Leisure and Society in Britain*, ed. M. Smith, S. Parker, and C. Smith (London, 1973).

20 The power relationship between the FA and the Football League is too complex an issue to be dealt with here. It is extensively covered in Green, *History of the FA*, and in Sutcliffe, Brierley and Howarth, *Story of the FL*.

21 FL, 7 Oct 1895; FA Emergency Committee, 23 Feb–8 Mar 1911.

22 FL, 3 Feb 1892.

23 Green, *History of the FA*, p. 396.

24 FL, 17 Apr 1888.

25 In 1907 several of the old amateur clubs, concerned at the growing influence of professional clubs in the FA, broke away from the FA and formed the Amateur Football Association. The FA persuaded all its affiliated associations, the other home national associations and those on the continent to refuse recognition to the secessionists. This prevented the amateurs from making tours and ruled many quality players out of consideration for the Olympic Games. In 1914 these amateurs decided once again to recognise the ultimate authority of the FA. See Young, *History of British Football*, pp. 159–60; Green, *History of the FA*, pp. 203–28.

26 Ibid., pp. 395–6; FA, *passim*.

27 FL, 11 Oct 1893, 11 Sep 1894 and 16 Oct 1894.

28 FL, 5 Dec 1897.

29 FL, 3 Feb 1908

30 FL 21 Jan 1892, 6 Nov 1903, 5 Sep 1904, 28 Sep 1909, 12 Aug 1910, 6 Jan 1911 and 9 Sep 1912.

31 FL circular, 13 Jan 1910.

32 For an interpretation of an American-football match as 'seen' by the rival supporters, see A. H. Hastorf and H. Cantril, 'They Saw a Game: A Case Study', *Journal of Abnormal and Social Psychology*, XLIX (1954) 129–34.

33 FL, 14 May 1909.

34 B. Dobbs, *Edwardians at Play* (London, 1973) p. 68.

35 FA, Report of Commission into Complaint against Middlesborough FC, 16 Jan 1911.

36 Edwardes, in *Nineteenth Century*, XXXII, p. 623.

37 This seeming reversal of normal legal practice was probably owing to the difficulties of establishing guilt where evidence on oath could not be insisted upon.

38 FL, 14 Oct 1892.

39 FL, 1 Dec 1893.

40 Young, *History of British Football*, p. 164.

41 Smith, in *Sport and Social Order*, p. 313.

42 FL, 15 Feb 1895 and 14 Apr 1898.

43 For a discussion of the law and gambling in the nineteenth century, see W. Vamplew, *The Turf* (London, 1976) pp. 199–212.

44 FA, 9 May 1892 and 6 Feb 1897.

45 Green, *History of the FA*, p. 149.

46 FL, 24 Feb 1913; Green, *History of the FA*, pp. 535–6.

47 Francis, *History of Blackburn Rovers*, p. 164; FA Emergency Committee, 9 Mar–12 Apr 1911.

48 For example, FA, 16 Dec 1895, 5 Feb 1896 and 29 May 1896; FL 15 Feb 1906.

49 Hutchinson, 'Some Aspects of Football Crowds', pp. 5 and 14.

50 FA, Manchester United FC – Report of Commission, 30 Sep 1910; Francis, *History of Blackburn Rovers*, p. 196; Keates, *History of Everton FC*, p. 129.

51 Everton's average league gate in 1913–14 was £957 (FA circular, 30 Sep 1914). The club's average gates in 1889–90 can be estimated as £236 and in 1897–8 as £509 (calculated from data in Keates, *History of Everton F.C.* p. 126). Both these are maximum figures, as they are simply total gate receipts divided by the number of league games played; no allowance is made for cup matches, and as Everton were FA Cup finalists in 1897–8 the average gate for that season is more likely to have been of the order of £430. League positions in the respective seasons were: second, 1889–90; fourth 1897–8; fifteenth, 1913–14.

52 S. Meacham, ' "The Sense of an Impending Clash": English Working Class Unrest before the First World War', *American Historical Review*, LXXVII (1972) 1343–64; J. Lovell, *British Trade Unions, 1874–1933* (London, 1977).

8 Charles Booth's Poverty Survey: Some New Approaches

MICHAEL CULLEN

'Chadwick's claims to the parenthood of modern sociological investigation have been brushed aside in favour of his successor, Charles Booth . . .': thus, in his Introduction to the Edinburgh University Press edition of Edwin Chadwick's *Report on the Sanitary Condition of the Labouring Population of Great Britain, 1842* (Edinburgh, 1965), Michael Flinn implies both the importance of the social investigations of the early Victorian period and the continuity of tradition from those inquiries to the work of Charles Booth and others at the end of the nineteenth century. Booth is now seen to be part of a peculiarly British approach to sociology – weak on theory (at least explicit theory) but strong on empirical research – which dates back to Petty, Graunt, King and Halley in the seventeenth century but reached its Rostowian take-off point in the work of Chadwick, Farr, Porter and the rest of the social statisticians of the 1830s and 1840s.[1] In terms of both method and conclusion, a feature of this tradition is the recurrence of certain themes and problems accompanied by a failure to provide entirely satisfactory solutions to those problems.

One of the most obvious recurring elements is a particular style of research and presentation which imparts to the reader an immediate and vivid impression of the people being described. An early example of what is meant here occurs in the Rev. David Davies's

The Case of Labourers in Husbandry Stated and Considered (1795):

> *No. 1.* A man and his wife, and five children, the eldest eight years of age and the youngest an infant. The man receives the common weekly wage of 7s eight months in the year, and by task work the remaining four months about 1s weekly more. The wife's common work is to bake bread for the family, to wash and mend ragged clothes, and to look after the children: but at beansetting, haymaking, and harvest she earns one week with another about 6d.[2]

This kind of brief description of families and households providing a sort of quantified line-drawing of the lives of the poor is best exemplified in the early Victorian period by the London Statistical Society's survey of Church Lane, St Giles, one of the most notorious streets in London.[3] Here one finds a brief description of the general characteristics of the area in terms of size, type of housing, sanitation and ventilation, landowners and domestic furniture, followed by a detailed description of sample houses. Just one of these detailed descriptions will serve to impart the flavour:

> *House, No. 4. – Two Parlours, on Ground Floor.* Size of front room, 14 ft. long, 13 ft. broad, 6 ft. high; size of windows, 3 ft. 4 in. by 2 ft. 2 in. Size of back-room, 11 ft. 2 in. long, 9 ft. 4 in. broad, less than 6 feet in height; 1 window with 4 whole panes; rent paid, 5s. 6d. weekly for 2 rooms; under-rent paid, 3d. per night each adult; time occupied, 2 years; number of families, 5; comprising 4 males above 20, 9 females above 20, three of them single, 2 males under 20, 4 females under 20; total 19. Number of persons ill, 2; deaths in 1847, 1, measles. Country, Irish; trade, dealers and mendicants. State of rooms and furniture, bad, dirty; state of windows, 6 whole panes, and 10 broken. Number of beds, 6; number of bedsteads, 6.
>
> The door of this room opens into the yard, 6 feet square, which is covered over with night soil; no privy, but there is a tub for the accommodation of the inmates; the tub was full of night soil. These are nightly lodging-rooms. In the front room one girl, 7 years old, lay dead, and another was in its bed with its mother, ill of the measles.[4]

This, indeed, fulfils the committee's aim of providing 'detailed and graphic pictures'. The image is much more stark and brutal than in the work of David Davies, but there is the same simple factual approach, the description of the basic experiences and determinants of the world of poverty. There is neither romanticisation nor exaggeration – even in the tableau at the end with its obvious sentimentalist potential. But the scene comes alive for the middle-class observer (now or then) with an immediacy and a force which a more 'engaged' approach might well smother in suspicions of distortion. Shock and outrage are not demanded of the reader and yet are inevitably generated.

It is just this approach which Booth uses with such skill, especially in the second volume of his great survey. Booth's work is on a much larger scale, but the method of presentation is derived from earlier models. As is well known, Booth produced some remarkable maps of London, with the streets shaded in seven different colours according to their prevailing social character. He then proceeded to describe typical streets in each of these colour divisions in a way which very largely mirrors that used by the London Statistical Society's committee of 1848. There is, however, a much greater degree of classification involved. The descriptions are of two kinds. At the start of each section are lengthy descriptions of each household in a small number of streets. These are followed (in most categories) by briefer descriptions of a larger number of streets. For example, Little Merton Street (coloured light blue, corresponding to what Booth calls 'standard poverty') is described as follows:[5]

Little Merton Street. This is a very short street connecting Merton Street with Balliol Square, and when the end houses which severally belong rather to the square or to the main street are dropped out of consideration little remains. That little looks like very decent and respectable outwardly. In detail the residents are described as follows, rather a rough lot:–

No.	Rms.	Pers.		
1 10 rooms	2	4	(B) Man, wife, and 2 children	A cripple (was waterside labourer). Wife an ironer.
	2	7	(B) Man, wife, and 5 children.	Labourer. Wife washes. One child has spinal disease. Very poor.

No.	Rms.	Pers.		
	2	4	(B) Man, wife, and 2 children.	Cabwasher. Wife consumptive. Very poor.
	2	4	(D) Man, wife and children.	Labourer. Wife chars. Used to drink. Now abstainers.
	2	5	(A) Man, wife, and 3 children.	Bottle gatherers. Man now in prison. Wife drinks. One girl trying for employment at Pantomime. Low people.
2		2	(E) Man and wife, no children.	Sweep.
		4	(D) Man, wife, and 2 children.	Respectable. Have a disreputable son not at home.
		7	(D) Man, wife, and 5 children.	Porter. Wife canes chairs. Respectable.
3		6	(E) Man, wife, and 4 children.	Respectable couple.
		4	(A) Man, wife, and 2 daughters.	Cabwasher. A drunkard. Beats his wife and was in prison for it. Wife out late. Daughter wild.
		4	(D) Widower and 3 children.	Labourer. Fairly respectable. Wife, lately dead, was often in prison through drink.
4		5	(F) Widow and family.	Coachman's widow. Occupy the house.
7		6	(E) Man, wife, and 4 children.	Carman. Wife washes.
		2	(E) Man and wife, no children.	Cabman.
			Another family.	Refuse to be visited.
8		6	(E) Man, wife, and 4 children.	Kitchen porter. Wife washes. Respectable.
		5	(E) Man, wife, and 3 children.	Labourer. Respectable.

The similarity to the 1848 survey is obvious. But there is also, at first sight, an important difference. In Booth's descriptions there seems to be a much greater amount of moralising. This is true if attention is confined to the descriptions of the individual households alone. However, once the conclusion of the 1848 report is studied, this difference quickly disappears. The London Statistical Society's committee were equally concerned with 'the ordinary decencies of life', with 'propriety and self-respect', and with 'religion, virtue, truth, order, industry, and cleanliness'.[6] The concepts mentioned here were central to the work of the early Victorian statistical movement. The early Victorian statisticians were preoccupied with the moral consequences of poverty (especially the lack of education and poor housing conditions associated with poverty) and their writings indicate a tension between a moralistic and an environmental explanation of the causes of poverty.[7] The same preoccupation and tension is to be found in the Booth survey. As John Brown has put it, Booth's 'unflattering descriptions of the poor perpetuated a concern for character in the discussion of policy'.[8] Booth's descriptive language is suffused with moral undertones: the problems of poverty are 'the evils with which society has to deal'; the poor (classes C and D) are differentiated from the very poor (classes A and B) by the fact that the former can just manage to sustain a 'decent independent life'; the registered lodging houses 'represent the principles of order, cleanliness, and decency'.[9] Above all, perhaps, is Booth's insistent use of the terms 'respectable' and 'disreputable'. If Booth invented the poverty line, usually seen as his greatest contribution to sociological method, he also, if at times unconsciously, invented a respectability line, which largely serves to differentiate the deserving from the undeserving poor (a concept which in one form or other dates back at least to Tudor times).

It may be objected that when Booth came explicitly to analyse the causes of poverty he assigned no more than 13 or 14 per cent of a sample of 4000 cases to 'questions of habit' (that is, drink).[10] The objection is only partially valid. Booth shows much more that tension between a moral and an environmental view characteristic of the early Victorian investigators. Thus, of the unemployed he says, 'lack of work is not really the disease with them, and the mere provision of it is therefore useless as a cure. The unemployed are, as a class, a selection of the unfit, and, on, the whole, those most in want are the most unfit.'[11] He in fact very largely ignores his own analysis of the causes of poverty among the members of class B and proceeds to discuss solutions to the problem of their existence in terms of imposing discipline and regularity upon a feckless leisure class.[12] Indiscriminate charity was no answer – as it also had not been for the early Victorians, supporters of the new Poor Law almost to a man. Moreover, some solution had to be found, not just on grounds of humanity, but also to prevent the growth of full-blooded socialism and a resort to revolution. Booth had little time for what he called 'agitators' who wished to destroy his beloved 'forces of individualism and sources of wealth'.[13] Here, again, he shows a remarkable affinity with his predecessors.

Where he goes most clearly beyond them is in certain aspects of his method. The origin and form of the investigation certainly build on early Victorian precedents. It has recently been established that Booth did not undertake the poverty survey in order to disprove the results of a survey by the Social Democratic Federation concerning the extent of poverty. But Booth was concerned, in E. P. Hennock's phrase, 'to refute all bold numerical assertions based on a minute piece of investigation' and did claim to have given the lie to the exaggerations of the 'sensationalists'.[14] Here we have, then, the 'scientific' investigator setting out to correct the false impression created by 'agitators': an exact parallel with a number of early Victorian surveys, especially the 1833 Factory Commission's work, which was designed to refute the conclusions of M. T. Sadler's 1832 Select Committee. Booth undertook a preliminary study of an area containing about 20,000 people in East London before extending his inquiry to the whole of the Tower Hamlets division and thence to the entire census area of London.

This approach had been pioneered in the 1830s by the Manchester Statistical Society in its survey of the moral and physical condition of the Manchester working classes.[15] The Manchester Statistical Society, however, like the other statistical societies of the 1830s, had used paid agents to carry out the actual work of collecting the data. Such an approach was impractical in Booth's case: it would take far too many agents to cover the population involved. Booth therefore had recourse to the school-board visitors, sometimes known as the school-attendance officers. It was the function of these people to check on absenteeism and, more significantly, to assess the claims of families to a remission of school fees on the grounds of hardship. They performed a house-to-house visitation and kept records of every house in every street, with details of each family in which there were children of school age. The scheduling of the children began two or three years before they reached school age and records remained in the visitors' books after the children left school. Booth felt that the visitors had 'a very considerable knowledge of the parents of the school children, especially of the poorest amongst them, and of the conditions under which they live'.[16] Undoubtedly the visitors varied in quality, but it is worth noting that those who appeared before the 1884–5 Royal Commission on the Housing of the Working Classes demonstrated their ability to answer specific questions about particular streets and houses.[17] Booth's use of field officers of this sort on such a scale and in such detail was highly unusual, though perhaps more in terms of detail than of scale, since earlier official inquiries of various kinds had made some use of civil servants to generate social data (indeed, in a certain sense, it could be argued, the census enumerators performed every ten years functions analogous to those of the visitors in the Booth survey).

Booth's real innovations were twofold: his system of classification and his concern for checking his data and verifying its accuracy. In his system of classification he went well beyond his predecessors. He divided the population into eight main classes containing four groups. The lowest group consisted of class A, 'the lowest class of occasional labourers, loafers, and semi-criminals', and class B, 'those on casual earnings'. Initially Booth identified the very poor with class B alone, but class A was so small that classes A and B may be conveniently combined as 'the very poor' (as Booth himself later did). Class C, those on what Booth called 'intermittent earnings', and class D, those on 'small regular earnings', formed 'the poor'. The four better-off classes, E, F, G and H, consisted of the comfortable working classes and the middle classes. Thus, those 'in poverty' comprised classes A to D inclusive, and Booth's famous invention, the 'poverty line', was drawn between classes D and E. It follows that the essence of Booth's taxonomy lies in the division between the very poor and the poor and, even more so, in the division between the poor and the comfortable working classes. Booth describes these divisions as follows:

By the word 'poor' I mean to describe those who have a sufficiently regular though bare income, such as 18s to 21s per week for a moderate family, and by 'very poor' those who from any cause fall much below this standard. The 'poor' are those whose means may be sufficient, but are barely sufficient, for decent

independent life; the 'very poor' those whose means are insufficient for this according to the usual standard of life in this
country. My 'poor' may be described as living under a struggle
to obtain the necessaries of life and make both ends meet; while
the 'very poor' live in a state of chronic want.[18]

Armed with this system of classification, Booth was able to deduce
from the data supplied by the school-board visitors that 8·4 per
cent of the population of London, excluding those living in institutions, were in classes A and B, 22·3 per cent in classes C and
D, 51·5 per cent in classes E and F, and 17·8 per cent in classes
G and H. Thus 30·7 per cent of the population not living in
institutions were stated to be living in poverty.[19] In fact this statement could be a little misleading, since the population surveyed
consisted of those families with at least one child in the age group
three to thirteen. Booth assumed that the whole population lived
in the same condition as the large proportion, perhaps two-thirds
of the whole, with which the school-board visitors were concerned.[20]
    There is something of a problem on this point. Booth was rather
vague and contradictory about the proportion the sample surveyed
bore to the whole population. In his first published paper on
poverty in London, covering the Tower Hamlets division, he estimated the proportion at 'from half to two-thirds of the whole'.
In the first volume of the survey this estimate drops to 'fully one
half'.[21] The lower figure seems scarcely credible in a high-fertility–
high-mortality society with few old people and large families.
This is an important question, for Booth believed, possibly correctly,
that the general condition of the population was somewhat better
than the condition of the tested part.[22] There is a worrying element
of doubt introduced here: what if the condition of the untested
part was substantially different from the condition of those dealt
with by the school-board visitors? The confusion is not diminished
by the fact that, whereas in the examples of streets given in the
first volume of the survey those families without children in the
specified age group had no classification assigned to them, those
in the second volume and the families in the sample blocks of
buildings described in the third volume were classified.[23] These
classifications were carried out only for the sample streets and
blocks of dwellings and were ignored in the final estimate, since
Booth reiterates that it was upon the school children (he includes

those of just pre-school age in this rather misleading term) that
the final figures were based.[24]

But the data on the sample streets and blocks of dwellings given
in the second and third volumes make it possible to resolve these
doubts. I took a count of 5822 classified persons,[25] of whom 4610
(77 per cent) belonged to families in which there was at least
one child aged three to thirteen. Of these 4610, 28·5 per cent
were classified by Booth as 'very poor' and another 41·2 per cent
as 'poor', making 69·7 per cent living in poverty. The corresponding
figures for the 1212 persons living in families with no such children
were 18·0 per cent, 39·6 per cent, and 57·6 per cent. Clearly
there is a significant difference between these two groups, but
the figures for all 5822 persons were 26·5, 40·9 and 67·4 per cent.
These figures are not substantially different from those of Booth's
'tested part'. Moreover, the sample is clearly not representative
and the direction of the error introduced by this fact is undoubtedly
towards exaggerating the difference between the two sets of figures.
It will be recalled that the figures for the total number of families
with children in the three-to-thirteen age range in London were
8·4, 22·3 and 30·7 per cent. Thus, in the selected streets and
blocks of dwellings there was a very high over-representation of
the very poor and a high over-representation of the poor. Among
these groups large families tended to be the rule and so the picture
is somewhat distorted. If the same relative reductions from the
'tested part' to the total population found in the sample streets
and blocks of buildings applied to the whole of London, then
the figure of 8·4 per cent for the very poor would be reduced
to 7·8 per cent, and the 22·3 per cent of the poor to 22·1 per
cent, giving 29·9 per cent living in poverty, or a reduction of
0·8 per cent. Furthermore, the difference in wealth between those
with school children and those without seemed most marked in
the poorest streets (which, it must be repeated, were greatly over-
represented in the sample) and less so in Booth's 'purple' and 'pink'
streets, which better represented the general run of London's working-class streets. This analysis of sample streets and blocks, therefore,
appears to show that even the small error of 0·8 per cent which
Booth's method appears to have introduced is probably an overesti-
mate of the actual error.

The last methodological hurdle has thus been cleared, but there
still remains the general question of the reliability of the figures

Booth presents. Here we find the second major aspect of Booth's originality, since he applied a number of tests himself. The first of these was an attempt to get the teachers in the elementary schools to classify their classes according to social status. Booth was hopeful that, from the 'regularity or irregularity of attendance, the condition in which the children come to school, the demands for remission of fees, and in many other ways, the teachers can, and usually do, acquire a very considerable knowledge of the parents, and a fair idea of the character of the home'.[26]

The results of this investigation (see Table 16) must have alarmed him. Excluding the small number of children from classes G and H present in the above sample and scaling the rest in order to total 82·2 per cent for classes A to F (the total derived from

TABLE 16   Classification of London children by teachers in elementary schools[27]

Classes	Board schools	Voluntary schools (Protestant)	Voluntary schools (Catholic)	Total
A and B (%)	15·3	6·5	23·5	13·2
C and D (%)	44·8	19·6	46·0	37·4
E and F (%)	39·9	73·9	30·5	49·4
Total (no.)	441,609	175,417	32,525	649,551

the visitors' reports), the teachers classified 45·0 per cent of the population as being in poverty and 11·8 per cent as very poor.[28] These figures, especially those for the poor, were substantially in excess of those derived from the school-board visitors. However, this is not as serious a situation as it may at first appear. First, the teachers were only asked to state the proportions of the various classes to be found among their pupils. As Booth said, 'in such general statements there will be a tendency to exaggeration'.[29] This is especially likely since the teachers brought to the school a set of middle-class values which ill fitted them to understand the working classes.[30] Clearly, Booth's test had failed. The difference between the estimates based on the information supplied by the school-board visitors, who were full-time officials working amongst the poorer classes, and the estimates of the schoolteachers is understandable, and it would seem incorrect to doubt the accuracy of the survey on the basis of the latter estimates. On the other hand, it cannot be claimed that the accuracy of the survey was confirmed by these estimates. But certainly we do not need to introduce the large element of doubt that Booth almost unconsciously did when he stated that 'the teachers in distinguishing between class and class may have drawn the lines of demarcation somewhat above the levels we have attempted to maintain. A very little change as to this would be enough to throw large numbers down from E to D and C, or from C to B.'[31]

Booth's attempt to give substance to his figures by examining thirty selected families and their income and expenditure was more successful. The first case was a family of five: a sick dock labourer, his consumptive wife, their eighteen-year-old son and their two daughters, aged eight and six. The family lived in two rooms, neither more than ten feet square, and their diet consisted largely of bread, margarine, tea and sugar. In five weeks only three pounds of meat was bought. Disturbing as it was, this case was by no means the worst that could be found in class B. The fifth case, also from class B, was that of a less unfortunate family. Yet even here 'the only luxury (?) [was] an occasional bottle of ginger beer'. The sixth case Booth regarded as fairly typical of those on the dividing line between class B and classes C and D. The man was a dock labourer earning 20s to 21s a week. His wife occasionally did some work but was usually busy with their five children under ten years of age. There was also a daughter, a domestic servant, who still received money and clothes from home. In five weeks the family consumed 40 pounds of meat, 25 pounds of fish, 150 pounds of potatoes, 172 pounds of bread, 15 pounds of flour, 6 or 7 pounds of butter and 36 pounds of sugar, 'besides minor matters. This may not be choice fare, but there is something like plenty about it'.[32] It might seem so to Booth when such a long period is considered, but, when broken down to the daily consumption of a family of seven (three ounces of butter, eighteen of meat, eleven of fish, sixty-nine of potatoes and seventy-nine of bread per day), there seems little of plenty about it except for the large consumption of bread and potatoes. The ten cases of class C and D families seem a little, though not much, better. Bacon, eggs and cheese were sometimes bought.[33] The proportion of the family budget spent on bread tended to fall. These tendencies increased in the ten cases of class E and the four of class F. In the six class B families 13·4 per cent of the total income was spent on bread alone, this figure dropping slightly to 11·5 per cent in the ten class C and D families and to 7·7 and 7·2 per cent for the ten class E and four class F families, respectively.

The general impression to be gained from the thirty budgets presented by Booth is that there existed definite differences between the classes, though with some overlapping in the various divisions of expenditure (food, rent, etc.). Most importantly, the family budgets show that the classification system used was flexible and was not merely an attempt to describe the distribution of income. Further than that it would be perhaps dangerous to go, except to state that by present-day standards it would appear unlikely that the original survey overstated the amount of poverty – it is apparent that 'the usual standard of life' in Booth's time was still a low one.

Booth himself was clearly dissatisfied with the tests of reliability that he was able to apply to the Poverty Series. The 1891 Census provided him with much additional information and it was this information which was to give him what he regarded as the conclusive test of the great survey.[34] In the census of that year the people were, for the first time, asked to state how many rooms they lived in. Although the word 'room' was not defined – and therefore different people probably placed different interpretations upon it – this is not the problem that it may appear, since the poor usually lived in only one or two rooms, with no extra rooms such as kitchen, laundry, bathroom or lavatory. Using the Census information Booth was able to construct the table displayed here as Table 17.

Thus, setting the level of 'crowding' at two or more persons per room, the percentage of the population, excluding those living in institutions, classified as 'crowded' (31·5) was very nearly the same as that classified as living in poverty (30·7). Moreover, those living three and under four per room were divided into two by Booth, one-half being added to those living four or more persons per room and one-half to those living two and under three persons per room and an even more startling connection emerged. The lower section of the crowded then totalled 340,000 persons (compared with 354,000 previously classified very poor) and the upper

TABLE 17 Accommodation conditions in London, 1891[35]

Description		Percentage of the population	
3 or more persons per room	12·0	} Crowded	
2 and under 3 persons per room	19·0	31·5	
Common lodging houses, etc.	0·5		
1 and under 2 persons per room	23·4		
Less than 1 person per room	3·7		
Occupying more than 4 rooms	23·9	56·4	
Servants	5·0		Not crowded,
Persons living in large shops, etc.	0·4		68·5
4 or more persons to 1 servant	5·5		
3 or less persons to 1 servant	6·0	12·1	
Inmates of hotels and boarding houses where servants kept	0·6		

section 934,000 persons (compared with 938,000 classified poor).[36]

The correspondence between the poverty figures and the crowding figures was impressive, but it must be emphasised that Booth had really been very lucky. Although the crowding level that he set became accepted[37] it was as arbitrary as any of the definitions used in the Poverty Series. It might well have been found that the percentage of the population in poverty corresponded to the percentage living more than 2·31 persons, say, to a room. It was convenient that the correspondence should come at an integer, but (and Booth never realised this) no great significance could be attached to this fact by itself.

Thus, criticism must be made even of the one test of reliability that it seems Booth felt was conclusive. To test his figures other methods will have to be adopted, though Booth himself provided some of the necessary data for the following analysis. This he did in the paper he read before the Royal Statistical Society in 1893. In this paper Booth presented a crowding index, which was the percentage of the population living two or more to a room in each of the registration districts of London in 1891; the average birth rate in each registration district for the ten years 1881–90; the average death rate in each district for the six years 1885–90; an early-marriage index, which was the number of married females under twenty-five per 10,000 of the population in each registration district in 1891; the surplus of unmarried males compared with unmarried females; and the rate of natural increase in the registration districts. This last was shown to bear no relationship to the percentage of poverty in the registration districts, but the other indices appeared to bear a relationship and thus could well have provided the independent tests that Booth had been seeking.

For some reason Booth dropped all these tests, except the version of the crowding index for the whole of London which has already been examined, when he came to write the Industry Series.[38] It is possible that he felt that he could not demonstrate as adequately as he would have wished the relationships between the indices. Booth was a careful tabulator of facts but in his statistical reasoning he often showed great naïveté. For example, as the percentage crowded and the percentage in poverty for the whole of London were very nearly equal, Booth seems to have felt that some such neat relationship of equality should hold for all the registration districts. This apparent naïveté is, of course, owing to the fact that he did not have at his disposal the necessary statistical tools to deal with the material that he had culled from the 1891 Census. Although theoretical statistics had made some advances by Booth's time, the major practical applications were yet to be made. The main theoretical interest of statisticians until the end of the nineteenth century still seems to have lain in the normal probability curve and its applications to hypothesis testing.[39] The principle of fitting a line to bivariate data had been discovered as far back as 1805 by the great French mathematician Legendre, but the term 'regression line' was not given to this technique of curve-fitting for more than a century after Legendre's discovery. Moreover, correlation analysis was not developed to any degree of sophistication until this century.

It is therefore interesting to carry Booth's analysis a stage further, though with some modifications to his indices. Table 18 sets out the necessary data.

A number of points in Table 18 need to be explained. To begin with, only twenty-seven registration districts are included, instead of the full thirty into which census London was divided. Following Booth, the City of London has been excluded, as 'its population is so abnormal as to yield no results useful for comparison'. The population of the City was declining at such a rapid rate that all other demographic factors were likely to be thrown

TABLE 18 The poverty index and associated indices in London, 1891[40]

District	Poverty (%)	Crowding (%)	Location index	Early-marriage index[a]	Marital-fertility rate[b]	Death rate (per 1000)
Holborn	48·9	55	1	21·1	27·8	26·6
St George's-in-the-East	48·9	57	1	27·4	31·4	31·3
Bethnal Green	44·6	49	1	22·9	30·1	23·9
St Saviour's	43·4	42	2	23·8	26·2	25·2
St Olave's	42·2	35	1	22·6	29·3	23·1
Shoreditch	40·2	49	1	21·4	27·6	23·1
Whitechapel	39·2	54	2	23·9	33·1	23·6
Stepney	38·0	39	1	22·4	27·8	26·7
Greenwich	36·8	19	3	17·7	26·3	20·6
Poplar	36·5	30	2	21·9	28·8	21·9
Islington	32·7	31	3	16·3	24·4	19·7
St Pancras	30·4	41	1	18·6	23·0	21·5
Camberwell	28·6	18	3	15·1	25·5	19·2
Strand, etc.	28·5	38	1	13·7	22·4	27·1
Wandsworth	27·4	17	3	13·2	24·0	18·1
Marylebone	27·4	40	1	12·7	24·0	23·3
Mile End Old Town	26·1	35	1	23·0	29·7	21·9
Lambeth	26·1	26	2	15·4	25·7	20·7
Woolwich	24·7	18	3	22·3	26·2	18·3
Fulham	24·7	24	3	16·9	25·2	20·1
Kensington	24·7	26	1	8·7	21·5	18·7
Chelsea	24·5	30	2	15·7	23·3	22·1
Hackney	23·1	18	3	13·1	25·4	18·4
Paddington	21·7	27	3	10·0	22·1	18·1
St George's Hanover Square	21·6	28	1	10·4	20·7	21·5
Lewisham	18·1	7	3	7·9	24·1	14·6
Hampstead	13·5	16	3	6·4	22·0	14·6

[a]Percentage of women aged 15–25 married.
[b]Number of legitimate births in 1891 per 100 married women aged 15–45.

out of joint. The other alteration that Booth made was to amalgamate the three registration districts of the Strand, St Giles and Westminster, because they were contiguous and small, and because he did not have a complete set of separate figures for each.[41]

While Booth has been followed on these two points, certain alterations and additions have been made. A location index has been added, since it is clear that crowding was likely to be highest, all else being equal, in those inner-city areas where growth was lowest, and lowest in outer suburban areas with the ability to absorb high growth rates. In other words, the growth rate may be seen as bearing, generally, an inverse relationship to location and the amount of pressure on housing resources. An index number of 1 indicates a growth rate of less than or equal to 2 per cent over the decade 1881–91; 2 indicates a growth rate above 2 but less than or equal to 10 per cent; and 3 a growth rate above 10 per cent. Booth's early-marriage index has been abandoned in favour of the one used in Table 18 since the former takes no account of the differing age and sex structures of each registration district. In the case of the birth rate, Booth did not make an adjustment for all the hospitals in London; only for Queen Charlotte's Hospital in Marylebone did he redistribute the births to their home areas, since he considered that the other hospitals served only the local areas.[42] Again, he took no account of the demographic determinants of the birth rate. Inspection of the reports of the Registrar-General for the period revealed that the latter could be a serious defect, while most of the peculiar figures which seem to arise out of the location of particular hospitals were connected with illegitimate births. It was therefore decided to use the marital-fertility rate. Booth did redistribute the deaths to their home districts, but his data have been further modified by standardising the figures for each district to a common population structure. The correlations between these various indices are given in Table 19.

TABLE 19   Correlation coefficients between the poverty index and associated indices

	Crowding	Location	Early marriage	Marital fertility	Death rate
Poverty	·789	−·478	·823	·730	·788
Crowding		−·732	·681	·572	·855
Location			−·380	−·244	−·708
Early marriage				·855	·703
Marital fertility					·521

Significant levels (one-tailed test): p ·005   ·0005
r ·487   ·597

Booth's poverty figures thus correlate significantly (at the ·0005 level on a one-tailed test) with the crowding index, the early marriage index, the marital fertility rate and the death rate. The crowding index is a better predictor of the death rate but substantially inferior as a predictor of early marriage or marital fertility. Predictably, the location index correlates well (with, of course, a negative slope) with the crowding index and also with the death rate. Two of the test indices – early marriage and marital fertility – are in fact so closely related that they do not provide independent tests. The partial-correlation coefficient between the poverty index and marital fertility, controlling for early marriage, is only ·089. This means that the variation in the poverty index explains no significant further variation in the fertility rate once allowance has been made for the strong positive relationship between poverty and early marriage. We are thus reduced to three main test indices: early marriage, the death rate and the crowding index. It is important to note that the multiple-correlation coefficient between the poverty index and the crowding and location indices is ·886, a higher correlation than that between poverty and crowding alone, which conforms to expectation and common-sense and strengthens the case for regarding Booth's poverty index as a valid one.

But if, on *a priori* grounds, we regard the crowding index as some sort of valid index of poverty we have to choose between it and Booth's poverty figures in terms of which seems the better. Taking London as a whole, Booth's figures have a distinct but far from great advantage. Breaking the data down into two subgroups, those with a location index of one (roughly corresponding to the Registrar-General's definition of the Inner Circle of London used in the 1891 Census) and those with location indices of two and three (roughly the Outer Circle) may help to clarify matters somewhat (see Tables 20 and 21).

Within the two sub-groups Booth's poverty figures retain their advantage, and this advantage is very clearly increased in the case of the 'outer' districts of London. It seems reasonable to conclude, therefore, that the poverty figures provide a valid index of poverty – that is, that the concept of the poverty line was applied with a fair degree of consistency across London. There remain some oddities: the suspicion must be that Holborn's poverty was exaggerated a little (St George's-in-the-East was almost certainly the poorest area in London) and Greenwich's by a more substantial

TABLE 20   Correlation coefficients between various social indices in
registration districts with a location index of 1

	Crowding	Early marriage	Death rate
Poverty	·848	·791	·656
Crowding		·706	·720

Significance levels (one-tailed test): p   ·01   ·005   ·0005
                                        r   ·658   ·708   ·823

TABLE 21   Correlation coefficients between various social indices in
registration districts with location indices of 2 and 3

	Crowding	Early marriage	Death rate
Poverty	·708	·843	·863
Crowding		·688	·835

Significance levels (one-tailed test): p   ·01   ·005   ·0005
                                        r   ·592   ·641   ·755

amount. Areas in which the extent of poverty seems to have been
underestimated are Mile End Old Town (as Booth himself noted)[43]
and, perhaps, Whitechapel, though in the latter case massive, recent
and continuing immigration of Jewish refugees from Tsarist oppres-
sion was a significant factor in causing unnaturally high levels
of crowding relative to the level of poverty.

With these major qualifications it can be argued that Booth
succeeded in applying a reasonably consistent standard of poverty
in extracting information from the school-board visitors. Beyond
that we can say very little – if for no other reason than because
the poverty line is a relative thing, defined in socio-historical terms.
Undoubtedly Booth's standard of poverty was a low one by present
west European standards; whether it was too low or too high
by the standards of his day it is really impossible to say. It seems
unlikely that it was wildly so: public reaction and criticism would
have been much greater in that case – especially since, in his descriptions of individual families, he provided ample ammunition for
any would-be attackers. Booth then, may be reckoned as one of
the most outstanding of the Victorian social investigators. He had

attempted the most ambitious survey of them all and had been remarkably successful. The Poverty Series remains as his master-piece, whatever the flaws in the second and third series of his great work. It remains, too, as a fitting culmination to Victorian social inquiry; a summary of much that had gone before as well as an initiator of new methods and new approaches.

Notes

1 See M. W. Flinn, Introduction to Edwin Chadwick, *Report on the Sanitary Condition of the Labouring Population of Great Britain*, 1842 (Edinburgh, 1965). pp. 26–9; Philip Abrams, *The Origins of British Sociology* (Chicago and London, 1968); M. J. Cullen, *The Statistical Movement in Early Victorian Britain: The Origins of Empirical Social Research* (Hassocks, 1975).

2 Rev. David Davies, *The Case of the Labourers in Husbandry Stated and Considered* (London, 1795).

3 'Report of a Committee of the Council of the Statistical Society of London to Investigate the State of the Inhabitants and their Dwellings in Church Lane, St Giles's, *JSSL*, XI (1848) 1–18.

4 Ibid., p. 5.

5 Charles Booth, *et al.*, *Life and Labour of the People in London*, 3rd ed (London, 1902), 1st ser. (Poverty), vol. II, p. 156.

6 In *JSSL*, XI, 17.

7 See Cullen, *Statistical Movement*, esp. pp. 135–49.

8 John Brown, 'Charles Booth and Labour Colonies, 1889–1905', *EHR*, 2nd ser., XXI (1968) 353. For a criticism of Brown's approach to Booth, see Trevor Lummis, 'Charles Booth, Moralist or Social Scientist?', ibid., XXIV (1971) 100–5, and, for Brown's reply, ibid., pp. 106–13.

9 Booth, *Life and Labour*, 1st ser., vol. I, pp. 5, 33 and 68.

10 Ibid., p. 147.

11 Ibid., p. 150.

12 Ibid., pp. 163–71.

13 Ibid., pp. 155 and 178.

14 E. P. Hennock, 'Poverty and Social Theory in England: The Experience of the Eighteen-eighties', *Social History*, I (1976) 70–2. Hennock's emphasis on Booth's distinction between the poor who 'lacked comfort' (classes C and D) and those 'in want' (classes A and B) is important though not entirely new. It is equally important not to underestimate the poverty of classes C and D, as many of Booth's individual cases makes clear.

15 Cullen *Statistical Movement*, p. 111.

16 Booth, *Life and Labour*, 1st ser., vol. I, p. 5.

17 Royal Commission on the Housing of the Working Classes, *Minutes of Evidence* (PP, 1884–5) vol. XXX, pp. 62–6, 142–6, 156–63 and 174.

18 Booth, *Life and Labour*, 1st ser., vol. I, p. 33.

19 Ibid., vol. II, pp. 21 and 24.

20 Ibid., vol. I, p. 5.

21 Charles Booth, 'The Inhabitants of the Tower Hamlets (School Board Division), their Condition and Occupations, *JRSS*, L (1887) 328; Booth, *Life and Labour*, 1st ser., vol. I, p. 5.

22 Ibid.

23 Ibid., vol. I, pp. 7–24; vol. II, pp. 46–225; vol. III, pp. 48–57.

24 Ibid., vol. II, p. 16.

25 Not all the streets could be counted, since some were described in greater detail omitting the classification and sizes of the individual families.

26 Booth, *Life and Labour*, 1st ser., vol. III, p. 195.

27 From ibid., p. 199.

28 From ibid., p. 200.

29 Ibid., p. 201.

30 For a study of this problem in grammar schools in the late 1950s, see Brian Jackson and Dennis Marsden, *Education and the Working Class* (London, 1962).

31 Booth, *Life and Labour*, 1st ser., vol. III, p. 201.

32 Ibid., vol. I, pp. 140–4.

33 Ibid., pp. 135–6.

34 See Charles Booth, 'Life and Labour of the People in London: First Results of an Inquiry based on the 1891 Census', *JRSS*, LVI (1893) 557–93.

35 From Booth, *Life and Labour*, 2nd ser. (Industry), vol. II, p. 10; Booth, in *JRSS*, LVI, 566.

36 Booth, *Life and Labour*, 2nd ser., vol. I, p. 13.

37 It was, for example, used in the 1931 Census.

38 See Booth, *Life and Labour*, 2nd ser., vol. I, ch. 1.

39 For example, see F. Y. Edgeworth, 'Methods of Statistics', *JSSL*, Jubilee vol. (1885) 181.

40 The first two columns derive from Booth, in *JRSS*, LVI, 592–3. The location index is derived from 1891 Census, (PP, 1893–4, CV) pp. 3–15; the marital fertility rate from the *Fifty-fourth Annual Report of the Registrar-General* (PP, 1892, XXIV) pp. 4–7; the early marriage index from 1891 Census (PP, 1893–4, CVI) pp. 7–8; the death rate from *Fifty-fifth Annual Report of the Registrar-General, Supp. Pt. I* (PP, 1895, XXIII, pt I) pp. xli and 97–126.

41 Booth, in *JRSS*, LVI, 572.

42 Ibid., p. 571.

43 Ibid., p. 568.

9 Social Conflict and Social Administration: The Conciliation Act in British Industrial Relations

ROGER DAVIDSON

I

The problem of industrial unrest featured prominently in late nineteenth- and early twentieth-century British political debate. Within the governing classes, there was growing concern at the inability of the existing machinery of collective bargaining to stabilise labour relations and at the consequent threat to social order and productive efficiency. In an effort to reinforce private dispute procedures, the Conciliation Act was passed in 1896. It provided the sole legal sanction for Government intervention in collective bargaining prior to the First World War, yet its administration by the Board of Trade and its impact during a critical period in the growth of British industrial relations have been superficially treated by historians.

Several explanations for this neglect can be advanced. First, research focused until recently upon the incidence, ideology and political implications of conflict within late Victorian and Edwardian society rather than the extent of social consensus and the agencies designed to secure its preservation. Secondly, the fact that additional measures to contain industrial strife continued to be advocated after 1896, and the stress of industrial sociologists upon the failure of State intervention either to eradicate the fundamental economic and social causes of industrial conflict or to provide an effective framework for its resolution have combined to produce the unmerited presumption that the Conciliation Act was ineffectual and had no positive role to play in the evolution of the norms and institutions of British collective bargaining. Misrepresentation has also arisen from a failure to recognise the degree to which labour policy was initiated at departmental rather than Cabinet level and determined by the Board of Trade's interpretation and implementation of the Conciliation Act. Even when the Board's initiative has been acknowledged, it has mainly been interpreted as a function of the political acumen and negotiating skills of Lloyd George, Winston Churchill and George Askwith – a hagiographical approach that ignores equally important structural shifts in the bureaucratic response to social conflict.

The objective of this essay is to provide a reappraisal of the Conciliation Act; to examine the logistical and attitudinal problems facing the Board of Trade in its administration; to delineate the strategies adopted to overcome them; to evaluate and explain the incidence and degree of the Act's impact upon industrial unrest, and to assess its more general significance in the development of twentieth-century industrial relations policy.

II

Despite the fact that, for the greater part of the nineteenth century, matters relating to industrial relations had been the responsibility of the Home Office, the enforcement of the Conciliation Act was entrusted to the Board of Trade. The problem of industrial unrest was viewed by late Victorian administrators as primarily one of economic dislocation rather than of law and order. It was therefore more logical that the Board should assume responsibility for dealing with it. Moreover, the Board's Commercial, Labour and Statistical Branch was uniquely informed on all matters relating to capital and labour. Finally, although the Home Office was responsible for regulating working conditions in many industries, and for framing legislation with regard to the legal status of trade disputes and combinations, it had little experience of collective bargaining. In contrast, the Labour Department of the Board of Trade contained several experienced industrial negotiators.[1]

The problems that confronted the Board in extending the role of the State in industrial relations were formidable. Under the existing system of collective bargaining, third-party arbitration and conciliation had never figured prominently in either the prevention or settlement of disputes. The overwhelming majority of strikes and lockouts had traditionally been settled by direct arrangement between the parties, and the bulk of the remainder had been resolved either by a return to work on the employers' terms without negotiation or by the replacement of the workpeople involved.[2]

Furthermore, the powers conferred by the Conciliation Act upon the Board of Trade were relatively limited. Schemes involving compulsory conciliation with a statutory cooling-off period and/or compulsory arbitration with legally binding awards had been widely canvassed since the early 1890s. At Westminster, a sizable group of Conservative backbenchers representing 'villa Toryism' and fearful of the threat to property and dividends from industrial stoppages had persistently advocated legal coercion to curtail trade disputes.[3] In addition, a small but vocal group of Liberal businessmen and even some elder statesmen of craft unionism had sought to contain rank-and-file militancy by investing existing voluntary collective-bargaining machinery with powers to enforce wage agreements.[4] In 1896, Joseph Chamberlain also pressed in Cabinet for compulsory legislation, on the grounds that it would enable the Conservative Party to monopolise the credit for relieving the problem of industrial unrest.[5]

However, the Board of Trade successfully resisted such proposals.[6] Its president, C. T. Ritchie, believed that, by distorting the labour market, compulsory arbitration would dislocate the cost structure of British industry and render it vulnerable to foreign competition.[7] Furthermore, the consensus of expert opinion favoured permissive legislation. Leading industrial negotiators such as Spence Watson and David Dale fully endorsed the view of the Labour Department that any system of dispute procedure involving 'overt' compulsion would prove unacceptable to the majority of industrialists and trade unionists and would be certain to produce a confrontation between labour and the State; that legal sanctions were inappropriate to the enforcement of wage agreements and that the only realistic course of action was for the Government to rely upon the 'moral sanction' of public opinion.[8]

As a result, the Conciliation Act was an extremely modest measure.[9] When an industrial stoppage occurred or was anticipated, the Board of Trade was empowered to inquire into its 'causes and circumstances' and to facilitate negotiations between the parties concerned. It might also appoint a conciliator or arbitrator at the request of the disputants. There was no provision in the Act for a compulsory cooling-off period and State arbitration could only be initiated by the voluntary submission of a dispute by both the parties involved. Moreover, arbitration awards were not legally binding.

Yet, despite the absence of compulsion from the Conciliation Act, many industrialists and trade unionists were opposed to its widespread application. Some sections of the working class, such as the dockers and railwaymen, welcomed the prospect of State intervention in industrial disputes as a means of gaining union recognition. The Fabian view that the Conciliation Act might prove a significant step towards State-regulated minimum wages, fixed according to human needs rather than those of the market, also appealed to a number of the more prominent leaders of New Unionism.[10]

However, the bulk of the trade-union movement did not regard the Act as a progressive measure, while the labour press dismissed it as at best an evasion of the fundamental problems of income inequality and at worst as a 'political confidence trick' designed to secure a cheap and servile labour force for industrial capitalism.[11]

This distrust was reinforced by the disillusionment in labour circles with the system of wage arbitration already operating in many sectors of British industry. The majority of umpires were from the professional or upper classes. They tended to adhere to the conventional view of political economy, to make their awards in line with short-run changes in the level of economic activity or with the selling price of the product involved, and to pay little regard to the standard of living of the working classes. As a result, during the depression in industrial prices between 1873 and 1896, the bulk of arbitration awards had given wage reductions.[12]

Furthermore, the Board of Trade's handling of industrial disputes since 1893 had given trade-union leaders little confidence that

State arbitration would be any less likely to sacrifice labour's living standards on the altar of free-market economics. The two major industrial settlements in which the Board had been involved had both represented major setbacks to the labour movement. The Coal Settlement of 1893 had entailed the ultimate abandonment of all the miners' main objectives, leading in subsequent years to an actual reduction in earnings,[13] while *The Times* had with ill-disguised relish described the outcome of the 1895 boot-and-shoe dispute as 'a charter of rights for the manufacturers'.[14] In 1896, with a trade revival, fuller employment and rising prices, the more militant leaders and rank and file of the trade-union movement not unnaturally gave a cool reception to legislation that threatened to restrict the power of organised labour to gain wage advances and protect its standard of living.

An equally serious obstacle to the success of the Conciliation Act was the attitude of employers. Many considered their labour relations to be a private concern of management and not a public issue. State intervention in industrial relations was viewed as an unjustified invasion of private enterprise which would impair business efficiency. Furthermore, in 1896, industrialists were not in a conciliatory mood. Confronted by growing demands from labour militants for industrial power as well as wage advances, and with the prospect of falling profit margins consequent upon foreign competition in home and export markets, the employers' associations were preparing for a major counter-attack on the trade-union movement. In their view, any extension of Government conciliation machinery was inappropriate at a time when 'it was essential in the country's interest to fight to the bitter end the attempts of the unions to usurp the powers of management'.[15] It was felt to be particularly inappropriate that the administration of industrial relations should be entrusted to the Labour Department of the Board of Trade, in that it was staffed by former trade unionists and middle-class radicals, many of whom had played a prominent part in the rise of New Unionism. Employers feared that the Labour Department would use the Conciliation Act to weaken their impending offensive against trade unionism, and that, in determining wage awards, State arbitrators would be influenced more by socialistic idealism than by the dictates of the market.[16]

Finally, in its efforts to reduce industrial unrest, the Board of Trade had to contend with Treasury control. Weaned on the

principles of free trade and Gladstonian economy, Treasury officials
questioned whether industrial relations were a legitimate area for
Government intervention and whether State conciliation and arbitration should become a public charge.[17] Although Ritchie convinced
the Cabinet that the threat to Britain's economic performance
and social stability posed by industrial stoppages fully justified
the provision of collective-bargaining machinery by the State, the
Treasury continued to assert its financial orthodoxy by starving
the Labour Department of money and staff. As a result, in implementing the Conciliation Act the Board of Trade had to rely
almost exclusively upon its existing establishment. No permanent
conciliation officers were appointed. Instead, labour correspondents
and statisticians had to assume the additional role of industrial
mediation. More seriously, the Labour Department was forced
to depend upon its part-time local correspondents for immediate
information on strikes and lockouts. As these were active trade
unionists, this reliance hampered the efforts of the Department
to gain the confidence of employers in its handling of industrial
disputes.[18]

III

Contemplating the future of the Conciliation Act in 1896, Llewellyn
Smith, the Labour Commissioner, concluded that its influence upon
industrial relations would be 'heavily dependent upon creative
and dynamic administration'.[19] This, he felt confident, the Labour
Department could provide. Its staff were highly motivated, thoroughly familiar with the machinery of collective bargaining in
British industry, and enjoyed an administrative environment in
which both their zeal and expertise could be fully utilised. Above
all, unlike other areas of late Victorian social administration, they
were committed to innovation in the pursuit of policy goals rather
than the routine application of a code.[20]

In implementing the Conciliation Act, the Labour Department
therefore interpreted its powers in the broadest possible fashion.
It took particular advantage of the fact that its powers of investigation and informal mediation, although not mandatory, were ill-
defined. In so doing, it inverted the intention of the Act that
the initiative in State conciliation and arbitration should rest with
the parties to industrial disputes rather than with Board of Trade
officials.

The Board had been authorised to inquire into the 'causes and circumstances' of industrial unrest in order that it might amplify its labour statistics and brief its conciliators and arbitrators subsequent to their appointment. However, the Labour Department viewed its investigative role in a far more positive light, systematically exploiting it so as to persuade, and on occasions, almost to compel employers and trade-union leaders to submit their differences for settlement under the Conciliation Act. Thus, in the Midland Colliery dispute of 1898, the Labour Commissioner adroitly transformed John Burnett's position as observer for the *Labour Gazette* into the more active role of industrial negotiator.[21] In the Leicestershire building stoppage of 1899, with the caveat that 'no impression should be given that the Board of Trade was initiating proceedings', he instructed the local correspondent of the Labour Department so to 'direct his enquiries' as to dispose both sides to make an appeal for State intervention.[22] Similarly, when confronted in 1901 by the prospect of a protracted mining stoppage in South Wales, Llewellyn Smith recommended that 'someone be sent to *make enquiries*'. 'Under the pretext of investigation', he anticipated that the Department might well 'prevail upon the coalowners and miners' leaders to defer to State conciliation'.[23]

In periods of acute industrial unrest, as, for example, between 1897 and 1900, the Labour Department was prepared to adopt an even more forceful policy. During the committee stage of the Conciliation Bill in 1896, the Board of Trade had been specifically denied the right to report upon the merits of industrial disputes for the guidance of public opinion, and the intention of the Act was that the Board should only authorise intra-departmental reports from its umpires and conciliators as to the progress of their negotiations.[24] In contrast, when labour disputes were exceptionally bitter and prolonged, involving severe social hardship, economic dislocation, or civil strife, the Labour Department interpreted its powers of inquiry as a mandate to exert public pressure upon capital and labour to resolve their differences. For example, in the Penrhyn quarry dispute, Llewellyn Smith secured the publication of correspondence between the Board of Trade and Lord Penrhyn in an attempt to expose his dictatorial refusal to negotiate with the quarrymen according to the accepted practices of collective bargaining.[25] In 1898, fearful that the intransigence of Colonel Dyer and the Employers Federation in the engineering lockout would precipitate industrial violence and strengthen the influence of socialist agitators, the Labour Department urged that a public inquiry be authorised 'to examine and report upon the merits of the dispute'. As Llewellyn Smith confided to his Assistant Commissioner, 'A formal enquiry is the last weapon in our armoury but if this immoderate attack upon trade unionism is not to degenerate into general class conflict, the full force of public and parliamentary opinion must be brought to bear upon the parties to submit to arbitration.'[26]

In this instance, such an initiative was rejected as politically inexpedient. None the less, similar tactics were to be employed against labour intransigence later the same year when the progress reports of the Board of Trade's conciliator in the South Wales coal strike were published as a calculated effort to discredit the claims of the more militant miners for a minimum living wage and to rally support for an amended sliding scale as recommended by the union executive.[27] Llewellyn Smith's conviction that these reports had represented a 'most important influence in bringing the strike to an end' encouraged him to repeat such tactics during the Taff Vale dispute of 1900.[28] In a revealing note to Sir Courtenay Boyle, the Permanent Secretary, he conceded that the employers' refusal to recognise the Amalgamated Society of Railway Servants was 'undoubtedly unreasonable' and their use of free labour 'provocative'. Nevertheless, the Labour Commissioner considered that Board of Trade negotiations were being 'deliberately aborted by a minority' of rank-and-file 'agitators' and that, if the 'men rejected the peace formula proffered by the Department' and recommended by their General Secretary, Richard Bell, 'it should be made known, for then either moderation [would] have to prevail or the public [would] turn against the strikers and the power of the union be in great danger of being smashed to bits'. Accordingly, a detailed account of the Board's efforts to settle the dispute was systematically leaked to the press by the Labour Department.[29]

The right of the Labour Department under the Conciliation Act to facilitate negotiations between parties involved in labour disputes was exercised in an equally forceful fashion. It was primarily designed to activate existing collective-bargaining machinery within British industry and to encourage recourse to State *conciliation* when local negotiating procedures proved ineffectual. In contrast, the Board of Trade deliberately exploited it as a means to promote State *arbitration*. Prior to 1906, the Labour Department normally was prepared to intervene in disputes only when the probability of securing a definite settlement was high, and it considered that, 'in general, where trade boards and other domestic bargaining procedures had failed, State conciliation was unlikely to succeed'.[30] In negotiating with management and unions it therefore concentrated its efforts upon obtaining a joint submission of their differences to arbitration. When only one party to a dispute was amenable to State intervention, instead of appointing a conciliator the Labour Department frequently delayed formal proceedings until either social hardship or declining profits or further negotiations by Board of Trade labour officials induced the 'intransigent' party to yield to arbitration.[31] Even when it received a *joint* application for the appointment of a conciliator, the Department seized every opportunity to extend his terms of reference to arbitration.[32]

Such tactics were particularly suited to three categories of industrial dispute. First, there were disputes, such as the 1901 compositors' strike, in which the levels of management concession and union expectation were so divergent that only informal negotiations by the Board of Trade to reduce the magnitude of disagreement between the parties, followed by the authoritative award of an independent umpire, could avert a protracted stoppage.[33] Secondly, there were disputes in which industrialists or union leaders entrenched themselves in unrealistic bargaining positions from which they were unwilling to retreat for fear of 'losing face'. At the same time, the prospect of social distress, depleted benefit funds and reduced profit margins rendered them equally anxious to secure a settlement. In such instances, as for example in the Welsh tinplate stoppage of 1903–4, Labour Department officials had little difficulty in persuading local negotiators of the desirability of State arbitration as a means of breaking the deadlock.[34] Thirdly, there were disputes in which collective-bargaining procedures failed to resolve essentially qualitative issues, such as conditions of work and labour discipline. On such occasions, the Board of Trade might persuade the parties to translate their demands into more tangible financial claims better suited to arbitration. Thus, in the 1904 London cigar-makers dispute, the Labour Commissioner induced the Imperial Tobacco Company and its employees to abandon their abortive negotiations over management and union prerogatives in favour of a straightforward submission to wage arbitration.[35]

In its efforts to initiate State arbitration, the Labour Department left nothing to chance. In each labour dispute, its strategy was based upon a detailed assessment of factors likely to determine industrial response to State intervention, from economic variables such as the cost structure and profit margins of the firm and the financial resources of the union involved, to social and bureaucratic determinants such as the previous history of labour relations and bargaining procedures within the trade and the structure of authority within management and union hierarchies. As a result, although State arbitration had been conceived of in 1896 by C. T. Ritchie as 'a last resort', it subsequently accounted for 72 per cent of industrial settlements achieved under the Conciliation Act prior to the First World War.[36]

Yet, however liberal its interpretation of the Conciliation Act, the Board of Trade retained its essentially voluntarist view of industrial relations. To protect the community against the more serious economic and social repercussions of industrial conflict, the Board was prepared to exercise a considerable degree of 'bureaucratic licence' in implementing its powers. In an effort to ensure that voluntary dispute procedures were fully utilised and the merits of protracted stoppages fully investigated and publicised, it was also prepared to endorse the various schemes for a National Conciliation Board advocated by the General Federation of Trade Unions, the Trades Union Congress and the Industrial Co-operation Movement between 1898 and 1904.[37] None the less, the Board of Trade vigorously opposed contemporary proposals for compulsory arbitration with legal sanctions canvassed by an 'unholy alliance' of right-wing politicians obsessed with the impact of strikes on Britain's cost-competitiveness in overseas markets, trade-union leaders in the engineering and transport sectors seeking legal sanctuary from the counter-attack of the employers' associations, and middle-class social engineers infatuated with Australasian collectivism.[38] In the opinion of the Labour Department, any attempt to impose legal coercion upon collective bargaining would 'forfeit the confidence of Capital and Labour' and render the Conciliation Act a 'dead letter'.[39]

The Department was equally fearful that, by politicising labour relations, its administration of the Conciliation Act might alienate industrial opinion from Governmental dispute procedures. Reflecting upon the Board's failure to intervene successfully in several of the more serious labour disputes of the late 1890s, the Labour

Commissioner observed that the appointment of 'its own permanent officers and political chiefs' as conciliators and arbitrators had been 'greatly overdone' at the risk of 'undermining industrial confidence in the department's impartiality and injecting party politics into the discussion of what ought to be pure economics'.[40] Sir Courtenay Boyle, the Permanent Secretary, was in full agreement: 'We ought to appoint good *officers* from outside, not attempt our own good officers save in a great emergency. The oftener we try the less chance we have of doing good. Every failure hampers us but *so* does every success.'[41] As a result, the percentage of disputes formally settled under the Conciliation Act by the mediation or arbitration of Board of Trade officials and political chiefs fell dramatically, from 62 per cent in 1897 to 4 per cent in 1905.[42] Instead, increasing reliance was placed upon a small pool of 'independent' umpires and conciliators.

The pool was very carefully selected. The Board of Trade realised that industrialists would reject State arbitration if awards were based on anything other than strictly commercial criteria. Accordingly, while it never prescribed any formal wages policy, the Labour Department ensured that the traditional criteria of wage determination (the state of trade, the competitive needs of a district, or changes in the selling price of the product involved) were broadly adhered to by recruiting its umpires almost entirely from among the professional and upper classes, whose economic orthodoxy could be relied upon.[43] Although this strategy was bitterly attacked in the socialist press and hampered the efforts of trade unionists to secure a more equitable distribution of industrial profits,[44] it did not in fact alienate the trade-union movement in general from State arbitration. Three main explanations can be advanced for this.

As the Labour Department appreciated, while the minority of the more militant trade-union leaders remained firmly committed to the attainment of a minimum living wage defined by social need rather than the dictates of the market, most labour negotiators, confronted by formal arbitration or conciliation proceedings, were content to abandon socialistic rhetoric and to bargain within the bounds of established relativities and comparative market criteria. Indeed, when, after the Board of Trade's cost-of-living inquiry of 1906, a few umpires *did* pay more attention to local variations in rents and commodity prices, their awards were by no means assured of a favourable reception from labour. Not untypical was the complaint of one union secretary that such 'novel considerations' were 'much too scientific to deal with a simple problem of work and wages. We are', he added, 'not so much interested in the price of butter and eggs in certain districts as in the price to be paid for a given quantity of work in our own – more, we want to be paid the same price as other people.'[45]

Secondly, although the Board of Trade's choice of umpires and conciliators was socially exclusive, it also favoured expertise and accorded a minimal role to employers. Contemporary observers of British industrial relations attributed much of the breakdown of trade-union confidence in the existing machinery of collective bargaining to the ignorance of many umpires and mediators of the techniques and organisation of the trades involved in labour disputes, and to the frequent appointment of industrialists.[46] In implementing the Conciliation Act, Llewellyn Smith endeavoured to avoid similar disenchantment. As a result, as Table 22 indicates, if one compares a breakdown of State arbitrators by occupation

TABLE 22 Breakdown of State and private arbitrators by occupation

Occupation	% private arbitrators[a]	% State arbitrators[b]	% State arbitrations[b]
Lawyer	48	32	30
Civil servant (administrator)	5	14	8
Civil servant (specialist)	–	20	24
National politician	10	5	4
Local politician	10	6	10
Architect/Surveyor	–	8	12
Employer	19	6	3
Trade unionist	5	7	6
Academic	–	2	3
Ecclesiastic	3	–	–

[a] 1865–1914.
[b] 1896–1914.

Sources. J. H. Porter, 'Industrial Conciliation and Arbitration, 1860–1914' (unpublished Ph.D. thesis, Leeds University, 1968) p. 502; Parliamentary Papers, annual Reports of Proceedings under the Conciliation (Trades Disputes) Act, 1896.

with a similar breakdown of umpires chosen in the course of domestic dispute procedures, a number of contrasts emerge.

Apart from the lower participation ratio of employers, the role of occupational groups with least industrial expertise, such as lawyers, national politicians and ecclesiastics, is significantly less in State arbitration. Equally marked is the very much higher representation of the industrial professions – such as the architects and surveyors chosen to deal with some of the many building stoppages that constituted nearly a third of the labour disputes dealt with by the Board of Trade. However, the most outstanding contrast is the extensive use made by the Board of the scientific and industrial expertise of the Civil Service inspectorate, former inspectors of mines being appointed to arbitrate in colliery stoppages, while mercantile-marine inspectors and nautical assessors were deployed in shipyard demarcation disputes. In fact, Table 22 substantially understates the degree of expertise possessed by State arbitrators, as lawyers were often selected by the Labour Department as much for their specialised knowledge of particular trades as for their professional status. For example, A. A. Hudson, who arbitrated in nearly 20 per cent of disputes settled under the Conciliation Act between 1896 and 1914, was not only an experienced barrister but also a qualified architect and specialist in engineering and building litigation.

Finally, the Board of Trade increasingly secured the confidence not only of the more powerful unions, but also of many employers' associations, by capitalising upon the outstanding success of George Askwith as an industrial negotiator. The reasons for this success have been amply discussed elsewhere.[47] Suffice it to say that a breakdown of the size and trade distributions of disputes settled under the Conciliation Act prior to the First World War clearly reveals that Askwith's talents were specifically reserved for the more important strikes and lockouts involving the staple trades and transport, where industrial relations were particularly explosive and the economic and social costs of a stoppage exceptionally high, or where an award might have industry-wide repercussions upon production costs and pay differentials.

IV

Just how successful was the Board of Trade in reducing industrial unrest after 1896?[48] At first sight, its achievements under the Conservative administrations from 1896 to 1905 appear impressive. It was involved in 189 disputes, affecting nearly a quarter of a million workmen. It intervened in a quarter of the 'major industrial stoppages' of the period (officially defined as those involving not less than 5000 employees and/or the loss of more than 100,000 working days). In addition, the Board of Trade was responsible for 40 per cent of industrial settlements effected by third-party arbitration and conciliation. The success rate of proceedings under the Conciliation Act was high, averaging 71 per cent. Moreover, the rate showed a marked upward trend, from 51 per cent in 1897 to 93 per cent in 1905. If one takes into consideration disputes such as the Taff Vale stoppage, in which the Board of Trade's proposals were rejected but subsequently formed the basis of private negotiations, the Board's record appears even more creditable. Furthermore, although labour militants and industrialists were often dissatisfied with arbitration awards, such awards were normally adhered to. Their life expectancy was certainly no shorter than that of private settlements, and in many instances much longer.

The Board of Trade also accomplished a certain amount of preventive work. In a number of settlements it contrived to establish new conciliation machinery or to improve existing provisions for collective bargaining. In addition, as the influence of the Labour Department in industrial relations spread, there was an increasing tendency on the part of voluntary conciliation boards to embody in their rules a provision for appeal to the Board of Trade to appoint an umpire in case of deadlock. By 1905, sixty such arrangements existed, in a variety of industries – some, such as those in the building and boot and shoe trades, affecting thousands of workmen. As a result, there was a steady rise in the percentage of disputes settled under the Conciliation Act without recourse to a stoppage.

However, a closer appraisal of the Board of Trade's early efforts in the field of industrial relations reveals a more dismal picture of its achievements prior to 1906. It was involved in only 3·5 per cent of industrial disputes and settled only 2·5 per cent, affecting a mere 5 per cent of the workforce involved in strikes and lockouts. Of the 'major industrial stoppages' in which it intervened, it resolved only one-quarter. In fact, most strikes and lockouts settled under the Conciliation Act were small both in terms of days lost and workmen involved, and Board of Trade officials were very conscious of their failure to intervene successfully in larger disputes.[49] After 1896, the vast majority of industrial stoppages continued to be settled by direct arrangement between the parties. The success rate of proceedings under the Conciliation Act for the period 1896–1905 was also less impressive than it appears, for after 1900 the Board of Trade was increasingly selective in its choice of disputes in which it was prepared to intervene. It carefully avoided the growing number of stoppages involving controversial issues of social justice and industrial power and concentrated instead upon simple wage disputes in which both sides were receptive to State arbitration. Moreover, if one compares the trade distribution of all disputes with that of proceedings under the Conciliation Act, it is evident that the Board's efforts to reduce industrial unrest were heavily overcommitted to the building sector, where disputes were small and the unions weak and disorganised, and that it made relatively little headway in staple industries such as mining and textiles, where stoppages were more protracted and damaging to the economy.

Viewed in relation to the achievements of local trade boards, the preventive work of the Board of Trade up to 1906 is also unimpressive. Although the Conciliation Act had empowered the Board to establish conciliation machinery in any district or trade where its provision was deemed inadequate, and generally to co-ordinate the private system of collective bargaining, such powers remained largely inoperative in the face of either apathy or hostility from industrialists and trade-union leaders. The growing resort to conciliatory agencies in many leading industrial sectors stemmed from the disillusionment in labour circles with arbitration boards and with the automatic dependence of wages on sliding scales,[50] rather than from any influence of the Conciliation Act. At most, only about 2 per cent of conciliation boards operating in 1905 can be said to have owed their existence directly to the efforts of the Labour Department.

It was only after 1906 that the Board of Trade began to make any real impact upon industrial relations. In the period 1906–14 it settled nearly 10 per cent of all industrial stoppages, affecting 25 per cent of the workforce involved in strikes and lockouts. Compared with the preceding decade, this represented a dramatic increase in the role of State conciliation and arbitration. The Board of Trade intervened in over 85 per cent of the 'major industrial disputes' between 1906 and the outbreak of the First World War and resolved nearly 75 per cent of them – a significant advance upon the corresponding intervention and success rates of 25 and 6 per cent previously attained. An analysis of the size distribution of disputes settled under the Conciliation Act reveals that up to 1906 only 15 per cent involved over 1000 employees. Thereafter, some 34 per cent were of similar magnitude. Furthermore, despite its involvement in larger and more intractable disputes after 1905, the Labour Department's mean annual success rate remained above 80 per cent, and the growing prominence of third-party intervention in British collective bargaining was primarily a reflection of this success. The trade distribution of disputes resolved under the Conciliation Act continued to be skewed away from staple industries, but the Labour Department secured far greater influence in the two industries traditionally most resistant to State intervention – coalmining and cotton textiles. Moreover, notwithstanding the deterioration in industrial relations after 1909, and the absence of legal sanctions, arbitration awards were generally observed and appear to have suffered no consistent fall in life expectancy.

While it is impossible to estimate with any degree of precision the extent to which industrial stoppages were averted by the Board of Trade after 1905, evidence would suggest that its preventive work also had a significant effect upon British industrial relations. By 1914, labour policy in many sectors of the economy was regulated by arbitration and conciliation schemes inspired by the Board's industrial negotiators, and often providing for appeal to the Board in the event of deadlock. Even in the coalmining, engineering, transport, and textile industries, many employers and trade-union leaders had been persuaded either to establish or reconstruct collective bargaining machinery with which they might resolve their differences. Such was George Askwith's success in this respect that Halévy was moved to picture him as the 'secret dictator' building up 'piece by piece throughout the United Kingdom a vast written code governing the relations between employers and employed'.[51] At a conservative estimate, some 17 per cent of the joint boards of conciliation and arbitration operating in 1914 had originated as a by-product of industrial settlements negotiated by the Board of Trade, and they affected some 27 per cent of the organised labour force. The significance of this achievement was very clearly reflected in the concern of socialist commentators. According to

Justice and the *Socialist Review*, in reducing the incidence of strikes
and lockouts the Board had proved itself 'to be a subtle enemy
of the proletariat', while the Independent Labour Party viewed
the Conciliation Act as 'the most effective device by which the
trade union movement [had] been humbugged by the dominant
class'.[52]

V

The increased significance of the Conciliation Act in British industrial relations after 1906 was determined by a variety of social,
political and institutional factors. The shift in the political context
of labour administration was clearly vital. In its efforts to extend
State conciliation and arbitration in the period 1896–1905, the
Board of Trade was severely constrained by the concern of Conservative policy both to preserve the free play of market forces in
the determination of labour costs and to secure the financial and
electoral support of the managerial classes.[53] In contrast, Liberal
policy after 1905 proved increasingly receptive to Government intervention in labour relations. In their concern with social utility,
radicals urged that the State adopt a more active role in the
determination of factor costs.[54] Even Liberal leaders of more orthodox persuasion, while 'reluctant to assume a central responsibility
for economic affairs', were none the less prepared to sanction intervention to protect the 'community interest' as the scale of industrial
confrontation escalated.[55]

   The shift of public opinion in favour of State intervention in
industrial relations after 1905 was equally marked. The effects
of nationwide stoppages in the mining and transport sectors upon
the supply of essential goods and services and on the level of
earnings and employment in related trades provoked a growing
demand for more stringent action to preserve industrial peace.[56]
Furthermore, a substantial number of industrialists and trade-union
leaders were receptive to an extension of Government conciliation
and arbitration. A growing proportion of the business community
shared the view of the Board of Trade that State intervention
in wage determination was compatible with productive efficiency
and that consensus strategies rather than industrial confrontation
constituted the most effective antidote to labour unrest. After 1905,
the value of State participation in collective bargaining was increas-

ingly accepted even amongst those managerial groups, such as ship-owners, dock-owners and railway directors, whose labour policy had previously been noted for its intransigence and resistance to Government interference.[57]

Meanwhile, although Lib–Lab theories of capital–labour interdependence were discredited in labour circles, the bulk of the trade-union movement was still prepared to adjust working conditions and remuneration within the traditional parameters of collective bargaining.[58] This inevitably led to a greater recourse to State conciliation and arbitration as the insistence by labour negotiators upon national wage settlements after 1906 highlighted the inability of private collective bargaining to effect industry-wide agreements on substantive issues.[59] Furthermore, such intervention was an integral part of the tactics of even the most militant unions. Thus, the Triple Industrial Alliance proceeded upon the assumption that, if employers refused to negotiate, the threat of massive strike measures would force the Government to impose a settlement upon management.[60]

The increasing impact of the Conciliation Act upon industrial relations was also a function of administrative factors. After 1905, the Board of Trade adopted a far more vigorous labour policy than hitherto. In contrast to its previous strategy of selective intervention, it was prepared to intervene in every major trade dispute, even where the concern of management and unions to preserve industrial self-government, the polarity of their respective bargaining positions or the intractability of the issues involved were such as to exclude the possibility of arbitration. Consequently, whereas only 7 per cent of settlements under the Conciliation Act in the period 1896–1905 were achieved by means of conciliation, in the subsequent decade it accounted for 19 per cent of settlements, affecting some 44 per cent of the workmen involved in disputes referred to the Labour Department.

In an effort to discredit the confrontation tactics of both right- and left-wing extremists, the Board also instituted a series of inquiries into labour relations in those trades worst affected by industrial unrest. For example, its report upon the 1912 Thames and Medway dock strikes was designed to discredit the victimisation of union officials and the provocative use of free labour by the Shipping Federation, as well as the syndicalist tactics advocated by the dock workers' leaders.[61] The Board initiated the court of inquiry into the Dublin transport workers' stoppage of 1913 for similar reasons. On the one hand, it wished to ostracise the hard-line anti-unionism of W. M. Murphy and the Dublin Employers' Executive Committee. On the other, by revealing the adverse income and employment effects of the stoppage, it sought to expose the anti-social aspects of sympathetic strike action.[62] In implementing a more forceful policy, the Board of Trade suffered some notable reverses, such as those experienced by Lloyd George in the engineering and shipbuilding disputes of 1908, when attempts to hasten the process of collective bargaining merely alienated industrial opinion.[63] Nevertheless, in the long run it enabled the Board to play a more influential role in the more critical areas of British industrial relations.

The proficiency with which the Board of Trade performed such a role was greatly enhanced by the establishment in 1911 of a separate department devoted exclusively to labour unrest and headed by George Askwith as Chief Industrial Commissioner. After 1905, senior labour officials had become increasingly preoccupied with a massive programme of commercial and welfare legislation. As a result, as Askwith warned Churchill in April 1909, insufficient manpower and resources were being invested in reducing the social costs of industrial stoppages.[64] Furthermore, because of this deficiency, the administration of the Conciliation Act had become more formalised and the strategy of the Board towards labour unrest increasingly determined by 'generalists' who lacked both the temperament and specialist skills necessary for successful industrial diplomacy.[65]

The establishment of an industrial relations department staffed by full-time negotiators therefore injected fresh expertise at a critical juncture. Askwith and his Assistant Commissioners were less constrained by the bureaucratic imperatives which now inhibited the older generation of labour administrators. They were more conversant with recent shifts in the ideology and tactics of management and labour, and therefore better equipped to modify State dispute procedures accordingly. In addition, the ability of the Board of Trade to deploy a specialist team of conciliation officers in any major dispute enabled it to determine the character and timing of departmental initiatives with greater precision. Indeed, Askwith's official correspondence clearly indicates that this was every bit as important as 'charisma' to the success of his celebrated shuttle diplomacy after 1910.[66]

Finally, at a time when labour unrest was becoming a highly sensitive political issue, the greater autonomy vested in the administration of the Conciliation Act was probably a significant factor in conserving industrial confidence in State conciliation and arbitration. While Lloyd George and Churchill had undoubtedly secured a more vigorous role for the Board of Trade in industrial relations, their personal involvement in disputes had, in the period 1906–10, also created 'the suspicion' that its peace formulas and arbitration awards were primarily determined by political expediency.[67] The low profile adopted in disputes by their successor, Sydney Buxton, coupled with the delegation of responsibility for industrial relations to a separate department, would appear to explain, at least in part, the small but significant upswing in the success rate of proceedings under the Conciliation Act between 1911 and the outbreak of the First World War.

VI

This study of the Conciliation Act seriously erodes the traditional view of early twentieth-century State intervention in industrial relations as a minimalist policy of negative voluntarism.[68] While the Act failed to eradicate the fundamental causes of industrial strife, it had a significant impact upon its incidence and degree, especially after 1905. It prescribed no formal code comparable to the statutory regulations that characterised other areas of social administration. Nevertheless, it enabled the Board of Trade to pursue a coherent and vigorous strategy of positive voluntarism designed to contain labour unrest and stabilise employment relations by reinforcing both the existing machinery of collective bargaining and the social and institutional norms upon which its success depended.

Furthermore, the administration of the Conciliation Act between 1896 and 1914 clearly demonstrated that, without recourse to legal compulsion, it was still possible to provide a statutory framework within which dispute procedures might be effectively developed, the interests of the community generally secured against the most serious economic and social repercussions of trade stoppages, and a capitalist employment structure protected by the institutionalisation of industrial conflict and the confinement of collective bargaining within the bounds of existing wage relativities and orthodox market criteria.

The Act therefore provided labour policy-makers with convincing testimony of the value of permissive legislation. While the Board of Trade wished to incorporate a 'cooling-off' period as part of dispute procedure in major stoppages and to extend its right to initiate public inquiries into the merits of such disputes, its overriding concern in advising the Government on the prevention of industrial strife after 1909 was to dissuade it from adopting policy options that involved compulsion.[69] The Reconstruction Committee on industrial relations and post-war labour administrators were equally impressed by the ability of the Conciliation Act to sustain a policy of positive voluntarism without formal sanctions and without undermining industrial self-government. In essence, the 1919 Industrial Courts Act merely codified the procedures that had grown up under the Conciliation Act between 1896 and 1914. Industrial-relations policy in the 1920s was explicitly founded upon the principle that, apart from minor modifications, 'the machinery for the settlement of labour disputes' should remain 'fundamentally the same as in pre-war times'.[70]

Indeed, until 1971, the Conciliation Act continued to provide both the legal base and procedural norms of government conciliation services.[71] Moreover, the major policy files relating to the Act were consulted by the Donovan Commission, and, although many industrial sociologists, incensed by its 'faith in voluntarism', criticised the Commission for its 'historicist' approach,[72] the subsequent fate of the Industrial Relations Act would suggest that the history of the Conciliation Act as administered by the Board of Trade can still provide valuable insights for present and future policy-makers intent upon the alleviation of industrial strife.

Notes

1 *Studies in the Growth of Nineteenth Century Government*, ed. G. Sutherland (London, 1972) pp. 227–62.

2 PP: annual *Reports on Strikes and Lockouts*; annual *Reports on Changes in the Rate of Wages and the Hours of Labour*.

3 See, for example, *Hansard* (Commons) 4th ser., xxxi, 395 (5 Mar 1895).

4 See, for example, ibid., xxxiii, 209–12 (30 Apr 1895); PP, 1893–4 (228) i, 187.

5 W. E. Gladstone Papers, BL Add. MSS. 44258, A. J. Mundella to Gladstone, 28 Dec 1896.

6 For a detailed account, see S. B. Boulton, *The Genesis of a Conciliation Act* (London, 1896) pp. 9–10.

7 PRO, BT13/26/E12293/1896.

8 Ibid.

9 PP, 1896 (307) I, 407.

10 E. H. Phelps Brown, *The Growth of British Industrial Relations* (London, 1959) pp. 187–8.

11 R. Davidson, 'The Board of Trade and Industrial Relations, 1896–1914', *Historical Journal*, XXI (1978) 592.

12 J. H. Porter, 'Wage Bargaining under Conciliation Agreements, 1860–1914', *EHR*, 2nd ser., XXIII (1970) 472.

13 J. E. Williams, 'Labour in the Coalfields', *Labour History Bulletin*, IV (1962) 26.

14 *The Times*, 25 Apr 1895.

15 H. A. Clegg, A. Fox and A. F. Thompson, *A History of British Trade Unions since 1889*, vol. I: *1889–1910* (Oxford, 1964) p. 177.

16 See, for example, *Liberty Review*, V (1896) 142.

17 PRO, BT13/24/E11856/1895.

18 See, for example, *Hansard* (Commons) 4th ser., XLV, 691–762 (28 Jan 1897).

19 PRO, BT13/26/E12293/1896.

20 *Studies in the Growth of Nineteenth Century Government*, p. 246.

21 PRO, Lab. 2/75/L1094/1898.

22 PRO, Lab. 2/9/L908/1899.

23 PRO, Lab. 2/75/L776/1902.

24 *Hansard* (Commons) 4th ser., LX, 75 (24 June 1898).

25 Hopwood Papers, Llewellyn Smith to Hopwood, 27 June 1901; PP, 1897 (31) LXXII.

26 Wilson Fox Papers, Llewellyn Smith to Fox, 30 Oct 1897.

27 PP, 1898 (C9031) LXXII, 7–9; PRO Lab. 2/101/L1312/1901.

28 Ibid.

29 Ibid.; Hopwood Papers, Llewellyn Smith to Boyle, 26 Aug 1900.

30 H. Llewellyn Smith, 'Arbitration and Conciliation in Trade Disputes', *Encyclopaedia Britannica*, vol. XXV (1902) p. 552.

31 See, for example, PRO, Lab. 2/75/L776/1902.

32 See, for example, PRO, Lab. 2/75/L1094/1898.

33 PRO, Lab. 2/102/L247/1901.

34 PRO, Lab. 2/98/L1463/1903.

35 PRO, Lab. 2/141/L1483/1904.

36 PP, annual *Reports of Proceedings under the Conciliation (Trade Disputes) Act, 1896.*

37 Clegg, Fox and Thompson, *History of British Trade Unions*, vol. I, pp. 177 and 265; D. Knoop, *Industrial Conciliation and Arbitration* (London, 1905) p. 114.

38 Phelps Brown, *Growth of British Industrial Relations*, pp. 187–8.

39 *Encyclopaedia Britannica*, vol. XXV (1902) p. 553; PRO, Lab. 2/1/L128/1902.

40 Hopwood Papers, Llewellyn Smith to Boyle, 1 Jan 1898.

41 Bryce Papers, Bodleian Library, P11/J63, Boyle to Bryce, 5 Jan 1898.

42 PP, annual *Reports of Proceedings under the Conciliation Act.*

43 Davidson, in *Historical Journal*, XXI, 605–8.

44 Ibid., 609; *Labour Leader*, 23 Oct 1908.

45 PRO, Lab. 2/29/C7067/1910, A. Smith to G. R. Askwith, 17 Sep 1910.

46 J. H. Porter, 'Industrial Conciliation and Arbitration, 1860–1914' (unpublished Ph.D. thesis, Leeds University, 1968) pp. 27 and 501.

47 See R. Davidson, Introduction to Lord Askwith, *Industrial Problems and Disputes* (Hassocks, 1974).

48 Unless otherwise stated, analysis in this section is based upon material contained in PP: annual *Reports of Proceedings under the Conciliation Act*; annual *Reports on Strikes and Lockouts*; annual *Abstracts of Labour Statistics*.

49 See, for example, PRO, Lab. 2/75/L776/1902, Wilson Fox to Llewellyn Smith, 14 Feb 1901.

50 Porter, in *EHR*, 2nd ser., XXIII, 460–75.

51 E. Halévy, *A History of the English People in the Nineteenth Century*, vol. VI: *The Rule of Democracy, 1905–14*, revised edn (London, 1952) p. 261.

52 *Justice*, 6 Nov 1913; *Socialist Review*, VII (1911) 248; *Labour Leader*, 24 Sep 1909.

53 Davidson, in *Historical Journal*, XXI, 597–8.

54 H. V. Emy, *Liberals, Radicals and Social Politics 1892–1914* (Cambridge, 1973) pp. 264 and 270.

55 Ibid., pp. 269 and 275.

56 PRO, Cab. 37/107/98 (9 Aug 1911).

57 R. Charles, *The Development of Industrial Relations in Britain, 1911–1939* (London, 1973) pp. 24, 39 and 51.

58 J. Lovell, *British Trade Unions, 1875–1933* (London, 1977, for the Economic History Society) p. 39.

59 H. A. Clegg, *The System of Industrial Relations in Great Britain* (Oxford, 1970) p. 203.

60 G. A. Phillips, 'The Triple Industrial Alliance in 1914', *EHR*, 2nd ser., XXIV (1971) 65.

61 PP, 1912–13 (Cd. 6229) XLVII.

62 PRO, Lab. 2/100/IC4614/1913.

63 E. Wigham, *The Power to Manage* (London, 1973) p. 78.

64 PRO, BT13/134, Askwith to Churchill, Apr 1909.

65 Ibid., Fountain to Smith, 13 Mar 1909.

66 See, for example, Buxton Papers, correspondence relating to the boilermakers' and cotton-spinners' disputes of 1910.

67 PRO, Cab. 37/107/98, 9 Aug 1911.

68 See, for example, Phelps Brown, *Growth of British Industrial Relations*, pp. 185 and 354; Charles, *Development of Industrial Relations*, p. 305.

69 See PRO, Cab. 37/107/70 and 98, Cab. 37/110/62–3, Cab. 37/118/14.

70 PRO, Lab. 2/921/IR190/1922. I am indebted to Dr Rodney Lowe for putting his transcripts of this file at my disposal.

71 *Industrial Relations Handbook* (London: HMSO, 1961) pp. 19 and 141.

72 J. R. Crossley, 'The Donovan Report: A Case Study in the Poverty of Historicism', *British Journal of Industrial Relations*, VI (1968) 298.

Part III
Scotland

10 The Creation of the Disablement Rule in the Scottish Poor Law

ROSALIND MITCHISON

It is generally thought, that the Scots and English laws concerning the poor are very different; but, if we carefully examine both, we shall find a very near resemblance. [John McFarlan, DD, *Inquiries Concerning the Poor* (Edinburgh, 1782) p. 46.]

The evils attendant on the *administration* did not arrive from any defects in the laws ... ; but entirely from the decisions of the Court of Session, who, being during the last century almost entirely composed of landholders, and having the dread of the English parochial burdens before their eyes, introduced the rule that the decisions of the Heritors and Kirk Sessions ... could not be reviewed except in the *Court of Session*. As this amounted to a practical abolition of the right of appeal in ninety nine out of a hundred, it left the ratepayers in reality judges without review in their own cause .... [A. Alison, *Essays Political, Historical and Miscellaneous* (London, 1850) vol. II, p. 640.]

The important distinction ... between the respective titles of able-bodied and impotent paupers, was held for centuries to be the distinguishing excellence of these laws. [*Report of the Royal Commission on the Administration and Practical Operation of the Poor Laws in Scotland* (PP, 1844, xx) p. xliv.]

This essay is an exploration of the creation of the rule of the Scottish Poor Law that 'disablement' as well as 'destitution' was a necessary qualification for relief. That there was no such rule in the early eighteenth century has been shown elsewhere,[1] and much of the development in the Poor Law between 1700 and 1780 was designed to make it an effective instrument to cope with the problems of harvest shortfall or other general emergencies, which, in the words of the East Lothian justices of the peace in 1773, meant that 'the price of grain has now risen to such a height that many persons now stand in need of assistance who were formerly in a condition to support themselves'.[2] The impulse therefore was to expand the scope of relief. This was often done by subsidising the price of grain (sometimes by funds raised by an *ad hoc* committee of heritors, sometimes directly from Poor Law funds), a method which blurred the distinction between able-bodied and disabled. It is true that there were efforts to reverse this expansionist trend. There survives correspondence of a land-owner in Angus and a lawyer, written before the landowners succeeded in gaining control of the local Poor Law in 1751 through the Humbie case, which shows the frustration of the landowner in the face of the generosity of the kirk session.[3] But the first description of the Scottish Poor Law which praised it for the opportunities it provided for meanness to the poor is a letter from James Anderson of Monk's Hill to Jeremy Bentham in 1781.[4] This account has three points of interest. First, it is the first to minimise the role of relief, stressing that every effort must be made by the parish to leave as much as possible to be done by the pauper, his friends and private charity. Secondly, it makes no direct reference to the fact that the parish's relieving actions are based on a body of statute law, the implication throughout being that Scottish parishes acted spontaneously in this benign and yet invigorating way. Only in minor asides is the shadow of a legal obligation allowed to show, as when Anderson suggests that there is a power of appeal to those who oppose payments. Thirdly, it states 'if any one is in a condition to earn his own Bread, he can expect no sort of supply': yet even this is not a clear statement that the unemployed or merely needy could not get relief.

Study of Anderson's own parish, Daviot, and presbytery, Garioch, suggests that in this matter he was describing local practice.[5] The

northern parishes in this area doled out small amounts of money
to cases of inescapable need, and where more was essential they
would send out an appeal to the whole presbytery for a special
contribution. But Anderson was a sophisticated and travelled man
and he is unlikely to have thought that this was the practice
everywhere in Scotland.

A more thorough description of the Scottish Poor Law at this
time comes from the work of John McFarlan, minister of the
Canongate, who produced a book of 494 pages on Poor Laws,
mostly referring to Scotland but also concerned with England,
drawing on the practice in the south of Scotland and also in
Perthshire.[6] An important theme in it is the resemblance of the
law in the two countries. Here again there is a striking omission:
at no point does he refer to disablement as a necessary qualification
for relief in Scotland. Since this was to come to the fore as the
difference between the two countries, it is difficult to avoid the
conclusion that at least in the parts of Scotland from which his
information came this rule was not yet established. McFarlan
touches on relief for the able-bodied inexplicitly: 'though worthless
people often make the want of employment a pretence for begging,
yet sometimes it happens that there is real cause for the complaint' – particularly, he adds, in a commercial or industrial society,
or during a hard frost. 'To grant . . . an occasional relief, answers
all the purposes of real charity, without discouraging a spirit of
industry.'[7] Aware of the problem of Highlanders walking the Perthshire roads after a poor harvest, ostensibly as harvest labour for
the south, but of necessity begging, he argued for distinctions in
law between the different types of beggar.

Anderson's letter indicates the existence of a desire to reduce
or abolish the legal structure of relief in both England and Scotland.
Bentham sent it on to Shelburne with the hope that it would
provoke some change in the law in England. At this date hostility
to legal relief was probably a view held by only a minority of
the propertied classes. In the 1780s there existed in Edinburgh
a self-appointed body of 'Noblemen and Gentlemen', who considered themselves in some way 'representative', the 'Monthly Club',
and in 1786 this body recorded its view of 'the danger of allowing
any Bill to pass in Parliament, that might tend to introduce into
this country Poors' Rates similar to those established in England'.[8]
Again the choice of language wrongly implies the absence of a

statutory base for poor relief in Scotland at a time when a considerable minority of parishes were already rated for this.

In 1793-4 a further discussion of poor relief, almost certainly
by Anderson, appeared in his own periodical, *The Bee*. On this
occasion he acknowledged that the system had a legal base.[9] His
aim was to belittle the past use of the law, so as to establish
its desuetude, or to gloss particular statutes, particularly that of
1663, to show that the cases for which assessment was demanded
were few. This statute of 1663,[10] in his eyes, allowed assessment
only for the support and control of sturdy beggars. The 'ordinary'
poor were to be supported only on voluntary funds, 'ordinary'
here meaning the infirm, aged or orphaned. So most places which
had set up poor rates, Anderson argued, had no legal basis for
them. In his efforts to keep down the obligatory nature of poor
rates, and in fact to abolish the compulsory element in the law,
he was driven to allow rating for able-bodied beggars.

There are points which both tie this publication to Anderson
and weaken its reliability as a source of either fact or contemporary
opinion. The tone of self-satisfied comparison with the sad state
of England is conspicuous. So is the determination to generalise
on matters on which it is most unlikely that the author could
be considered to have firm knowledge – for instance, the comment
on the post-Reformation period:

> almsgiving continued to be considered as a meritorious thing
> in Scotland, while it fell into total disrepute in England. . . . And
> though the clamours from disorderly persons in Scotland, who
> were strictly excluded from sharing in the poor's funds, continued
> for some time to be so great as to induce precipitant ministers
> of state to make some rash laws on that head, yet as the nation
> at large were at all times perfectly satisfied that the *real* poor
> were abundantly cared for . . . .[11]

This remark lies in such direct conflict with a large body of
seventeenth-century comment, in kirk-session registers, in the *Register
of the Privy Council* and by intelligent observers such as Sir Robert
Sibbald, that it cannot be justified by the general argument of
the difficulty of proving a negative. More importantly, Anderson
not only takes a free hand in abolishing the various Acts of Parliament of which he disapproves, the product of 'precipitant ministers',

by declaring that they were never operative, but also adds regulations which are not supported by either case or statute law. For instance, he states a regulation that 'no money can be *legally* issued from the poor's funds . . . unless legal proof can be brought that public intimation has been given from the pulpit . . . a full fortnight before', and that nobody but the treasurer of a kirk session can legally give out relief. In the way in which it freely interpreted the existing law, or invented it, this first attack on the legal base of poor relief foreshadowed the attacks of the nineteenth century.

The food crisis at the end of the eighteenth century, resulting from the bad harvests of 1799 and 1800, brought out a reassertion of the attitude of the 1770s. As the *Farmers' Magazine* declared in 1801, wages bore 'no affinity to the common prices of the necessaries of life'.[12] As a result, 'many country parishes have assessed themselves in considerable sums for the support of the working people', though there were doubts about the legality of this practice. This statement is borne out by the famous case of *Pollock* v. *Darling* of 1804,[13] in which the parish of Duns was confirmed in its action of raising rates to sustain wages, the 'Speenhamland' policy of England. The same practice was to be found in other places, particularly in East Lothian.[14] It is one of the more surprising untruths in the historiography of the Scottish Poor Law that in 1819 the Rev. Robert Burns should have declared that 'in Scotland we know nothing of the very impolitic and pernicious practice of making up the deficiency of wages for work done to private individuals by grants out of the parochial funds'. If Burns did not know of the practice, then he had not looked very far. Elsewhere, in the same spirit of generalisation, Burns can be found stating that the distinction between 'the industrious poor and the disabled' can be found in every parish.[15] There is no reason to think that he had searched for it in more than a handful of the near 900 parishes of Scotland.

The judges declared in the case of *Pollock* v. *Darling* that 'inability to earn subsistence, is the true and only distress which it is the object of a code of poor's law to relieve', but this decision came in the Inner House and by one vote only. In the *Farmers' Magazine* for 1804 and 1805 there is a series of letters signed 'Agricola', a pseudonym often, but not exclusively, used by Anderson, querying such a use of poor relief, except in emergencies, and generally arguing against any use of poor rates.[16] Many of the sentences, such as the comment on Scotland that there is 'no country in the world where the poor are more humanely and carefully attended to' echo sentences in *The Bee*. There appear to have been at this time two streams of thought about what should be the nature of the Poor Law: a modern political-economy opinion that rates were pernicious and unnecessary, and an old-fashioned view that rate-based relief was often a necessary fall-back in an agrarian emergency. Neither school of thought was prepared to deny categorically that rate-based money could be used on the support of the able-bodied.

That the Scottish courts, in *Pollock* v. *Darling* and in other cases, adopted what may seem a high-handed attitude to both statute and precedent should not surprise. Scots law, from its virtual 'creation' by Stair, had had to abandon some statutes, enlarge others, create whole topics from almost nothing, and to do this with the claim that it was merely stating the law as it had always been. Hence the importance of the Scottish principle that statutes not used lose all validity. This principle, in turn, gave to lawyers a vested interest in misrepresenting legal history, a practice which continued long after it ceased to be necessary as a mechanism of adaptation. Lawyers lied about the history of the law and came to believe their own lies. 'What I tell you three times is true' might have been their motto.[17]

The period after the Napoleonic war was one of economic stress and discomfort in Scotland as well as in England, and also, not unconnected with this, of vocal and organised radicalism. Sound comparative figures for the national level of relief do not exist to enable us to discern whether, in real terms, the burden of relief was heavier than it had been during the war,[18] but there is no doubt that certain sections of the nation felt threatened by its level. This was partly because of inequalities in the burden. Not only was the distribution of assessment uneven, so that landowners in the south were paying more than in the north (in 1818 the Church of Scotland stated that the relief per pauper came as £5 15s 3½d in the synod of Merse and Teviotdale, £2 2s 2¾d in the synod of Aberdeen and only 16s 11d in Ross)[19] but also absentee landowners even in assessed parishes could avoid the burden altogether. The compromise that some landowners had reached of 'voluntary assessment', which brought home their obligations to absentees and made funds available in emergencies without

allowing the expectations of the workforce to rise, had the disadvantage of not being legally enforceable. Individual landowners might
break rank. In any case, the burden could not be forced on the
tenantry, as could assessment, though the Church's 1818 report
stated that it was 'not unusual' for tenants to contribute.[20] In
some parishes, until recently rural but now highly urbanised, where
stood the new factories of industrial Scotland, a system of rates
based either on real or valued rent left considerable concentrations
of wealth untaxed. For instance, in Paisley burgh 'one-half of
the real property of the burgh does not pay a farthing'.[21]

It may seem a puzzle how there could be uncertainty about
the right of the able-bodied to relief after *Pollock* v. *Darling*. If
rate-based relief could be given to those able to work and working,
then clearly it was not prohibited for the others. Also, the provisions
for dealing with vagrants, always though often incorrectly assumed
to be 'sturdy', would cover the unemployed. It was generally
accepted, except by Anderson, that all parishes had some discretion
and could dribble out small sums from voluntary funds to cases
not acceptable for the list of 'ordinary' poor, even though by
the Humbie decision of 1751, when the heritors established control
over the voluntary funds, the distinction between the kirk sessions'
discretionary money and that administered by heritors and kirk
sessions together had become obscured. But *Pollock* v. *Darling* has
to be seen not only in the context of the unacknowledged fluidity
of Scots law and the traditions of independent action by kirk
sessions: there is also the problem of the difference in the nature
of destitution in urban and in rural settings. 'Speenhamlanding',
which *Pollock* v. *Darling* declared to be not only legal in emergencies
but also customary, the 'known and indisputed usage to give relief
to the industrious poor under circumstances of temporary distress',
was likely only to be adopted in agricultural areas, where the
session could have intimate knowledge of the family circumstances
of individual labourers and the employment prospects. Indeed, the
variety of it discovered in some East Lothian parishes, where the
allowance decreased as the family got larger, suggests close attention
to the availability of work for juveniles.[22] In industrial areas, where
the problem was severe bouts of cyclical unemployment, it could
not be worked, and, in the years after the war, destitution was
an industrial problem on a new scale, though, particularly in
1817–18, high prices made for very tight budgets for the agricultural

labourer.[23] It seems that in many parishes the past policy of the parish was what the administrators regarded as the law.

Thus, there are conflicting statements about the rights of the unemployed. Burns, who cannot be treated as a legal authority, states,

> if through stagnation of trade or other casualties in the course of Providence, a number of tradesmen and labourers have been thrown out of employment, and cannot by any exertion of their own obtain it, in such a case, the system of poor laws is not brought forward as a scheme of relief. It does not appear to have been designed for such a purpose.[24]

A writer in *Blackwood's Magazine* for April 1818 took a similar stand. In contrast to these stand two legal textbooks: G. Hutcheson's *A Treatise on the Offices of Justice of the Peace, Constable etc. . . . in Scotland*, though regarding relief as normally for the disabled, adds, 'it has always been the practice to assist persons who, by misfortune, or disease, or other circumstances, are disabled, for a time, from maintaining their families' and 'parochial aid is afforded to those who, though willing to work, yet with their utmost exertion cannot earn enough';[25] and the advocate G. Tait in *Summary of the Powers and Duties of a Justice of the Peace in Scotland* says, on the subject of begging, 'poor persons who beg, even in their own parishes, are to be punished as vagabonds; as provision is made for supporting them without begging, if they cannot find work'.[26] Robert Davidson, professor of law at Glasgow University, was quoted by the Paisley operatives in 1820 as stating that the 'industrious poor' had, by *Pollock* v. *Darling*, a right to relief, but, 'the allowance must necessarily be moderate'.[27] (The qualification was not in the judgement.)

Some of the confusion of opinion may well come from the fact that to lawyers this was not an important branch of law: nobody was going to earn substantial fees in it. But there was a genuine difference of opinion, reinforced by differences in local practice, and this explains the indignation expressed by Cockburn in November 1821 at the plea 'that people *out of work*, though in perfect health, have a legal right to be maintained', which he described as a claim for a 'constitutional right' in a man 'to ruin his own morality, and pick my pocket at the same time'.[28] This view was modified later when he wrote for the *Edinburgh Review* stating that it was lawful to assess for the support of persons 'who, though in ordinary seasons, able to gain their livelihood, are reduced, during a dearth of provisions, to . . . charitable supply'.[29] But these were probably the agricultural poor, so much more the cause of sympathy than the industrial, and he was unsure whether the demand of the Paisley unemployed in 1819 that this be extended to them had been 'well founded'. As late, however, as 1830, Dr Thomas Chalmers, asked by the Royal Commission investigating the need for a Poor Law in Ireland, assumed rather hazily that *Pollock* v. *Darling* had shown the Scottish unemployed as having a right to relief.[30]

Cockburn's remark about the ruin of character shows a new line of thought about relief: that it was bad for the recipient. This opinion seems to start with Thomas Chalmers in 1808, when he commented publicly on 'the power of charity to corrupt its object'.[31] It became a standard element in the opinion of those who opposed the expansion or the extent of poor relief, and its expression on any occasion does not mean that the speaker was consciously indebted to Chalmers. The poor would, in the long run, be better spiritually, and hence happier, without State aid. That this was a convenient theory to those who did not wish to be rated need not mean that it was not sincerely held. Chalmers had enormous influence, first of all in his period in Glasgow (1815–23) as a leading preacher, and later as an academic, when in his lectures he welded together evangelical religion and the individualist political economy of Malthus. An important element in his thought was the combination of hostility to the Poor Law on moral grounds with hostility on economic grounds. This can be seen reflected in an early number of *The Scotsman*: 'the principle of the poor laws is radically bad and decidedly prejudicial to the lower classes themselves', declared this new, Whiggish paper.[32] This theme gained strength from the manifest unease of the English propertied classes at the level of poor relief in that country. Chalmers's famous 'experiment' on poor relief in St John's parish, Glasgow, 1819–23, has recently been critically examined.[33] It was embarked on not to find out truth but to prove it. It confirmed the opponents of poor relief in the view that they were not really advocating any increased hardship for the poor, for Chalmers appeared to show that, even in the heart of a big city, rate-based relief could be replaced by the help of relatives and neighbours and a small amount of charity.

As the Rev. Robert Burns said of the Poor Law, 'as the heritors themselves are the persons to be assessed, they may be supposed to exercise the greatest care in the allocation of the assessment. . . . There is in every parish a legally constituted court, consisting of minister and elders . . . controlled to every extent by the committee of heritors.' Cockburn said the same thing, that the Poor Law was administered by those 'who are steeled against profusion by their being themselves its immediate victims'.[34] There was little in the way of appeal. Appeal to the Court of Session was difficult (because the parish was not a court of record) and costly; it has not left many cases in the standard repositories of case law. It was less clear whether, and under what circumstances, any lower court could revise decisions.[35] Eighteenth-century justices of the peace had often constructed schemes of poor relief and vagrancy control, with or without pressure from sheriffs, and in the course of these had put pressure on parishes to fulfil their legal duties; but they had not directly ordered either assessment or the payment of a specific sum by a parish to an individual. In 1772 there had been a decision in the Court of Session against the power of a sheriff to fix a level of relief in the first instance.[36] In 1824 Cockburn referred to twenty-six cases where sheriffs had insisted that kirk sessions increase inadequate allowances, and to another thirty threatened appeals to sheriff courts.[37]

Eighteenth-century heritors had valued the existence of an appeals system because it was easier for them than it was for a kirk session to manipulate the legal system, at least as long as the Cambuslang case was regarded as of authority.[38] But, as Cockburn pointed out, there was now an appeal 'of so expressive a character, that it throws all the rest into the shade'. This was the appeal, starting in 1819, of *Richmond and others* (variously stated at between 825 and 1000) v. *The Heritors and Kirk Session of the Abbey Parish of Paisley*.[39] To appreciate its significance an understanding of the force of the 'New Whigs' in Scottish history is necessary, as well as of the explosive nature of the issue of urban radicalism in a severe depression.

The New Whigs were the young men in a hurry. They were the *Edinburgh Review* group. The politics of the *Review* have been analysed by John Clive, and can be summarised as being against all forms of privilege and prescriptive right except that of money.[40]

The *Review*'s own words were that as a 'general proposition' it was against all restrictive laws which excluded 'certain classes of men from political stations'. It was therefore in favour of Catholic Emancipation, 'popular' or semi-popular elections and burgh reform. The *Review* was Benthamite and Malthusian. In general it held for free trade and against monopoly. In particular it supported Malthus's attack on the Poor Laws[41] and wished for law reform, including penal reform and reform of the structure of the courts. In the post-war period the names particularly associated with the *Review* are those of Francis Jeffrey and John Archibald Murray. Cockburn gives a list of his Whig friends, which adds George Cranstoun, Thomas Thomson, John McFarlan, George Joseph Bell, James Moncrieff and James Grahame.[42] Jury trial was a New Whig fetish, and the lawyers who served in the jury court should be regarded as tied to New Whiggery. This, besides re-emphasising Jeffrey and Cockburn, brings forward the name of an older man, David Monypenny, Lord Pitmilly. There were two other figures, of significance because they came early into Parliament: Cockburn's friend T. F. Kennedy, and James Abercromby, who often acted as political adviser to the group. Henry Brougham, though of Whig and radical opinions and closely associated with the *Review*, cannot be included, because the only cause he stood for in any sustained way was that of Henry Brougham, and because he rapidly transferred his concern from Scottish to English political affairs. A younger lawyer, Alexander Dunlop, whose views Cockburn considered 'right' on reform,[43] should be considered as a latecomer to this party.

Most of these men were lawyers. Law was the most prestigious of professions, and the bulk of advocates and judges were drawn from landed society. Legal practice gave men opportunities to see the need for legal change, and in the Scottish legal system of the day there was no sharp demarcation between the concept of what the law ought to be and what it was in a particular decision. Malthusian thought held that the able-bodied unemployed should not receive poor relief, and that relief even to those disabled should be on a small and restricted scale. It was easy to assert in Scotland that this was already the case.

Burgh reform was the most pressing issue of the post-war period and was linked to Parliamentary reform. But there was also, as was shown in the radical trials of 1819 and after, an important issue in free speech and in the selection of juries. T. F. Kennedy, even before he entered Parliament, had been considering the need to 'reform' the Poor Law,[44] but when he entered, in 1818, he was also concerned over jury selection. In 1819 he introduced into Parliament a Bill to remove all right of appeal by Scottish claimants of poor relief from the decision of the parish.[45] He claimed that 'a new class of person, as poor, had been introduced, by some denominated "the industrial poor" '. 'The Courts of Justice had of late interfered and perverted the old law. . . . For a long period Scotland had been greatly indebted to the ignorance of a great part of the society that there were any laws compelling a relief to the poor.' Here Kennedy showed that his ultimate aim was to dissolve the legal basis of relief, but for the present he concentrated on local independence. The courts might favour the 'new' idea of relief for the able-bodied, and so he wished to see the parish left supreme. 'As the local jurisdiction was the only safe one', he wanted it made 'final and absolute'.[46]

It is not an accident that the main agent in the achievement of a recognised New Whig cause, the opening of the jury system, should also have attacked the Poor Law. Kennedy was also deeply involved in plans for Parliamentary reform.[47] He claimed, with some truth, that there was considerable uncertainty whether justices of the peace or sheriffs could hear appeals from decisions of kirk sessions. There was no doubt, though, that the Court of Session could do so. R. Clark *A View of the Office of Sheriff in Scotland*, sets out the sheriff's position:[48] he has power to order a parish to act, but 'no power to fix the quantum of parochial aliment'.

Cockburn's *Letters* show that Kennedy's Bill provoked 'provincial abuse'.[49] It failed during the summer. But judicial decisions achieved most of its aims in the course of the next two years.

The crucial Richmond case sprang from the sharp trade depression of 1819. Attention has focused on the disturbances and radical meetings in the west of Scotland, on the unease arising from Peterloo in August, and finally on the Scottish 'Radical War' of 1820, recently ennobled into a nationalist movement.[50] There has been less notice of the cautious attempt of a large body of Paisley cotton operatives to establish that the unemployed in Scotland were entitled to poor relief.[51] On refusal of relief, an appeal was brought to the sheriff, who decided in favour of the unemployed. The parish appealed to the Court of Session. Lord Pitmilly, as

Lord Ordinary, decided against the unemployed and this judgement was confirmed late in 1821 in the Inner House, with one of Cockburn's New Whigs as advocate for the parish, on the grounds that the sheriff did not have an appellate jurisdiction.[52]

It is difficult, on the pleadings, not to feel that this decision bent the law, but it also seems that the clarity demanded by the operatives involved bending too. The powers of justices of the peace seem more clearly established than those of sheriffs by the Act of 1661, but Morison's *Dictionary of Decisions* implies that the sheriff had some appellant right.[53] The parish's case was based on the 'intentions' of the early Acts of Parliament, a very shady area of mingled law and history, most of the history being bad, and on the fact that an obligation on a kirk session to relieve did not give an enforceable claim to the poor to be relieved. The cases cited – for instance, *Paton* v. *Adamson*, which is not about an appeal – seem mere window-dressing. But the weakness of the operatives' case, that 'there are serious, if not insuperable, difficulties against the proceedings of the heritors and kirk sessions being reviewable directly by this Court, without having previously gone through the sheriff court' was an attempt to argue on the principle of what, in the best of all possible worlds, the law would be, and to argue it in a hostile environment.

The Richmond case might seem to have tightened up the Poor Law enough for Kennedy and his friends. That it did not is clear from Kennedy's correspondence. From 1821 Kennedy was planning a new Bill.[54] Sir Henry Moncreiff Wellwood wrote to him about the Richmond judgement: 'from what passed on the Bench I think it probable that if it had been taken up on the merits it would have infallibly been given in favour of the paupers. Such are our judges!'[55] Continued nervousness is understandable in the light of the numbers involved in such claims, the underlying threat of violence and the wayward attitude of the Court of Session to its own decisions, and still more in the widespread practice of many parishes which can be seen in the 1844 report giving relief to the able-bodied. Some of these added a further gloss to their view of the law by stating that they gave relief to the able-bodied only in cases of 'protracted illness'.[56] The uncertainty of the law remained. Alexander Dunlop was, thought Cockburn, far too generous to such claims in his draft work on the Poor Law.[57] Kennedy manifested the growing hostility of landed society to the claims of the Church in his fear that kirk sessions might 'pack' themselves with extra elders to outvote heritors in the joint committee, though it was far more likely at this time that, in parishes undergoing development, changes in landownership would increase the number of heritors.[58]

For personal reasons, and to leave a clear run for his jury reform, Kennedy did not move again on the Poor Law until 1824, when, in the middle of the session and at midnight, he introduced a second Bill which would eventually have removed all compulsory elements from the Poor Law. The kirk sessions were to have nothing to do with assessment, managing only voluntary funds, and the existing system of combined sessions and heritors managing assessment was to be maintained only for cases already supported, and provided that the sessions could not take on the burden on their own. In assessed parishes claimants could appeal to the Quarter Sessions to make the heritors, who would have complete control over rate-based money, consider their cases. Otherwise there were to be no appeals of any sort to any court. It was a model Malthusian scheme.[59]

The opposition to this Bill can be easily seen in the press. At various dates *The Scotsman*, which was favourable to restriction of the Poor Law, reported protests and speeches in presbyteries and county meetings, and itself pronounced 'we do not see any great necessity for abolishing the slender provision now levied'.[60] If the Parliamentary timetable had allowed Kennedy to act later in the year he would have had exactly the instance he needed. Clerk of Eldin, the unpredictable Whig who had recently become a judge, acting as Lord Ordinary in the case of an Irishman of Barony parish, Glasgow, who was indeed disabled but of indubitable nationality, had rebutted the argument put forward for the parish by Cockburn among other advocates, that 'the heritors and kirk session, when assembled on business regarding the poor . . . are not required to keep any record; and . . . their resolutions, being expressed verbally, do not admit of being received by a court of law', and declared that relief was not confined to natives. The Inner House had sustained this reaffirmation of an attenuated appeals system.[61] Clerk had already, in a Midlothian county meeting, stated that the interpretation that left the kirk session to settle both 'the quantum of allowance' and also the qualification was new; clearly he did not hold with it.[62] The tide of opposition to the Bill swept through the General Assembly when it met. Chalmers took a leading part in the debate on a motion that the Bill was 'inexpedient'.[63] He would have supported 'permissive' change (though it is difficult to see how the removal of all compulsion from the Poor Law could be permissive) but not such a drastic and comprehensive measure. After various draft motions every member of the General Assembly voted for this except for John Archibald Murray, who sat as an elder. All public bodies in Scotland, said the Lord Advocate in the House of Commons, were against the Bill. Kennedy withdrew it with expressions of surprise. The surprise may have been genuine. Cockburn said that the opposition was based on ignorance: 'the whole fools in the kingdom are up against the Poor Bill'.[64] But the General Assembly and the presbyteries were largely composed of people with active experience of the working of the Poor Law.

Kennedy did not, therefore, manage to destroy the Poor Law, but in practice the parishes could interpret it as they saw fit. A further weakening, however, took place in legal textbooks. The New Whigs assumed a monopoly of authoritative interpretations, and their position was not disputed, since this was an unpopular, because unremunerative, area of legal practice. Alexander Dunlop moved from his 1825 position to take a more decisive line in his textbook *Parochial Law*:[65] on *Pollock* v. *Darling* he stated that

its soundness has been much questioned. Moreover, since the period when it was pronounced, the inexpediency of the system sanctioned by it, has been more generally acknowledged; and the dread which was then entertained of persons in such circumstances incurring the danger of starvation, if not supported by compulsory provision, has been completely removed, by the greater knowledge which has been acquired, as to the true causes and remedies of pauperism.

George Joseph Bell, who became the leading authority on the laws of Scotland, printed as a textbook the contents of his university lectures in 1829. In these, he stated simply that supply was 'restricted to the *actual* necessity of the disabled and impotent poor', and ignored *Pollock* v. *Darling*.[66]

In 1834 Pitmilly, in *Remarks on the Poor Laws*, a work which, since it was designed as an essay and not as a textbook, gave him considerable freedom of expression, described it as a solitary case: 'in these circumstances, great doubts may reasonably be entertained, whether this judgement would now be repeated, if a similar case should occur'. He went on to call assessment 'for able-bodied labourers, in time of dearth', illegal; 'All those who are able to work, but who, by temporary and accidental circumstances, are reduced to indigence, must be supplied from other sources', by which he meant that the only parish money they could receive must be from that half of the voluntary contributions over which the session had a fairly, though not totally, free hand.[67] In 1835, Dunlop, in his second edition, reaffirmed his criticism of *Pollock* v. *Darling* and also criticised Pitmilly for having contended that there was 'an inherent right in the poor who have not the means of subsistence to be supplied'. It is true that Pitmilly had used the word 'right', but he had taken a great deal of space to point out that this did not mean right to supply from the Poor Law. Any statutes which suggested support for the unemployed could be dismissed, as they were by Dunlop, as 'regulations of police intended for the security of the public, and not for the benefit of the individual'.[68] An occasional lone voice, such as that of the Rev. Patrick Brewster, stating 'that the Poor Laws of Scotland made provision for the Unemployed must be evident to all'[69] could get nowhere against this battery of Whig legal opinion. When, in December 1841, events in Paisley, again the hot centre of trouble, forced Peel and Graham reluctantly to consider a liberalisation of the Scottish Poor Law, they assumed that the law as established by the Whigs had been going for 200 years and allowed nothing but alms for the able-bodied.[70] In the Royal Commission report of 1844 it was Pitmilly who was quoted as authoritative on the question 'the important distinction ... between the respective titles of able-bodied and impotent paupers, was held for centuries to be the distinguishing excellence of those laws'.[71] The Whigs resemble a cricket team who had found it more advantageous to nobble the umpires than to make runs.

The main legislative achievements of the English Whigs in the 1830s were Parliamentary reform, the reform of towns and Poor Law reform. It has long been known that the Scottish Whigs stood for Parliamentary and burgh reform. It is the theme of this paper that they also stood for, and achieved, a Poor Law reform which, like the English, was in the direction of increased stringency. Since this was carried out in the courts and textbooks and was complete before they came to power, it did not need to be part of the legislative programme of the governments of Grey and Melbourne.

Notes

1 Rosalind Mitchison, 'The Making of the Old Scottish Poor Law', *Past and Present*, no. 63 (1974).

2 SRO JP 2/2/2 (16 Jan 1773).

3 Edinburgh University Library MSS., La III 746, 1 and 2, 'Answers to and Queries from the Parishes of Kineff and Grange, 1738 and 1744'.

4 *The Correspondence of Jeremy Bentham*, ed. I. R. Christie, vol. III (London, 1971) pp. 18–39.

5 SRO, CH2/549/1 and 3, Daviot kirk-session register and accounts, and CH2/166/4–6, Garioch presbytery register.

6 John McFarlan, *Inquiries Concerning the Poor* (Edinburgh, 1782).

7 Ibid., pp. 302–3 and 338.

8 NLS, MS. 196, 'Minutes of the Monthly Club'.

9 *The Bee*, XVIII (1793–4), contains a series of pieces on Poor Laws, signed 'J. A.' It is known that Anderson published a pamphlet on the Poor Law in Scotland in 1793, which cannot now be traced, and since he was both editor and owner of *The Bee* his authorship of these seems likely, even though these initials are not among the ten listed pseudonyms he used. See C. F. Mullett, 'A Village Aristotle and the Harmony of Interests, James Anderson (1739–1808) of Monk's Hill', *Journal of British Studies*, VIII (1968).

10 *APS* (Edinburgh 1844–75) vol. VII, p. 385, 'Concerning Beggars and Vagabonds'.

11 *The Bee*, XVIII, 28.

12 *Farmers' Magazine*, II (1801) 84.

13 *Decisions of the Court of Session* (Edinburgh, 1808, and serially at other dates) (*Faculty Decisions*), 17 Jan 1804.

14 Graham M. Birnie, 'Tradition and Transition, The Scottish Poor Law, Harvest Failure and the Industrious Poor' (unpublished MA thesis, Department of Economic History, Edinburgh University, 1976) ch. 5.

15 Rev. Robert Burns, *Historical Dissertations on the Law and Practice of Great Britain and Particularly of Scotland with Regard to the Poor* (Edinburgh, 1819) p. 62.

16 See, for instance, *Farmers' Magazine*, V (1804) 20, and VI (1805) 139.

17 What understanding I have of the general process of the development of Scots law I owe to conversations with Dr N. T. Phillipson.

18 D. A. Baugh, 'The Cost of Poor Relief in South-East England, 1790–1824', *EHR*, 2nd ser., XXVIII (1975), shows that this was the case in one area.

19 *3rd Report from the Select Committee of the House of Lords on the Poor Laws*, appendix containing *Report of the Committee of the General Assembly of the Church of Scotland* (PP, 1818, v). Caution is necessary in handling all figures in this report, not only because of the considerable number of parishes that did not make returns to the inquiry, but also because the view of the Committee, expressed on p. 32, that 'average' means the mean of the highest and lowest figures suggests weaknesses in numeracy.

20 See, for instance, SRO, CH2/543/6, memorial by Sir James Montgomery and others over poor relief in the parish of Newlands, 1832.

21 *Report of the Royal Commission on the Administration and Practical Operation of the Poor Laws in Scotland*, vol. I, evidence of the Rev. Robert Burns (PP, 1844, XX) p. 562.

22 Birnie, 'Tradition and Transition'.

23 Alexander Somerville, *Autobiography of a Working Man* (London, 1848) p. 17: J. D. Post, 'Famine, Mortality and Epidemic Disease in the Process of Modernization', *EHR*, 2nd ser., XXIX (1976).

24 Burns, *Historical Dissertations*, p. 62.

25 G. Hutcheson, *A Treatise on the Officer of Justice of the Peace, Constable, etc. . . . in Scotland* (Edinburgh, 1815) vol. II, p. 54. This is the work of Sir H. Moncreiff Wellwood and the Rev. Dr Finlayson.

26 G. Tait, *Summary of the Powers and Duties of a Justice of the Peace in Scotland* (Edinburgh, 1815) p. 368.

27 NLS microfilm, Anonymous, *Process of the Poor Operatives of the Abbey Parish against the Heritors and Kirk Session of the Said Parish* (Paisley, 1820) pp. 45-7.

28 H. Cockburn, *Letters on the Affairs of Scotland* (London, 1874) p. 35.

29 *Edinburgh Review*, XLI (Oct 1824) 240.

30 *2nd Report of Evidence from the Select Committee on the State of the Poor in Ireland*, Question 3353 (*PP*, 1830, VII).

31 W. Hanna, *Memoirs of Dr Chalmers* (Edinburgh, 1849) vol. I, p. 381.

32 *The Scotsman*, 29 Mar 1817.

33 R. A. Cage and E. O. A. Checkland, 'Thomas Chalmers and Urban Poverty', *Philosophical Journal*, XIII (1976) 37–56.

34 Burns, *Historical Dissertations*, p. 64; *Edinburgh Review*, XLI (Oct 1824) 234.

35 See on this the *Edinburgh Magazine and Literary Miscellany* (a new series of the *Scots Magazine*) II (June, 1818) 506, reviewing the Church of Scotland's 1818 *Report*.

36 *Paton vs Adamson, Faculty Decisions*, 30 Nov 1772.

37 *Edinburgh Review*, XLI (Oct 1824) 246. An instance of a sheriff court appeal which later went on to the Court of Session is the case of James Brand, weaver, of Dunnichen, 1800, Court of Session papers, 416; 56.

38 For this case, see Mitchison, in *Past and Present*, no. 63, p. 86; and Hutcheson, *Treatise*, vol. II, pp. 52–4, footnote.

39 *Faculty Decisions*, 29 Nov 1821. The Richmond here was not Alexander, 'the Spy', but William.

40 John Clive, *Scotch Reviewers* (London, 1957) *passim*. In using the phrase 'New Whigs' I make clear my debt to conversation with Dr N. T. Phillipson.

41 Ibid., p. 132.

42 Henry Cockburn, *Memorials of his Time* (Edinburgh, 1856) p. 260.

43 Cockburn, *Letters*, p. 127.

44 This is clear from unpublished letters to him, to which I have had access by kindness of his descendant Lt Col T. K. MacFarlan.

45 PP, 1819, IB (180).

46 *Hansard* (Commons) XXXIX, 1264, 1472 and 1475; *Caledonian Mercury*, 1 May 1819.

47 Cockburn, *Letters*, p. 7.

48 R. Clark, *A View of the Office of Sheriff in Scotland* (Edinburgh, 1821) p. 274.

49 Cockburn, *Letters*, p. 5.

50 See W. L. Mathieson, *Church and Reform in Scotland* (Glasgow, 1916) pp. 152–9, and B. W. Ellis and S. Mac á Ghobhainn, *The Scottish Insurrection of 1820* (London, 1970).

51 See NLS microfilm, Anon., *Process of the Poor Operatives*.

52 *Faculty Decisions*, 29 Nov 1821.

53 'Commission and Instruction to Justices of the Peace and Constables', *APS*, VII, 311b; W. Morison, *The Decisions of the Court of Session from its Institution until the Separation of the Court into Two Divisions in the Year 1808, Digested under Proper Heads in the Form of a Dictionary* (Edinburgh, 1811) p. 10,577.

54 Cockburn, *Letters*, p. 338 and unprinted letters in the Kennedy papers from Abercromby.

55 Letter in the Kennedy papers dated 2 Dec 1821. Moncreiff Wellwood came of a landed and clerical family and was a lawyer active in Church affairs and Whig politics. As the Cockburn *Letters* show, he acted as adviser to the New Whigs. In 1826 he became Dean of the Faculty of Advocates.

56 PP, 1844, XXIV, answers to Question 49.

57 Cockburn, *Letters*, p. 127. Alexander Dunlop, *The Law of Scotland relative to the Poor* (London, 1825), is clearly the work referred to.

58 Cockburn, *Letters*, p. 38.

59 PP, 1824, II (217); letters from John Archibald Murray in the Kennedy papers.

60 *The Scotsman*, 1, 3, 6, 10 and 15 May 1824; *Caledonian Mercury*, 1 May 1824.

61 *Luke Higgins vs the heritors and kirk session of the Barony Parish of Glasgow*, 9 July 1824.

62 *Caledonian Mercury*, 3 May 1824.

63 SRO, CH1/1/79; and John Archibald Murray to Kennedy, 31 May 1824, in the Kennedy letters.

64 *Hansard* (Commons) new ser., I, 900; Cockburn, *Letters*, pp. 117 and 118.

65 Alexander Dunlop, *Parochial Law* (Edinburgh, 1830) p. 190.

66 G. J. Bell, *Principles of the Law of Scotland* (Edinburgh, 1829) p. 281.

67 David Monypenny, Lord Pitmilly, *Remarks on the Poor Laws* (Edinburgh, 1834) pp. 39–40.

68 Dunlop, *Parochial Law*, pp. 343–5; Pitmilly, *Remarks*, p. 309, footnote.

69 Rev. Patrick Brewster. *The Seven Chartist and Military Discourses* (Edinburgh and Glasgow, 1843) p. 71.

70 BL, Add. MS. 40446, fo. 251, Graham to Peel, 26 Dec 1841.

71 PP, 1844, XX, xliv.

11 The Strange Intervention of Edward Twistleton: Paisley in Depression, 1841-3

T. C. SMOUT

I

This essay deals with an episode in the local history of Paisley; yet the story it has to tell touches at many points on themes familiar in the wider social history of Britain in the 1840s.[1] It is rooted in the need, common to many industrial cities, to relieve the unemployed in the face of an inadequate Poor Law during a uniquely savage depression; it deals with the problems of local politics and public order in the age of the Chartists; it illuminates the strength of community as opposed to class feeling in confrontations between the provinces and the State. But above all it is about the subterfuges of Sir Robert Peel's administration, simultaneously drawn by a mixture of humanity and fear to intervene in a local crisis, yet repelled from doing so openly by foreboding about the precedents it would set for central-government action. It demonstrates at once the reality of a *laissez-faire* ideology and the pressures to modify it in practice. It is a case study in the efforts of rulers to maintain social stability in one locality on the long and bumpy road through industrialisation.

Paisley was a large town, virtually the same size as Dundee, but exceeded in Scotland by Glasgow, Edinburgh and Aberdeen. It had about 60,500 inhabitants according to the Census of 1841, of whom some 48,400 lived within the boundaries of the Parliamentary burgh. It was a highly specialised, one-industry, textile town. At the time of the *New Statistical Account* of 1837 there were stated to be three factories engaged in the manufacture of cotton thread and another making cotton cloth for the local printfields. But these mainly provided female employment; the men were handloom weavers: 5350 harness weavers (most of whom would have had drawboys to help them) and 650 plain weavers, as well as forty weavers who were women, making 6040 looms in all.[2] An 1838 calculation found 5599 looms, and on in October 1841 5746 handloom 'steads'.[3] Therefore probably nearly half the population consisted of the families of handloom weavers; many of the remainder were directly dependent upon them as designers of the patterned cloth, or as the flower-lashers who prepared the harness looms by tying the coloured threads before weaving commenced. Others were engaged in subsidiary employments (such as the manufacture of starch, or of weavers' reeds), or in the service sector, providing food, drink and housing for the weavers and marketing the cloth they produced.

The famous staple of Paisley was the shawl, though the weavers also made great quantities of clothing and dress material – two firms in the town were said to employ 4000–5000 women in Ayrshire and in Ireland sewing dresses.[4] The manufacture of shawls had been introduced into Paisley from Edinburgh around 1805 by manufacturers anxious to tap new sources of labour, and the product was originally a close imitation of the Kashmir shawls that had been introduced as luxury goods into Europe at the end of the eighteenth century.[5] From that date until after 1870 (when the invention of the bustle at the back of the skirt and possibly some deterioration in the quality and exclusive reputation of the shawl brought the trade to a sudden collapse) there was vigorous competition between Paisley, Edinburgh, Norwich and Lyons, the principal European centres of the trade, and Kashmir itself. Edinburgh probably dropped out at a relatively early stage, but, despite a series of technical advances in the West, Kashmir went on until the end as the market leader, carried by the extraordinary quality of her workmanship, the almost unbelievably low wages of the Indian weavers, and the special characteristics of the raw material – Kashmir goat's wool – which was not obtainable in large quantities outside India. It is certainly not a case of Indian manufactures ruined by European competition.

In this situation it behoved the Paisley weavers themselves to work with great skill and for small returns. The Paisley shawl was woven in designs embodying Indian motifs (especially what became known as the Paisley 'pine') in a mixed fabric, at this period generally of silk warps with cotton or fine wool wefts: some were printed on fine wool, or on a very high-quality cotton gauze reinforced with silk. Until the Jacquard method of automatic thread selection was developed for shawl manufacture (and, though Jaquards had been introduced into the town around 1825, this probably did not occur on a wide scale until the later 1840s – perhaps because of the continuing heavy duty on the thick cards), Paisley shawls were woven on a large harness loom, with a male weaver at the pedals and a drawboy at the right-hand side picking out the coloured threads of the weft which formed the pattern, to the shouted orders of the weaver. It was a process that demanded much expertise in execution by the weavers. The most significant modification to the harness loom was the introduction in 1812 of the 'ten-box lay' from Manchester, a device that allowed five shuttles to be held at each side of the loom simultaneously and which made the weaving of multi-coloured patterns much easier. Otherwise one is aware – from examining the splendid collection of shawls in Paisley museum – of constant adaptations of patterns and design from the end of the Napoleonic Wars through to the 1840s and beyond, as Paisley rose to the whims of fashion and tried to outsmart or to pirate the innovations of Norwich and Lyons.

The results were textiles often of wonderful beauty, aimed at a market probably still rather outside most working-class incomes in the early 1840s. It is suggested that a Paisley shawl at the beginning of the century might cost between £3 and £9 (though at the top end of the market they might fetch £20). It would have cost a skilled farm worker in most parts of Scotland some six weeks' real earnings to buy a £3 shawl in about 1815. In 1832 'Cashmere shawls with deep borders' were priced at 25s to £3. By 1843, 'Paisley shawls' were selling at 21s 6d, those with scarlet grounds at 31s 6d. By 1860 one could be bought for as little as 17s 6d.[6] The latter represented the earnings of only about ten days' work for a farm worker. There may by the 1840s, therefore, have been some purchase of shawls by workers, but the main market must have lain in the middle-income brackets, with the highest fashion attuned more to French or Indian imports. Nevertheless, the demand for Paisley's staple wares was highly volatile, partly because fashion was liable to sudden alteration even among the bourgeois, and partly because buying a shawl represented marginal spending by the wives of many tradesmen, who would cease to purchase when the downturn of a trade cycle cut into the family purchasing power. There were also seasonal irregularities, with peaks of employment in autumn and spring, as was common in all branches of the clothing trade: it was the failure, in any one year, of these peaks to occur that usually signalled the onset of a severe depression.

Such depressions had occurred, according to Sheriff Campbell in 1843, 'half a dozen times' in the course of the previous forty years: contemporaries remembered before 1841 especially 1816, 1819, 1826, 1829, 1831 and 1837.[7] Each occasion had placed a great strain on the ability of the town to support the weavers when they were out of work, more particularly since the Scottish Poor Law did not admit of any clear right of the unemployed to demand relief – a point that had been tested (if ambiguously resolved) in the famous case of *Richmond and others vs the Heritors and Kirk Session of the Abbey Parish of Paisley*, following an unsuccessful attempt by the Paisley able-bodied poor to compel the kirk session of one of the two main parishes in the town to come to their assistance in the distress of 1819.[8] The usual way of relieving the unemployed was, in consequence, by a voluntary subscription raised inside and outside the town and county. The depression of 1837, for example, had cost £13,600 in voluntary subscriptions, at least half coming from outside Renfrewshire. That of 1826–7 had cost £22,000, of which £8000 had been provided by a committee in London.[9]

The fact of the matter was that each depression saw more and more weavers fall into a worse plight, as the general trend of their earnings could not escape the dizzy plunge from prosperity that affected handloom weavers all over Britain in the 1820s and 1830s. In Paisley 'a fair average weekly wage' for a weaver fell from 30s early in the century to 7s in the late 1830s, and the plight of the town much exercised the Handloom Weavers Commission that reported in 1838. Their *Report* was full of accounts of growing poverty, of a falling standard of living represented by worse food and ragged clothes, of a deteriorating physical and moral environment, and of doubt about the future.[10]

Nevertheless, it would be quite wrong to suppose that the traditional culture of the weavers – a proud and radical one that had had encompassed both poets and Paineites in the late eighteenth century – was broken by the 1840s. The weavers, though now a very shabby aristocracy, remained literate, religious, politically well organised: certainly rendered neither apathetic nor inarticulate by their economic misfortunes. The Paisley 'Literary and Convivial Association' was wont still to meet and discuss the works of Shakespear, Franklin, Paine and Sir Thomas Moore, or to hear essays by the weavers on such subjects as whether prosperity or adversity were worse for a man, on the uses and necessities of holidays, and the causes for the undue veneration of political leaders.[11] The *New Statistical Account* had described the inhabitants' religious allegiance as 45 per cent Established Church of Scotland, 39 per cent dissenting Presbyterian churches, 6 per cent Catholics (indicating how few southern Irish there were), 2 per cent Episcopalian and 8 per cent of no religious denomination. Dr Burns, the minister of one of the two main Established churches, plainly regarded the weavers as a backbone of church life, and described how even the drawboys would buy the scriptures as soon as they had a little cash.[12]

On the other hand, the weavers were also the backbone of the local, and very strong, Chartist movement – here as elsewhere in west and central Scotland. The religious and political allegiances met in the fervent support given in Paisley to the minister of the other principal Established church, the Rev. Patrick Brewster of the Abbey. Brewster was the leader of the Scottish moral-force Chartists, an enthusiast for temperance, an arch-opponent of the physical-force leader Fergus O'Connor. He was rebuked by his presbytery for his Chartism but replied at a public meeting of his allies, 'the Church and the aristocracy were against them, but thanks be to God they had the Bible and the people on their side'.[13] No wonder he was described by a Tory opponent (the unknown annotator of *Fowler's Paisley and Johnstone Commercial Directory for 1841–2* in Paisley Museum) as 'a firy, furious Blockhead. A pest to the town. A learned Man and an excellent preacher, which increases his power to do Mischief.' He was not, however, without rivals: the weavers themselves threw up Chartist leaders, such as Robert Cochran: 'wee Clearhead in a flurry', he was described in a poem by another weaver – 'As proud and game as any rooster,/And ready, too, for Patrick Brewster.'[14] Though Cochran later became a successful businessman in his own right, he was at this stage very much the champion and spokesman of the unemployed.

The more orthodox politics of Paisley can be described as middle-class Liberal and radical. The 1510 voters of the burgh had chosen as their MP Archibald Hastie, a London merchant and Liberal; 300 voters in that part of Abbey parish that lay beyond the Parliamentary burgh had chosen Patrick Stewart, a local man and Liberal, as their county member. William Wallace, the Liberal member for the neighbouring burgh of Greenock, was also active in Paisley through his involvement in the Renfrewshire Political Union, 1829–35. The town was ruled (under its reformed municipal constitution) by a provost, four baillies, a treasurer and ten ordinary councillors elected annually (traditionally the Provost served for two years). The complexion of the council was small-tradesman radical. The results of the municipal elections in November 1842 were succinctly described by the Tory *Paisley Advertiser* in these terms:

Polemically, the council now consists of 10 dissenters, and 6 churchmen. Politically, of the whole number, 13 fall to be divided among whigs, chartists, and sturgeites, the former having the largest share; of the remaining three, the conservatism of the one is deemed pure, that of the other two is dashed, but not drenched, with whiggism.[15]

The Provost was John Henderson, a Quaker cutler by trade, who in the year of Peterloo had had to fly to America to avoid arrest (according to the Tory annotator) 'for radicalism or pike-making': by the 1840s he was a proprietor and editor of the *Glasgow Saturday Post*, which always had a Paisley section and strongly reflected his views as a Liberal, an Anti-Corn-Law Leaguer and advocate of the Complete Suffrage Association, which was attempting (unsuccessfully, even in Paisley) to build an alliance between the middle-class League and the working-class Chartists. Other present and

recent magistrates included paper-hangers, joiners, shawl manufacturers and grocers: virtually all were free traders and enthusiasts
for the League, and in this they were joined by the Established
Church in the person of Dr Burns.[16]

The Liberal radicals were not, however, quite the only political
presence in Paisley, as the *Advertiser* pointed out. The principal
Tory councillor was William Barr, a writer, who occupied the
important position of Clerk of Supply to the County. The Sheriff
Depute and the Sheriff Substitute were also Tories (being government appointees). Alexander Campbell was the Sheriff Substitute,
described by the sour annotator of *Fowler's Directory* as a 'good
but lazy judge highly respectat, and keeps aloof from the public'.
This was possibly as true and as false as his comment on the
Provost: 'Is a plodding character without education, of coarse
manners', and of Dr Burns, 'Forward-bustling-Meddling body'.
These were the leaders of the community on which a catastrophe
of unparalleled proportions was about to fall.

II

The depression that began in Paisley in the late spring of 1841
lasted for almost exactly two years and was described by more
than one commentator as the worst ever to have afflicted a British
city.[17] Before the spring of 1843, sixty-seven out of 112 businesses
operating in Paisley in 1841 had failed; twenty out of forty merchants ('and those the leading men') had gone bankrupt; the
Corporation itself had to suspend payment, because of the collapse
of the Cart Navigation Trust, into which it had invested much
of the town's money; of thirty-six friendly societies, eighteen were
dissolved and fourteen obliged to suspend their constitutions during
the crisis; and two savings banks got into trouble. 'A gentleman
who was then in the midst of the trade of the town and who
took correct notes of the failures' calculated the total amount of
liabilities at £640,000, and the average dividend paid to creditors
at 4s in the pound. At the peak of the distress almost 15,000
people – a quarter of the population – were dependent on relief
funds. By no means all of these were workers: Dr Burns described
how this depression, the worst in thirty years, had affected a class
of persons not affected before, 'considerably above the level of
the working classes'.[18] For many weavers, however, the destitution

was total. Provost Henderson described how

> I have visited a very great number of families and found many
> of them without any single article which they could dispose
> of in any form; without anything in the shape of bedding, without
> anything in the shape of furniture, without anything in the
> shape of clothes to cover themselves; and several of the petitioners
> who have come to state their case to me have had to borrow
> some piece of upper clothing from a neighbour to enable them
> to appear on the street.[19]

Even the pawnbrokers began to go bankrupt in large numbers,
as their customers ran out of goods to pledge.

Paisley was not, of course, the only depressed town: England
and Scotland suffered a severe trough in the trade cycle, and
this, which was at its deepest in 1842, fed the fires of Chartism
from end to end of the kingdom; but Paisley, from what Lord
Cockburn called 'the precarious nature of its fancy manufactures'[20]
was more seriously affected than any other large town. Its plight
left a deep impression. More than any other factor, it led to
the Royal Commission on the Scottish Poor Laws (which reported
in 1844) and to the subsequent legislation of 1845 that basically
amended the old Scottish Poor Law. Sir James Graham, the Home
Secretary, plainly had Paisley in mind when he declared to the
House of Commons that 'nothing but a conviction of the great
sufferings that had prevailed in the manufacturing districts had
induced him to disturb a system which, on the whole, had acted
well'.[21] Indeed, he first broached the matter of Scottish Poor Law
reform 'with reluctance and hesitation' in a letter to Peel of 26
December 1841 at the height of the Paisley crisis, when he was
receiving weekly letters from the Provost, and in it he related
the need for reform to the problems of the new large towns.[22]
Only three months before, they had been considering English and
Irish Poor Law reform alone, assuming the Scottish system still
to be excellent; it needed the deepening urban crisis of that autumn
to focus attention on the north. The root of Scottish Poor Law
reform must surely be sought here (and in the well-orchestrated
campaign of the medical lobby led by Professor Alison) rather
than (as is sometimes stated) in the Disruption of the Church
of Scotland in 1843: the Commission was established several months

before the Disruption occurred.[23]

How did Paisley seek to relieve the distress?[24] At first, in the traditional way of relying on local resources. The first distress was noticed in April 1841, the first bankruptcies a month later, and the first meeting to arrange formal relief for the unemployed took place at the Court Hall, Paisley, on 29 June (though some sort of *ad hoc* relief committee had existed since 10 June). It was a general meeting of the inhabitants, the first of several that were to be called during the crisis, and it brought into being a General Relief Committee composed of twenty-nine lay individuals (including the five elected magistrates of the town) and twenty-five clergy: this body was to grow steadily in size, and was to number nearly 100 by the spring of the following year, though not all attended regularly. Among the laity, 'county gentlemen' were at least as numerous as the inhabitants of Paisley, a testimony to the degree to which the problem was seen as involving not merely the Whig or Radical urban leaders of the 'new middle class' but also the traditional and often Tory rural leaders of the old paternalism. Town–country antagonism was hardly prominent in the crisis (though it was certainly present); possibly the antagonism was muted because the county of Renfrew was dotted with weaving villages, such as Elderslie, Kilbarchan and Johnstone, which had industries related to those in Paisley. The General Relief Committee raised a fund and immediately set about distributing money (without making the individual submit to a labour test) to about 2000 recipients and their dependants. At first they seemed to contain the problem (see Figure 2), as the numbers on relief did not increase for several weeks. October, however, brought a sudden surge in distress: the number of those on relief leapt in a month to over 6000, and were nearly 12,000 by December: the peak of almost 15,000 was reached after the catastrophes of the town's, the friendly societies' and a savings bank's bankruptcies, by the middle of February. No charitable organising committee in any British city had ever been faced with such problems.

Where could they turn for help? As well as the town fund, the county of Renfrew started a subscription in August 1841, and a second one in March 1842; London merchants connected with Paisley contributed a substantial sum in October 1841, and subscriptions were also opened in Edinburgh and Glasgow. There was in addition an appeal to congregations all over Scotland. The

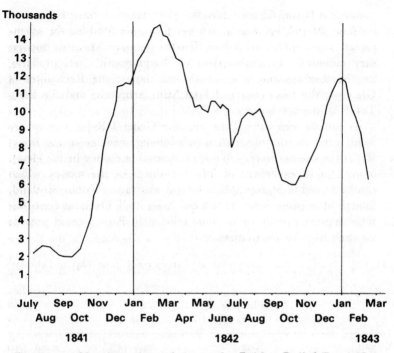

FIGURE 2   Numbers dependent on the Paisley Relief Fund, July 1841 to February 1843

local press carried detailed reports of the subscriptions, which came from a remarkable variety of places and people. For example, in February 1842 the *Paisley Advertiser* announced contributions to the Operative Relief Fund from (among others) the Catholic congregations of Lochaber, Glenlivet and Elgin, from the Episcopalians of Montrose, the United Secession Churches at Bristo Street, Edinburgh, and Queensferry, and the Methodists of Nantwich in Cheshire; help came from Orkney, from Saltoun in East Lothian, Kilniver in Argyll, Dunoon (sixteen bags of potatoes), from Galashiels and from Berwick-on-Tweed. Many of these places were extremely poor themselves, and had little ostensible connection with Paisley. Not the least remarkable was a subscription of $200 from Richmond and Petersburgh in Virginia, which was paralleled at other times by subscriptions from such unlikely sources of charity for a Scottish town as India and New York. In addition, in the same month the *Glasgow Saturday Post* reported contributions to the Rev. Patrick Brewster's own much smaller fund for the unemployed, which presumably had Chartist sympathisers as its donors: they included the boilermakers of 'Teignmouth' (but probably the Northumberland, not the Devon, town); the Rechabites of Glasgow; the flax-dressers of Pool Mill, Arbroath; and the Elgin Total Abstinence Society.

As can be seen from Table 23, the General Relief Committee (with a few minor independent relief-giving agencies such as Brewster's) disposed of over £28,000 of charitable money in the eleven months of its existence: of this, two-thirds of the money which can be traced to a geographical origin was raised within Scotland, though little came from the stricken town itself. Overseas contributions, indeed, accounted for more relief than Paisley could provide for itself from its own citizenry.

TABLE 23   Source of charitable funds for Paisley relief, June 1841 to February 1843 (£)

	Period 10 June 1841– 9 May 1842	Period 9 May 1842– 7 Feb 1843	Total
Paisley	1,692 (6%)	748 (4%)	2,440 (5%)
Other Renfrewshire	4,143 (15%)	1,457 (8%)	5,600 (12%)
Other Scottish	8,376 (30%)	537 (3%)	8,913 (19%)
Manufacturers' Relief Committee	– (0%)	15,081 (79%)	15,081 (32%)
Other English	4,914 (17%)	87 (0·5%)	5,001 (10·5%)
Overseas	1,990 (7%)	294 (1·5%)	2,284 (5%)
Miscellaneous and unknown	7,118 (25%)	964 (5%)	8,082 (17%)
	28,233	*19,168*	*47,401*

Source. Report of the Select Committee on Distress in Paisley, appendices (*pp,* 1843, VII).

As the relief list lengthened and the weeks went by with the situation steadily deteriorating, the Paisley authorities cast around for other forms of help. Perhaps the highest in the land could be prevailed upon to give a lead in fashion, and thus revive the flagging demand for Paisley goods? The first, inept attempt in this direction occurred as early as 8 September 1841, when a deputation of Paisley men led by a Mr Giblett approached the Duke of Wellington and tried to persuade him to wear light clothes (which wore less well than the dark greens and blacks then favoured by the nobility) and to get the Prince Consort to do the same. The Duke replied with some asperity, 'it was not part of his duty to suggest the colours which Prince Albert should choose for his spring clothes'.[25] More successful was the acceptance by Queen Victoria early in 1842 of a number of shawls. The local press reported in February that eighteen had been sent, 'the finest description of India imitation shawls [and] . . . some very rich satins, merinos, velvets and a tartan of a rare and beautiful make'.[26] Both the *Advertiser* and the *Saturday Post* agreed that the Queen's example had helped to revive demand at the fancy end of the trade, and whether it was coincidence or not the number on the relief list did drop sharply (for the first time since the crisis had begun) between mid-February and the end of March. But this still left over 10,000 on relief in mid-April.

The main effort of the Paisley leaders, however, was bent towards trying to obtain direct financial help from the Government, on the grounds that the crisis was too large for any town to hope to relieve unassisted. The first deputation to meet Sir Robert Peel's administration left in October 1841 and spent four or five weeks 'pressing the state of matters upon the Government' and raising a voluntary contribution mainly from Londoners with a Paisley commercial connection; the deputation was received by Sir Robert Peel himself, by Lord Stanley and by Sir James Graham. The Home Secretary, according to David Murray, the town Treasurer,

> threw off a great deal of the official reserve and was not only quite prepared to listen to our statements but started the question of our one pound notes, and too great banking facilities, as the cause of our distress, by promoting and encouraging over-trading. Then he took to the habits of the people. He said that the people in the large towns of Scotland drank too much whisky.[27]

The impetuous Paisley minister Dr Burns unfortunately also threw aside his reserve and for his part began to denounce the Corn Laws as a main cause and aggravation of the distress: for at least six months thereafter, Graham and Peel harboured a suspicion that the clergy and magistrates of Paisley were all fanatical Anti-Corn-Law Leaguers exaggerating the distress to make political propaganda. The reports they received of the contents of Provost Henderson's *Glasgow Saturday Post* were hardly calculated to allay these fears. The Prime Minister himself dismissed the delegation with the remark that the Government itself could do nothing, but that it would use its influence to support any charitable appeal. It was in effect a flat refusual to intervene.

Peel was not, however, as officially unconcerned as he appeared. On 19 October he called for a confidential report on Paisley and district from the Sheriff Depute (now unfortunately lost), and Provost Henderson was encouraged to keep in touch with the Home Office by sending regular returns of the numbers relieved and covering letters explaining the situation. By the new year, the Provost was writing of the distress being 'fearfully on the increase ... our state and condition are very alarming'.[28] There were some minor disorders, and signs of reluctance by the magistrates to put them down: the Tory *Advertiser* reported the Provost as saying that he would never call out the troops to stop people from looting who would otherwise die of want.[29] By 12 February the local MPs Wallace and Hastie had inaugurated a debate on Paisley in the Commons. By 19 February the General Relief Committee had decided to memorialise the Government again, asking it to patronise a national subscription 'or to adopt such other means as they might judge necessary', as the destitution was so severe and the funds of the committee practically exhausted.

The Government returned another cold answer but privately decided to ask for another confidential report. Graham made it the first task of a newly appointed Sheriff Depute, H. J. Robertson, who had been welcomed by the *Saturday Post* with the comment that, though a Tory, he was a moderate and a 'sound and judicious lawyer – a gentleman who can think and act independently'.[30] Had the Provost been able to read his report to the Home Office, he might not have encouraged his editor to write so warmly.

The secret report, dated 24 February 1842, was in every sense a critical document.[31] Robertson began by confirming that the situation in Paisley was grave: he believed that up to 17,000 were 'in a condition of destitution', supported by 'contributions from all parts of the united empire; and dependent for the means of supporting life upon the weekly distributions of the Operative Relief Committee'. Unfortunately, the Committee had adopted a system of relief 'rather too liberal and somewhat liable to abuse'. It was,

he said, so large and unwieldy a body that effective control had
fallen into the hands of 'about a dozen of acute and dextrous
members . . . intimately connected with the Operative Classes.
Their politics are in general radical; and their opposition to the
Corn Laws violent and inveterate.' He suspected them of engineering discussion on the Corn Laws in Parliament to synchronise
with 'a high degree of distress in Paisley', in order to highlight
the plight of the town, so that 'the exhibition might be made
available for political effect'. On the other hand, he said, the
sway of this faction (which plainly included the Provost and the
magistrates, though he did not name them) might be eroded by
the recent modifications to the Corn Laws which Peel had steered
through Parliament in February, and, more seriously, 'by the
approach of insolvency in the Committee's finance; and the steady
continuance of the public distress'. They were running out of funds,
and a minority on the Committee interested in tighter administration and in enforcing a labour test was gaining ground. (This
was probably led by Sheriff Campbell, but again Robertson did
not say so.) He proposed hinting to the secretaries of independent
fund-raising committees in Glasgow and Edinburgh ('without
appearing to interfere') not to give any more money to Paisley
until it had reformed its way of providing relief.

He had, he said, no immediate fears for the public peace unless
there was 'an utter failure of funds'. Then it would 'be for the
Government to give me decisive instructions, for this is an event
in which it is utterly impossible to expect the people to remain
quiet'. He was trying to get the reluctant magistrates to raise
'a large force of Special Constables': the town police were untrust-
worthy, the rural police amounted to fewer than twenty men and
there were perhaps 170 'effective men' commanded by Major Riach
at the Paisley Barracks. In short, he believed the situation to
be potentially explosive and the relief fund in incompetent hands.

It is very difficult to assess the justice of his allegations of slack
administration, but Graham and Peel were impressed. It was at
this stage that they hit on their remarkable subterfuge, and des-
patched Mr Twistleton north.

III

Edward Twistleton was a civil servant, an Assistant Poor Law

Commissioner for England. Of his previous career it is difficult to discover much. Having finished his stint of duty in Paisley, he was chosen to serve on the Royal Commission investigating the Scottish Poor Law in 1843, and became the sole signatory of a minority report which, had it been followed, would have made the new Scottish Poor Law a much more generous instrument for social provision than it actually was. Subsequently he headed the Irish Poor Law Commission during the Great Famine, from which he ultimately resigned in disgust at the indifference of the House of Commons and at being asked to carry out 'a policy which must be one of extermination'. He told the Earl of Clarendon that he had been 'placed in a position . . . which no man of honour and humanity can endure'.[32] While he was at Paisley Twistleton proved himself manifestly clearheaded, humane, hard to intimidate and prepared to carry out his instructions. Even those who crossed swords with him, such as Provost Henderson, testified generously to his straightforwardness and efficiency: 'He did his duty as ably and effectively as any man could do . . . he was one of the most earnest and industrious men in the discharge of his duties likely to be found in the country.'[33]

Twistleton arrived in Paisley on 7 March and made himself known only to Sheriff Campbell.[34] On 23 March he received instructions, the exact nature of which he refused to divulge even to a later Parliamentary Committee, and which are evidently missing from the Home Office Papers in the Public Record Office and from the Peel and Graham collections. The next day he attended a meeting of the General Relief Committee and announced that he had a substantial sum of money in his custody subscribed by Queen Victoria in person and the Marquess of Abercorn (each of whom gave £500), and by certain members of Her Majesty's Government (Peel, Graham and Lord Stanley, each of whom gave £225) *acting as private individuals*: Paisley could have it if and only if able-bodied male applicants for relief were made to work under supervision for at least ten hours a day, and if the existing system of giving money or tickets on grocers was abolished in favour of giving all relief in kind through stores that the Committee itself would run. In other words, Peel and Graham were interfering but the State was not interfering: the Prime Minister and the Home Secretary were laying down exactly how relief should be administered (in a way that conformed with best English Poor

Law practice of 'economy'), but they were not committing the Government itself to any action or to providing any money.

Not surprisingly, these subtle distinctions were largely lost on the populace of Paisley, however scrupulously Twistleton insisted upon them at public meetings. To them it was gross Government interference without the clear promise of effective relief. The General Relief Committee itself (conscious of dwindling resources and rising debts) was deeply divided, especially over the issue of giving all relief through stores: Sheriff Campbell and the country gentlemen were willing to agree to it, believing that the tickets were exchanged for whisky, or used for paying rent and redeeming pawns rather than on food for starving children; Provost Henderson and the inhabitants of Paisley who served on the Committee (especially the clergy) were worried by the effect it would be likely to have on the small provision dealers (to say nothing of the poor). A letter to the *Saturday Post* on 2 April asked, 'what is to become of the grocers? Where is the public burden to be raised? Has it been from the manufacturers this last year, or the flower drawers, foremen of warehouses, the weavers or even the landlords? We say, no; but it has been from those whom they now intend to ruin.'

To the clamour of the tradesmen was added the voice of the unemployed themselves. A public meeting of the inhabitants summoned 'by tuck of drum' on 6 April was chaired by the Chartist leader Robert Cochran, who called for an orderly protest: 'By conducting themselves with decorum they would strike more terror to the hearts of their enemies than by any other course they could pursue'. They called for more generous allowances and rejected the proposed stores system 'with horror and astonishment'.[35]

As April progressed the confusion grew. The General Relief Committee at first reluctantly agreed to open stores, initially for the women, then for the men; the men refused to accept the store system when they discovered they could only obtain potatoes, meal and bread, and there was a frightening impromptu demonstration by a thousand unemployed. Fourteen out of eighteen captains of the special constables called upon to act refused to serve (many were themselves provision dealers) and the overseers of the poor went on strike. At a public meeting Cochran declared it to be 'a time that would try men's souls'; another speaker said 'British society was diseased and undulating like the waves of a tempestuous sea'.[36]

Provost Henderson assured a deputation of the unemployed that 'he would throw the mantle of his official authority over them and grant them their wishes so far as he could'. Privately he wrote to Sheriff Robertson, 'If weavers must earn a subsistence by breaking stones at the labourers' rate I conceive their case hard enough indeed, though they should be paid in cash and left free to select their own food.' He asked the authorities if perhaps a quarter of the relief could be paid in cash. Graham replied that it could not. He described what he was doing as a 'painful process, by which alone habitual dependence on Charity can be checked, and able-bodied men brought to make exertions for finding the means of subsistence for themselves', and he expected the magistrates and the sheriffs to do their duty in maintaining public order.[37]

By the beginning of May the remaining funds were all but exhausted, the General Relief Committee was running into debt but was now more opposed to the store system than ever, and there were still 10,000 needing suport. Sheriff Robertson told Graham that the only possible course of action was to disband the old committee while providing Twistleton with new funds to carry on relief. Otherwise public order would simply collapse. His letters at this stage had a quite different tone from his first report, for while he was alarmed at Provost Henderson's hesitation in supporting Twistleton and the store system (and wrote to him rebuking him for condoning the demands of the demonstrators) he appreciated his basic desire to keep order and his willingness to compromise.[38] Henderson indeed came to accept the stores because he could see no alternative way of keeping the people alive.

Graham then took two steps. On 9 May Edward Twistleton in Paisley 'announced the intervention of the Government, not of the individual members', and for six weeks he and another civil servant had sole charge of distributing relief, through the stores and after a labour test. There were protests but no further disturbances, mainly because there was no chance whatever of money being made available from other sources or on other conditions, and Twistleton could at least give a promise that the Government would not let the unemployed starve. The General Relief Committee simply vanished like the last of its funds.

Graham's other step was to reactivate a moribund body, the London Manufacturers' Relief Committee, first set up in 1826, when Peel had been Home Secretary, in order to co-ordinate and regulate the distribution to the provinces of charitable funds raised in England as the result of a royal appeal read in all churches during a similar period of industrial distress.[39] It had not operated since the end of that crisis, and had fifty-six very ornamental members, ranging from the archbishops and the Prime Minister to Lord John Russell, Lord Ashley, Dr Kay Shuttleworth and a clutch of merchant bankers; the real work was done by its secretary, William Henley Hyett, in close collaboration with Graham. Its task was to administer funds to be raised in England to relieve industrial distress, especially those received in response to a letter from Queen Victoria which was to be read in all churches in July. Plainly much of this money was destined (with strings) for Paisley. Meanwhile Twistleton had a bridging loan available from the Treasury. The idea of raising money by a royal appeal was not new (the old Paisley committee had urged it two months before), but Graham's deft footwork made the best use of it. He at once imposed conditions for 'economical relief' on Paisley by blatant interference (which he could still tenuously pretend was not *Government* interference), found fresh funds to carry on the relief from charitable, not Government, sources (thus setting no precedents), and established another seemingly independent body for the on-going supervision of this relief (which he could nevertheless use as he pleased). Nor is it unreasonable to see the hand of Peel behind Graham: there were precedents when he had been Home Secretary in 1829 for giving noncommittal answers to distressed Lancashire towns that applied for aid, but sending down agents secretly to investigate and relieve by stealth if they found it necessary.[40]

The take-over by Twistleton and the Manufacturer's Relief Committee inaugurated a new and quite different phase in the relief of the Paisley crisis. Henceforth (see Table 23) four-fifths of the money spent was to be raised through the London committee, and Scottish contributions fell sharply. Twistleton's administration, while strict in many ways, provided more generous relief (except for single women) than its predecessor (see Figure 3): perhaps this was necessary if heavy labour was to be exacted. The reduction in the number on relief in early June from 10,000 to 8000 was owing to a closer inspection and definition of those who were entitled to relief as dependants, but the number soon crept back

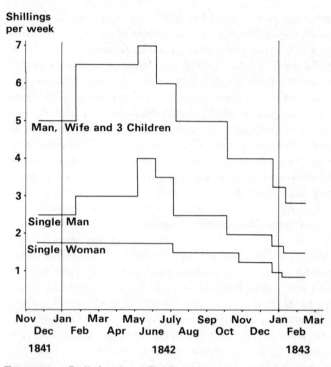

FIGURE 3   Relief scales at Paisley, November 1841 to February 1843

to its old level (see Figure 2). If the intention had been to make economies by frightening away imposters and the work-shy, it was evidently a failure, because there were none left to frighten.

After six weeks in which Twistleton had been the virtual dictator, Graham recalled him: it was clearly embarrassing to have a civil servant in charge of a situation where there was supposed to be no Government intervention. Already Wallace in the House of Commons was quoting Dr Burns's description of what he had done as 'an uncalled for interference with the local administration of charitable relief, and had rather effected mischief than been productive of benefit'.[41] Before he left Paisley, Twistleton selected a Local Relief Committee to replace him and to liaise with the Manufacturers' Relief Committee: it included Sheriff Campbell, Provost Henderson and the other magistrates, but very pointedly omitted Dr Burns, Brewster and the other clergy, who had been

his most eloquent opponents on the old committee ('it was certainly
an unpopular measure', he remarked later). In reply to a vote
of thanks for the 'great attention, unwearied application and uniform urbanity' with which he and his assistant had carried out
their duties, Twistleton laconically summed up what had happened:

> In strict compliance with specific instructions I had to urge
> the adoption in Paisley of certain alterations in distributing
> relief. . . . These alterations raised the honourable opposition of
> those who conscientiously preferred the previous system, they
> deeply affected the pecuniary interests of an important class
> of shopkeepers, and they modified the diet of several thousands
> of individuals. The new system, although intended solely for
> the benefit of the operatives, was inevitably unpopular.[42]

He left Paisley on the last day of June 1842. Graham wrote him
a note expressing his 'certain satisfaction with the prudence which
marked his conduct in the discharge of a very difficult and painful
duty'.[43]

IV

What happened thereafter must be more briefly told.[44] The new
Local Relief Committee came under intense pressure from two
opposing sides almost immediately. On the one hand, there was
a renewed series of 'meetings of the inhabitants' where the unemployed called for the abolition or modification of the stores: the
Committee agreed to pay at least a fifth of the allowance in cash.
On the other, the Manufacturers' Relief Committee became increasingly concerned about the proportion of their funds that were
being spent on Paisley alone. After all, they were charged with
co-ordinating relief to all the distressed manufacturing districts
of England and Scotland, but Paisley had, as Graham reminded
Stewart, the county MP, by December absorbed 'a sum exceeding
£12,500 within the last seven months, a sum more than one-third
of the Charitable aid granted in the same time to the whole of
Great Britain'.[45] The Manufacturer's Relief Committee progressively reduced the sums they forwarded to Paisley in the hope of
compelling the town to raise more locally; the Local Relief Committee in turn reduced the allowances to the unemployed, but

proved quite unable to gather more than very small sums from the town or the county.

The Queen also did her bit once more by ordering (in June) a special Paisley shawl, to be produced at a moderate price and called the 'Prince of Wales' Feathers', made of goat's wool and based on a design of 'Gracefully drooping feathers intermingling with the emblems of the nation'.[46] Her first visit to Scotland in the summer of 1842 greatly helped to popularise tartan shawls, and though the weavers were 'quite unaccustomed to such work' they took it 'with avidity'.[47] There was indeed a substantial drop between mid-August and mid-October to 6000 dependent on relief. Finally, in December, the Queen allowed herself to be persuaded by the daughter-in-law of Paisley's first MP, Lady Maxwell of Pollock (through the good offices of the Duchess of Buccleuch), to buy eleven 'shawl dresses' and cloaks from a Paisley firm in an attempt to popularise yet another new fashion – this time less successfully.[48] By the end of the crisis she must sometimes have felt like a tailor's dummy.

The revival of trade did not last beyond mid-October; but 1 December there were 10,000 back on relief, and 12,000 by the New Year – more than there had been when Edward Twistleton had arrived the previous March. Relations between the Local Relief Committee and MPs, on the one hand, and the Manufacturers' Relief Committee and the Home Office, on the other, became increasingly strained as a stream of letters and petitions calling for more money or a direct Government grant were met by accusations that the Paisley area was too mean to relieve its own poor and was content to live off English charity, and by threats to cut off aid completely. Graham in an internal Home Office note revealed the duplicity of his position on one such occasion by instructing his secretary to reply to Paisley 'in general but cautious terms, not implying my control over the decision of the Manufacturers' Relief Committee' but also to send an emissary to the secretary of the Manufacturers' Committee to tell him 'either the remittance ought to be augmented, or the distribution, if defective, improved. Sheriff Campbell is quite trust-worthy; and he declares the grant to be insufficient and the management well regulated.'[49]

It was solely owing to Graham's intervention that the money did keep dribbling through to Paisley, though in decreasing amounts as the funds held by the Manufacturers' Relief Committee were eroded by the many calls upon them. By the New Year the allowance for a man, his wife and three children had been reduced to less than 3s a week – the sum which the old General Relief Committee had judged enough for a single man (but which Twistleton had augmented) the previous spring. This terrible deprivation caused a further threat to law and order. Provost Henderson resigned from the Local Relief Committee on the grounds that its duty was not to starve but to relieve the people, and offered to open the prisons to the unemployed, because they would obtain better relief as felons inside than as citizens out.[50]

Sheriff Campbell and the others struggled on. By a controversial decision in January they decided to refuse relief to all Irish who had not been resident in the town for ten years: it created immense ill feeling, and effected a miserly saving of expense, as only 208 individuals were struck off the list.[51] This led to a Parliamentary inquiry chaired by Wallace, the Greenock MP, into the whole conduct of the relief in Paisley. This exonerated those concerned. The Local Relief Committee was saved from worse disasters by the revival of trade that began to become evident in January 1843, and the Committee was ultimately dissolved in May as having served its purpose. For the unemployed it had been a searing experience. The following summer, despite excellent trade, the weavers were wishing to emigrate in large numbers for fear of another winter like the last two.[52] The depression, along with the onward march of the powerloom and the Jaquard, sealed the fate of the old-style handloom weaver.

How can one assess what had occurred? The Government had held to its formal position of *laissez-faire*, though it also ultimately organised the relief in a way that prevented the poor from actually starving. The manner of Twistleton's intervention, however, exacerbated the humiliation of the poor, added to the distress of the tradesmen and was probably bad for the economy of Paisley, since the provisions for the stores were purchased at a distance (sometimes in Liverpool) to prevent anyone locally from making a profit from the distress.[53] The local authorities, though divided between themselves as to how to give relief, were increasingly united in their common effort to persuade the Government that it had a responsibility to produce it from somewhere.

Order was kept only because everyone wished to keep it: plainly the Government did, and the sheriffs; so did Provost Henderson and the magistrates, despite the former's occasional inflammatory statements and his manifest wish to keep the sympathy of the populace. But order was maintained mainly because the unemployed and the Chartist leaders believed in moral force. Cochran said that peaceful demonstrations were more terrifying to their enemies than any disorder could be; Brewster described the Chartists as 'an ornament to a community which but ill-requited them for their high moral worth'. And he was capable of filling Paisley Abbey during a sermon in aid of the unemployed in which (to quote the *Saturday Post*) 'the wealthiest aristocrats' sat with the 'most destitute of the humble poor', the 'lengthened faced and well spread loof'd Cameronian' by 'the laughing faced irreligious disciple of Owen' and the 'most sanctimonious Anti-burgher' with 'the disciples of Voltaire'.[54] Here we have no crude example of social control, no plausible clergyman in the pocket of the Establishment washing the minds of a simple-minded and passive audience. Rather it is the expression of one aspect of the radical tradition: the belief in the superiority of persuasion over force, of education over prejudice, of temperate behaviour over violence. The rulers (outside the town) misunderstood it and expected the streets to run with blood. Historians, too, have sometimes misunderstood comparable situations and tried to explain the absence of blood and revolution in the 1840s in terms of crude control.[55] But the community of Paisley at least had a basic will to be orderly, and its voluntary nature was emphasised by the continuing refusal of the town's special constables to serve throughout the latter stages of the crisis.

Paisley and Peel's Government eventually learnt a kind of mutual respect, which was symbolised by the congratulations the corporation sent to Peel when in 1846 he was eventually responsible for the repeal of the Corn Laws, and his acknowledgements which referred to the fortitude and exemplary orderliness with which they had withstood their miseries of earlier years.[56] There is, indeed, some sign that their experiences deeply touched that most austere and remote of British Prime Ministers. 'I shall never forget as long as I live', he told Parliament in a debate on the Factory Acts, 'the situation of Paisley in 1841 and 1842.'[57]

Notes

1 I am deeply grateful to Maureen Lochrie of the Paisley Museum both for the generosity with which she put her great knowledge of nineteenth-century Paisley at my disposal, and for introducing me to the beauty of the shawls. Professor Norman Gash, Lady Longford, Brenda Mitchell and Rosalind Mitchison also provided me with valuable information. The Social Sciences Research Council and the Moray Fund of Edinburgh University helped with finance. I thank them all.

pp. 261–75.

3 *Report of the Select Committee on Distress in Paisley* (*Report on Distress*) (PP, 1843, VII) p. 6.

4 Ibid., p. 102.

5 For an introduction to the shawl industry, see C. H. Rock, *Paisley Shawls* (Paisley Museum and Art Galleries, 1966); J. Irwin, *The Kashmir Shawl* (London: HMSO, 1973); M. Blair, *The Paisley Shawl* (Paisley, 1904).

6 Rock, *Paisley Shawls*, p. 11; and Maureen Lochrie, personal communication.

7 David Murray, *Reminiscences of Sixty Years in the History of Paisley* (Paisley, 1875); *Report on Distress*, p. 5; Robert Brown, *History of Paisley* (Paisley, 1886) vol. II, pp. 220–3.

8 See Rosalind Mitchison, ch. 10 above; L. A. Saunders, *Scottish Democracy* (Edinburgh, 1950) p. 205.

9 Brown, *History of Paisley*, vol. II, p. 221; *Report on Distress*, p. 95.

10 *Handloom Weavers: Assistant Commissioner's Report from South of Scotland* (PP, 1839, XLII). For a general discussion of the weavers, see Norman Murray, *The Scottish Handloom Weavers* (Edinburgh, 1978).

11 The minute books up to 1834 survive in Paisley Museum, but the Association placed an annual advertisement in the commercial directories until the mid-1850s, and there were occasional press reports of meetings in the late 1840s and 1850s. My thanks to Maureen Lochrie for this information.

12 *Report on Distress*, p. 110.

13 *Paisley Advertiser*, 30 July 1842.

14 John Rentoul, *Reminiscences of a Paisley Weaver*, c. 1878.

15 *Paisley Advertiser*, 5 Nov 1842.

16 *Fowler's Directory* is an admirable source for these details.

17 *Report on Distress*, p. 101; Murray, *Reminiscences*. For the details, see these sources, *passim*; the files of the *Paisley Advertiser* and *Glasgow Saturday Post* (in Paisley Public Library); and Home Office papers in the PRO, file HO/345/X/K5625 (henceforth cited as HO file; xerox now in Edinburgh University Library).

18 *Report on Distress*, p. 110.

19 Ibid., p. 56.

20 Cited in J. G. Fyfe, *Scottish Diaries and Memoirs, 1746–1843* (Stirling, 1942) pp. 388–90.

21 Quoted in Jean Lindsay, *The Scottish Poor Law* (Ilfracombe, 1975) p. 211.

22 Peel Papers, BL, Add. MS. 40446/251-6, especially a letter of 26 Dec 1841 from Graham to Peel. My thanks to Rosalind Mitchison for this reference.

23 The Royal Commission was signed on 26 Jan 1843, the Disruption took place in May.

24 See *Report on Distress*, *passim*; PRO, HO file, *passim*.

25 Elizabeth Longford, *Wellington, Pillar of the State* (St Albans, 1975) pp. 428–9.

26 *Glasgow Saturday Post*, 12 Feb 1842. There is a tradition that one was used for the christening of the Prince of Wales earlier in the year, but I could find no confirmation of that.

27 Murray, *Reminiscences*.
28 PRO, HO file, letters from Provost Henderson, Jan 1842.
29 *Paisley Advertiser*, 22 Jan 1842.
30 *Glasgow Saturday Post*, 19 Feb 1842.
31 PRO, HO file, Report on the State of Paisley and its Neighbourhood, by the Sheriff Depute of Renfrewshire, 24 Feb 1842.
32 Ian Levitt and Christopher Smout, *The State of the Scottish Working Class in 1843* (Edinburgh, 1979), reveals some of Twistleton's attitudes on the Scottish Poor Law Royal Commission.
33 *Report on Distress*. p. 66.
34 See ibid., pp. 9–30, for Twistleton's own account, and PRO, HO file. The *Paisley Advertiser* and *Glasgow Saturday Post* are also helpful.
35 *Glasgow Saturday Post*, 9 Apr 1842.
36 Ibid., 23 Apr 1842.
37 Ibid., PRO, HO file; *Report on Distress*, esp. appendix, pp. 163–4.
38 PRO, HO file, letters from Robertson 25–9 April 1842.
39 For this see *Report on Distress*, esp. pp. 1–8 (evidence of William Henry Hyett).
40 Norman Gash, *Mr Secretary Peel* (London, 1961) p. 603.
41 *Paisley Advertiser*, 9 July 1842.
42 Ibid.
43 PRO, HO file, note appended to Twistleton's letter of 4 July 1842.
44 *Report on Distress, passim*; PRO, HO file, *passim*.
45 Ibid., Graham to Stewart, 14 Dec 1842.
46 *Paisley Advertiser*, 4 June 1842.
47 *Report on Distress*, pp. 75 and 156.
48 See the Morgan Letters held in Paisley Museum MSS. department.
49 PRO, HO file, note appended to a letter from Provost Henderson, 11 Oct 1842.
50 *Report on Distress*, appendix, p. 166.
51 Ibid., pp. 92–3.
52 *Report of the Royal Commission for Inquiry into the Poor Laws* (Scotland) (PP, 1844, xx), evidence of the Rev. Dr Robert Burns.
53 PRO, HO file, Ramsay to Home Office, 22 June 1842.
54 *Glasgow Saturday Post*, 21 May 1842. See also ibid., 5 Feb 1842.
55 Esp. John Foster, *Class Struggle in the Industrial Revolution* (London, 1974).
56 Murray, *Reminiscences*.
57 Norman Gash, *Sir Robert Peel* (London, 1972) p. 441.

12 The Poor Law and Health: A Survey of Parochial Medical Aid in Glasgow, 1845-1900

STEPHANIE BLACKDEN

In the afternoon of 15 December 1846, a group of thirty-three Glasgow businessmen met in the Town's Hospital in the city. These sober men of affairs did not look like pioneers, yet as the first members of the City Parochial Board to be elected under the terms of the Poor Law Amendment (Scotland) Act of 1845 they were in a very real sense breaking new ground in Scottish social administration.[1] The Act had only been passed after considerable controversy and several of the new members themselves disliked the new legislation. At their second meeting, at which the real work of administering poor relief was set in motion, the Board listened to one of their number recalling the depths to which poor relief in Glasgow had sunk by 1845, with over a thousand of the poor, including the infirm, the aged, prostitutes and small children, besieging the kirk door and clamouring for relief until late at night. The members were urged to assess outdoor relief at the lowest point at which human existence could be supported in order to turn away the undeserving and reawaken the instinct of self-respect in the poor, so preserving as much of the spirit of the old Scottish Poor Law as possible while administering the new.

This spirit had been rooted in ideals of thrift and self-help on the part of the poor and of reform by encouragement, personal example and contact on the part of the members of kirk sessions dispensing relief. The old Poor Law had been the product of a series of Acts of the Scottish Parliament dating from the sixteenth century, but had differed from its Elizabethan counterpart in several important respects. There was no compulsory provision for the raising of rates, the collection at the church door augmented by additional revenue such as the hiring of mortcloths providing sufficient funds for most parishes. The distributors of parochial charity remained the kirk session and heritors of the parish and there was little attempt to grapple with the problem of involuntary unemployment. The able-bodied who were out of work had come to be regarded as undeserving of poor relief – an attitude which was to persist until after the end of the nineteenth century.[2] This refusal to confront the problems of unemployment simplified Scottish Poor Law administration. Those left as recipients of charity were the obviously deserving: the sick, the old and infirm, orphans and the mentally ill.

However, rapid urbanisation from the beginning of the nineteenth century onwards and the flow of immigrants into Glasgow from central Scotland, the Highlands and ultimately Ireland completely outstripped the ability of the old Poor Law to cope with the demands made upon it. The populations of individual parishes in Glasgow had grown to such an extent that no kirk session could organise the distribution of poor relief adequately, particularly in a city so prone to epidemic disease and where social contact between parish official and the individual pauper, normal in a country parish, had dwindled to vanishing point. By 1825 comparatively few of the slum dwellers had actually been born in Glasgow, immigration increasing the number of rootless, shifting strangers, to whom the established parishes were as alien as the city itself. Quite apart from the large number of destitute who failed to fulfil the residential qualifications for relief, many belonged to congregations too small or too poor to cope with their own paupers, while thousands admitted to no particular religion at all. Increasing concern about destitution, disease and the condition of the urban masses, particularly after the publication of Chadwick's *Report on the Sanitary Condition of the Labouring Population of Great Britain* in 1842, helped bring about a change of attitude towards the relief of pauperism and ensured that the protagonists of Scottish Poor Law reform would get the better of the debate.

The arguments used against the new Poor Law as opening up the public purse to the undeserving and work-shy could be rephrased to provide very conclusive arguments for some sort of supervised medical care for the pauper sick. Even Chalmers, the former Glasgow minister who led the movement against Poor Law reform, had recognised that 'no system, no multiplicity of funds or hospitals ... will tempt a man to become voluntarily diseased. No man will break a limb for the sake of its skilfull amputation or put out his eyes for the benefit of admittance to a blind asylum.'[3] Such an argument restated in contemporary terms a recognised connection between parish relief and the sick poor which preceded the Reformation in Scotland. This connection enabled the medical side of parochial relief to find specific inclusion in the 1845 Act, through sections binding the parishes to supply medicines to the sick poor, to give medical attendance to sick inmates of poorhouses and permitting subscriptions to established hospitals.

Generally speaking, a limiting factor to the service provided was the exclusion of all those who were not paupers from entitlement to relief, medical or otherwise. In the post-1845 period, where a particular parochial board was prepared to invest a considerable amount of time and money in the treatment of pauper sick – as for example in the two northern Glasgow parishes – then it was possible for a remarkably comprehensive medical-relief service to be established. Once the pauper had received his 'ticket' qualifying him for relief, he was entitled to domiciliary visits from the parochial surgeon, free medicines and cordials, removal to hospital and in-patient care when necessary and discharge under the care of the surgeon once again until he was fully recovered. At any time he could attend the surgery free or could call for medicines at a parochial dispensary. If mentally sick, he would be treated either at a private asylum at parochial expense, in the lunatic wards of the poorhouse or, a post-1870 development, in one of the parish mental hospitals in the country, such as Woodilee near Kirkintilloch. All this was available exclusively to paupers, giving rise to a situation where only the wealthiest and the poorest sections of society received medical care, the vast majority of the population being too poor to afford private doctors yet not poor enough to be classified as paupers. Later in the period it became the habit in all the

Glasgow parishes for district surgeons and apothecaries to give treatment first and ask for the inspector's line second.

Although catering for the individual pauper as a first priority, parochial health care came to be extended to the community at large in areas where there was a medical vacuum which the ubiquitous parochial boards could best fill. In districts where no other authority existed, they were responsible for sanitary measures as diverse as nuisance removal and checking for adulterated foods. They provided a public vaccination service after compulsory vaccination of infants became law. Finally, through their historic role as dispensers of medical relief they were largely responsible for control measures during periods of exceptional infectious diseases. Parochial health care can thus be more accurately regarded as consisting of two main branches from the same root: the one a general health service to the individual pauper; the other the provision of a public health service affecting the pauper and non-pauper population alike.

By the mid-nineteenth century, Glasgow must have been a potent argument for Poor Law reform. The population had risen by leaps and bounds, from 83,769 at the first census, in 1801, to 255,650 by 1841. Originally much of the immigration had been absorbed by the suburban burghs of Calton, Anderston and Gorbals, but by 1845 any open space between city and suburbs had disappeared and there was little to choose between ancient Royalty and suburban burghs for squalor and ill health. The key to Glasgow's appalling mortality lay in the city's housing. Building ground within Glasgow was at a premium and the only way to house newcomers was by 'making down' existing dwellings into smaller units. The customary four- and five-storeyed tenements typical of Scottish burghs lent themselves to multiple occupancy. One stair in a tenement block in McLaren's Land off the High Street in 1846 led to more than forty-one two-roomed dwellings, housing 360 persons. The tenements were built round a central courtyard and an added health hazard was the practice of retaining all the refuse and manure from piggeries, stables and domestic housing alike in huge dungsteads occupying the centre of each courtyard, emptied at intervals of six months or more with great difficulty, as the only means of removing the manure was by handcart through the narow closes leading from the wynds to the tenements. The only water supply to the more densely populated parts of the town was by public well, unless some enlightened landlord paid rent for the installation of a standpipe. Thousands of immigrants sought accommodation in the innumerable common lodginghouses of the Saltmarket and Gorbals, where conditions were so bad that they attracted statutory controls as early as 1841. Overcrowding, primitive sanitation and the lack of an adequate water supply had their concomitant in alarming epidemics of infectious diseases, which recurred with greater frequency as the century wore on. Although the average death rate in the early 1850s, when records first begin, was high at 28·74 per thousand, this could shoot up in epidemic years to even higher levels. In 1848, for example, a cholera year, it rose to 35·08 per thousand, and in 1847 during the great typhus epidemic it reached 52·63 per thousand, the highest death rate of the century.[4]

Although infectious epidemic diseases always attracted attention and received maximum publicity through the panic they were likely to cause, particularly to threatened middle-class areas, tuberculosis and bronchitis were more deadly and insidious killers, as they frequently caused a prolonged period of chronic illness which put an immense strain on the sufferer's family as well as himself. The major diseases of childhood were responsible for almost half the total number of deaths in Glasgow every year, but, as these carried off an unproductive and dependent section of the population which might otherwise be a burden on the poor rates, this could be regarded by the parish authorities as a help rather than a hindrance.

The practicalities of doing something to relieve poverty were already a discussion point in municipal circles, the frequency of epidemics having sufficiently aroused the instinct of self-preservation in the minds of the better-off to make sanitary improvement a necessity. The elected Police Commission had incorporated in the Police Act of 1837, after a particularly severe epidemic of typhus had swept the city, procedures for nuisance removal and improved cleansing, and it followed this a few years later with controls over common lodginghouses. The kirk sessions had established a system of compulsory rating quite early in the century and employed parochial surgeons throughout the city. Municipal and parochial health authorities had already learned co-operation even before the 1845 Act replaced the *quoad sacra* parishes by elected parochial boards.

The Act set up four parochial boards in Glasgow, following

closely the existing parish boundaries, two on the northern bank
of the river Clyde and two to the south. The City parish in
1845 was the most densely populated and urban of the four, covering
the area of the ancient Royalty and including well-known plague-
spots such as Bridgegate and the wynds. Its population in 1841
had been 120,183 and its situation in the heart of the city gave
it to some extent the leadership in parochial matters. It was the
only one to have an existing poorhouse, inheriting the Town's
Hospital in Parliamentary Road, the inmates of this institution
being pauper infirm, lunatics and orphans. The Barony parish
was extremely large and encircled the City like a giant horseshoe.
It included the burghs of Calton and Anderston and several villages
later to be included in the city, such as Maryhill and Shettleston
to the north and east and the wealthy Blythswood district, from
which came the rates to pay for the more ambitious schemes
hatched by the parochial board. Its population in 1841 was 106,075,
but this was to leap to 289,457 by 1875. Of the two southern
parishes, Gorbals was unique, both in size and in the extent of
its poverty. The parish covered only twenty-eight acres, being
confined to the old village of Gorbals (the remainder of the barony
of Gorbals – the wealthy districts of Hutchisontown, Laurieston
and Tradeston – formed part of Govan parish). Old Gorbals was
the very poorest and most dilapidated district south of the Clyde
and the parochial board laboured under the immense handicap
of having to maintain a large pauper population from rates raised
from a non-pauper population only marginally better off than
the paupers their rates supported. The entire rateable value of property in Gorbals in 1872 was around £20,000 and assessments
of 17½ per cent had to be imposed on the wretched inhabitants
in order to raise the paltry sum of £3000 to spend on poor relief.
In these circumstances it is hardly surprising that the contribution
of Gorbals to medical progress was minimal, and the parish amalgamated with Govan in 1873.

Govan, a large parish, covered the thriving industrial portions
of Gorbals, took in the village of Govan and a large landward
area south of the Clyde, and then straddled the river to take
in the small burgh of Partick on its northern bank. The inclusion
of so much of the barony of Gorbals in Govan parish had the
effect of putting parochial affairs into the hands of prominent
Glasgow businessmen, particularly as the principal landowners were

the Town Council, the Trades' House and Hutchison's Hospital. Its wealth did not make it lavish in its spending on medical relief for paupers, the medical services in 1869 accounting for £815 out of a total expenditure of £23,765. Its population in 1841 was 45,885, but Govan was to be the growth point of the urban area in the last quarter of the nineteenth century. It eventually built a fine parochial hospital, but it was not medical considerations so much as the need to have an efficient testhouse for the safeguarding of ratepayers' money which induced the parochial board to build the poorhouse at Merryflats with a hospital and lunatic asylum within the complex. Although the poorhouse has long since gone, the hospital was destined to have a long and distinguished career, forming the nucleus of the present-day Southern General Hospital. As Gorbals parish's contribution to a study of parochial health care is necessarily limited, and Govan, apart from those portions of it belonging to the barony of Gorbals, was not strictly within Glasgow until 1912, this study will concentrate chiefly on the two northern parishes.

Taken as a whole, the four parishes covered all aspects of parochial health care. The cornerstone of the service, common to all parishes, including Gorbals with its single district surgeon, was the provision of medical out-relief through the medium of parochial doctors and dispensaries. Each parish was divided up into districts of roughly equal populations, although financial considerations might expand or contract their number. The surgeons were bound to attend the pauper patients within their districts, to keep a surgery where they might be consulted and from thence they dispensed medicines, although both Barony and City later established central dispensaries of their own from which prescriptions were made up. The doctors had also to attend the paupers in their own homes both day and night if summoned and were obliged to include maternity cases among their responsibilities.

To ordinary Glaswegians, the outdoor medical service was by far the most important provided by the parish. They came near to accepting this as a right and were quick to complain if a surgeon had failed to respond when summoned. Surgeries and dispensaries were crowded with patients, many with dubious entitlement, and the number of patients a surgeon might treat in a year was very large. In 1875, when the average number of paupers throughout the urban area was 35·5 per thousand, the City parish employed one surgeon to every 20,000 of the population, Barony one to every 18,600, while Govan only one to every 30,000. It was known for a surgeon to have over 3000 home visits and surgery consultations in a year and yet no surgeon was employed full-time. The time spent on each individual patient must therefore have been very brief. Part of the difficulty was the antagonism felt by paupers towards indoor relief, even in the sick wards of a poorhouse. Outdoor medical relief was more easily camouflaged and preserved the dignity of the individual, while in the case of pauper housewives their reluctance to leave their homes and families was an added disincentive to hospital admission. Attempts were made to channel would-be patients without entitlement to other medical charities in the city, and by the end of the century the parishes paid charitable nursing organisations to provide home nursing to seriously ill pauper patients and relieve the overworked doctors.

The parishes were responsible within their own areas for the vaccination of infants under the terms of the Vaccination (Scotland) Act of 1863, although the City parish had provided free vaccination at its dispensaries for some years previously. The parochial vaccinators worked in conjunction with the district registrars, providing a certificate on successful vaccination for notification on the birth certificate. The procedure involved at least two examinations of the infants concerned, the first to carry out the vaccination and the second to ensure the success of the operation and provide the necessary certificate. The service ran into difficulties in Glasgow from the first – predictably in a city with a large, shifting population whose members rarely stayed long in one lodging. The City parish was particularly badly affected by the problem of defaulters, or the need to hunt for those families who had moved house between the two stages of the operation. The parish faced the additional hazard of hostility from the Faculty of Physicians and Surgeons of Glasgow, which also ran a vaccination clinic and which regarded the practice of directing parents to the parochial vaccinator through notices slipped by the district registrars into the birth certificates as an attack on private practice. Their opposition resulted in the cessation of this simple but effective way of encouraging the poorer parents to visit the parochial dispensaries, and in 1869 the parochial vaccinator reported that only 300 vaccinations had been carried out by the parochial authorities that year. As the population of the City parish was around 220,000 in 1869 and the birth rate for the whole city was 40·29 per thousand, the number of babies born in the parish must have been around 8800, so there must have been many thousands of children born whose parents failed to avail themselves of the parochial vaccination service provided by law. As the Registrar General for Scotland in his 1869 *Annual Report* claimed a 96·02 per cent vaccination rate, it has to be presumed either that the City parish of Glasgow went contrary to the national trend or that the majority of parents preferred to pay a modest fee and take their children to private dispensaries, rather than a Poor Law dispensary, however slim their financial resources. The parochial board itself was sufficiently alarmed by the poor performance of the vaccination service to institute administrative reforms designed to publicise it more widely and improve the detection of defaulters.

On the surface there appeared to be no cause for immediate alarm, deaths from smallpox having plummeted from 302 in 1864 to only nine in 1869. However, mortality from the disease shot up again to 180 in 1871 and 226 in 1873, not falling below 200 again until 1875, when it sank once again to single figures. A large part of the responsibility for the return of smallpox to the city was not, however, failure to vaccinate infants, but a generally low level of vaccination among the adult population and among those born before the Vaccination Act became law. The proportion of deaths in children under ten during the 1871–2 smallpox epidemic was 38 per cent of all deaths from the disease, which compared favourably with 88·8 per cent in the previous epidemic, in 1855–7. The need to carry out vaccination of the older population prompted the municipal Committee on Health to seek parochial assistance, but the request was rejected on the grounds that the law required only infants to be vaccinated by the parishes and it was left to the Committee to undertake a very thorough programme on its own. The result of poor parochial performance in this emergency was a gradual slackening of responsibility by the parishes for vaccination within the city, a responsibility that passed to the Committee on Health which already provided hospital accommodation for the treatment of the disease.

Another responsibility of all parishes was the care of the mentally sick. For some years after 1845 the Town's Hospital was the only parochial establishment for the insane, most being left either in the care of relatives or sent to asylums in various parts of Scotland. Once the parishes had established poorhouses, they provided wards for pauper lunatics, particularly the severely disturbed. Having taken this step, the in-patient care of the mentally sick became an important part of the parochial health service and taken very seriously by the parishes themselves – only the children in parochial care being treated with as much concern. In the early 1860s the establishment of a General Board of Lunacy and district asylums threatened the parochial asylums with closure, but after determined resistance they were allowed to continue under parochial management but with the close supervision of the General Board of Lunacy. Barony, against some opposition from ratepayers, pioneered the establishment of a large mental hospital in the country at Woodilee, with gardening and farming provided as a therapy. The first patients were admitted by 1873. The risk taken by the Board was well rewarded, for Woodilee became a nationally famous mental hospital and by the end of the century covered 459 acres with accommodation for 600 patients. The City was to follow suit with its smaller Gartloch mental hospital in 1893. The existence of these large mental institutions did not end the system of boarding out, which was a peculiarly Scottish method of treating the less severe cases of insanity. Up to four paupers would be boarded in the country under the care of a guardian, regularly visited by parochial officials to ensure their continued happiness and well-being.

Only the Barony and Govan parochial boards were, owing to their large landward areas, directly responsible for the provision of a sanitary service, which involved the maintenance of a staff of sanitary inspectors and other employees under the relevant sections of the Nuisance Removal (Scotland) Act of 1856 and the Public Health (Scotland) Act of 1867. However, all the parishes were involved in municipal public health up to the establishment of the Sanitary Department by the Police Board of the Town Council in 1863. The Glasgow Police Act of 1837 had brought in new procedures for detecting nuisances and prosecuting those responsible. No prosecution could be brought before the magistrates without a certificate signed by the district parochial surgeon certifying that a nuisance dangerous to health existed. The parochial officials as a whole were the people most likely to come across cases of fever, deposits of refuse and polluted water and thus became a major channel by which information on nuisances flowed back to the municipal authorities for their attention.

The most significant development of the post-1850 period was the provision of in-patient facilities by the three major parishes. This will be discussed more fully later. All the parishes, including Gorbals, were responsible for providing hospital accommodation for their paupers where this was necessary. Before the development of poorhouse sick-wards, the destination of most pauper patients was the Royal Infirmary, unless specialised treatment was needed in one of the specialist institutions, such as the Lock Hospital for venereal diseases.

Finally, the parishes were expected to provide a general medical relief service when epidemics broke out. In the first decade after the passing of the Poor Law Amendment Act it was this aspect of parochial health care which occupied most of the boards' time and effort on medical aid. In fact probably the greatest influence on the early development of parochial health care was the eight-year period of exceptional epidemic disease which began with typhus in April 1847, when the parochial boards had only just begun their duties and had not really had time to settle into a routine of medical administration. Not only were the parishes new to their responsibilities, but in addition a radical alteration in munici-pal administration had taken place in 1846 through the Extension Act, which had brought the smaller suburban burghs into Glasgow and had replaced the independently elected Police Commission with a Police Board of the Town Council. This could not excuse the fact that representatives of the parishes, the Police Board and Royal Infirmary did not meet to discuss joint control measures until July 1847, by which time the epidemic had been raging for three months.

Some sort of co-ordination was badly needed, particularly as the parochial boards had inherited the responsibility for providing medicines, hospital accommodation or attendance at home, while the municipal authorities limited their activities to cleansing and scouring the wynds and closes where infectious diseases had been detected, leaving it to the parish to whitewash and fumigate the interiors of houses from which fever sufferers had been removed and to fumigate or destroy their bed and body clothing. This strange partition of responsibilities was maintained with the tenacity of modern trade unions in demarcation disputes. In practical terms, it meant the parishes' superimposing onto their normal parochial responsibilities a complex range of duties, including domiciliary treatment of fever patients, the provision of extra dispensary facilities, hospital accommodation, convalescent care and isolation facilities for families, and finally a cleansing service. In practice the parishes either engaged a contractor to perform this or paid the bill after the Police Board's scavengers had undertaken the necessary operations.

Throughout the epidemic of 1847 only the City parish had a creditable record. Its Clyde Street fever hospital, housed in the historic Town's Hospital buildings, which the parish was at the point of selling when the epidemic broke out, was fitted up in record time and was responsible for treating a total of 5724 patients. By comparison, the Barony Parochial Board had belatedly erected a temporary wooden hospital of 100 beds, while Govan and Gorbals provided no accommodation of their own at all and relied entirely on the Royal Infirmary fever hospital or treated their patients at home.

The typhus epidemic was to claim over 4000 lives and attack some 30,000 of the population. Before it was finally over, another menace had arrived to occupy the energies of the overworked administration and terrify the unfortunate citizens – cholera. About the only favourable circumstance on this occasion was the inability of the local authorities to run down their disease-control procedures between epidemics to an irreversibly low level, although the process had begun. The 1848 cholera epidemic was the subject of a detailed report to the General Board of Health in London, made by Dr John Sutherland, who had been sent north to supervise control procedures in Glasgow and Edinburgh under the Cholera Act of 1848.[5] Sutherland insisted on a thorough programme of house-to-house visitations in the likely cholera districts, sixty-eight visitors, mostly medical students, being engaged for the job. The parishes had also to provide dispensaries open day and night for the emergency treatment of early symptoms; hospital accommodation for victims, with convalescent wards for those lucky enough to recover; and a house of refuge for the isolation of the victim's family. Thanks to the typhus epidemic of the previous year, the City still had its Clyde Street fever hospital staffed and operational. Barony, which had dismantled its small fever hospital, had to make do with twelve beds run jointly with the City in the west end of the town and otherwise relied on the Royal Infirmary for the treatment of its cholera victims. Many thousands of cholera patients suffered and, in numerous cases, died without any medical aid at all from parishes and charities alike, according to the reports of the house-to-house visitors making their hazardous way round their districts.

The result of so much activity through three exceptional years of mortality was the establishment of a definite disease-control procedure which could be followed in the likely event of further epidemics and could form the basis of a permanent system. Although four years were to elaspse between the decline of cholera in 1849 and its return in December 1853, a rudimentary system of notification of cases of typhus and other fevers was still being operated, by which the municipal cleansing authorities were alerted when cases had been discovered in order to undertake routine cleansing and fumigation, at parochial expense, of the lodgings concerned. The municipal authorities, for their part, kept together their staff of fumigators instead of paying them off at the end of the current epidemic, which had been previous practice. This system of notification made it possible to chart districts where typhus persisted and pay particular attention to cleansing within them in an effort to prevent an epidemic from breaking out.

When cholera returned in 1853 the local authorities were administratively more prepared to meet the threat. The City Parochial Board had extended the Town's Hospital in Parliamentary Road to include sick wards, while Barony had opened its new poorhouse at Barnhill with accommodation for infectious diseases. The direction of operations was much as before, with Dr Gavin arriving from London to supervise control procedures. The two south-side parishes, inexplicably omitted in 1848, were now included in his brief, but, although the three larger parishes grudgingly co-operated in the expensive measures he recommended to them, Gorbals refused to initiate any of the administrative and medical procedures. Nor did Gavin's measures prevent the death rate from being more severe than in 1848, although the presence of an external authority did maintain the parishes in a state of preparedness and enforced expenditure until the epidemic was declared over.

Few parochial administrations could experience such a prolonged public-health crisis without undergoing some change in procedures for the better. By 1854 both City and Barony had established permanent sub-committees specifically to handle medical and sanitary matters. Wards for sick paupers and dispensaries with a qualified staff had been set up where none had existed previously and procedures for epidemic control had been operated in conjunction with the municipal cleansing service. Put together, although rudimentary as a health service for a community of 350,000, these efforts made a considerable advance on what had existed prior to 1847, when a dozen or so parochial doctors were all that the parishes could muster between them by way of medical aid to the sick poor. It is arguable that, without the aid of typhus and cholera as catalysts of public-health reform, little progress would have been made in improving the medical service.

The experiences of the epidemic years also showed up the inadequacies of parochial public-health administration. The parishes had been saddled largely through tradition with a responsibility which by their nature they were ill equipped to fulfil. Parochial boards dealt with paupers and their planning was directed towards the pauper population and limited by the need to keep within the money provided by the poor rates. Although they were not expected to meet the cost of cholera epidemics from their ordinary revenue, setting up the apparatus for effective treatment and control of infectious diseases, as the municipal authorities were to do towards the end of the century, was well beyond their financial capabilities or the original intentions of the Act. Contemporary thinking on the origins of epidemic disease had blurred the edges between cleansing and epidemic control through the belief that disease was caused by decaying animal and vegetable refuse. The effect of this erroneous theory was to draw the municipal authorities from the side-lines into the centre of the struggle against epidemic disease, by the need to clean up the city more effectively and so prevent epidemics from occurring at all. The logical corollary to the assumption that cleansing was the first line of defence against disease was to have every stage in the fight against epidemics controlled by a single authority, rather than split between two. In 1862 the Glasgow Police Act set up a Sanitary Department, with Glasgow's first medical officer of health at its head and directed by a Sanitary Committee of the Police Board. Over the next ten years the Department worked with untiring energy to get a municipal public health service off the ground. In the early years it was to receive the same unwelcome assistance as the parochial boards had done when they first commenced their operations in 1846. An epidemic of typhus broke out in 1864, to be followed by cholera in 1866 and finally relapsing fever and smallpox in 1870. This hastened reforms which otherwise might have taken years to develop, the most important being the establishment of municipal fever hospitals. The first of these, in Parliamentary Road, was a collection of unprepossessing wooden huts erected while the Police Board debated its permanency. The second was an undeniably permanent institution in the grounds of Belvidere House on the eastern edge of the city. Belvidere became the headquarters of the municipal infectious-diseases service, being expanded to include a separate smallpox hospital and convalescent wards. Later sanatoria for tuberculosis and the large infectious-diseases hospital at Ruchill were to be added to the establishment.

This diversion into the realm of municipal health administration is justifiable because of the profound effect these developments had on parochial health care. Involvement with infectious diseases took up a disproportionately large amount of time, money and effort. At the beginning of the 1864 typhus epidemic, the parishes were still the only agencies capable of detecting fever cases, treating victims at home, providing them with hospital care, together with the Royal Infirmary, and dealing with infected bed and body linen. By the end of the epidemic in 1865, a parallel system of municipal district surgeons had removed much of the field work in detecting cases of fever and all the nuisance certification performed by the parochial surgeons. A municipal washing house coped with infected linen and a municipal fever hospital was responsible for in-patient care. Until Belvidere was fully operational, in 1871, the parochial boards were still requested to co-operate during periods of exceptional infectious disease by taking in the surplus of patients in their own parishes, but by 1873 all fever cases within the urban area were treated by the municipal authorities and even the Royal Infirmary closed down its fever wards. Barony and Govan, with their large landward areas, maintained fever accommodation for a few more years, but the wards at Barnhill were finally turned over to other uses in 1875.

With their responsibility for epidemic diseases removed, the parishes in the 1870s were able to concentrate on providing a medical service more suited to the care of the individual paupers. Stricter rules were drawn up for the guidance of the district surgeons (requiring them to find substitutes should they be absent or ill themselves), the number of dispensaries was increased, particularly in Barony, and a staff of qualified apothecaries was engaged to make up medicines.

This outdoor medical relief service was of great value, but it was a continuation of a very old tradition. Where the parishes were to break new ground was in the provision of a general hospital service which in the twentieth century would parallel that of the great charity hospitals of the city, if lacking their glamour. The central Board of Supervision had encouraged the establishment of sick wards in poorhouses from the first, but, once again, it was the great typhus epidemic of 1847 which had contributed most to effecting this innovation. The City Parochial Board was the first to appreciate the advantages of treating medical and surgical cases in their own poorhouse rather than paying for them to be treated in the Royal Infirmary. They discovered after the epidemic was over not only that each patient had been treated 3s cheaper than by the Infirmary, but that they were left with accommodation and furnishings for a 700-bedded hospital. As the beds were vacated by typhus patients, medical and surgical cases were put into them. Throughout the 1850s both Barony and City maintained wards for pauper patients in their poorhouses, but much of their effort went into the fever wards. With the 1870s this obligation was removed, and Barony had the added advantage of Woodilee from 1873 onwards for the mentally ill, so releasing further accommodation for the chronic and acute sick.

At the beginning of the 1870s the standard of parochial hospital care was extremely low. Wards were cold, draughty and damp; meals were monotonous, badly prepared with inferior-quality food-stuffs and rarely served hot; bread was carried up to the wards from the kitchens in nurses' aprons. Children sometimes slept two to a bed in the general wards, venereal patients used the same washing and lavatory facilities as other cases and bed linen was changed infrequently. There were reports of patients' being ill-treated, left without medical attention when seriously ill and allowed to remain verminous. On the medical side, antiseptic techniques were not introduced into the City wards until 1879[6] and the Barnhill hospital in Barony still performed operations either in the ward in hearing of the patients or in the ward kitchen as late as 1884. In both parishes the most senior medical officer held his appointment on a part-time basis with one full-time qualified assistant, while most of the nursing was performed by female paupers under the supervision of two paid nurses.

None of this mattered in the 1860s, when nursing standards, particularly in fever hospitals, were not high in any but exceptional hospitals. To some extent the treatment of pauper patients was affected by the generally intolerant attitude towards paupers and from the constraints put upon expenditure through the need to placate ratepayer opinion. Nor was Glasgow as a whole well served by medical charities until the last quarter of the nineteenth century, the largest up to 1874 being the Royal Infirmary, the Lying-in Hospital and a medical mission providing a domiciliary service to the sick poor. In the last quarter of the century a tide of medical reform swept over Glasgow, beginning with the establishment of the municipal fever hospitals. In 1874 a second major general hospital, the Western Infirmary, was opened, to be followed before the end of the century by the Royal Hospital for Sick Children and the Victoria Infirmary as a general hospital for the south side. The parochial boards in the same period were to contribute Woodilee and Gartloch mental hospitals and the Merryflats poorhouse hospital and asylum. New methods of antiseptic sugery and nursing care were introduced into the larger charity hospitals, and the atmosphere of innovation and reform affected the parochial hospitals no less than the charity institutions.

Management procedures at the poorhouse, for years accepted without criticism by the members of the parochial boards, were now called in question. The routine fortnightly inspection became the occasion for bringing to light abuses such as soured bread and damp food stores. The Town's Hospital (the poorhouse of City parish) was investigated by Dr Henry Littlejohn, the Board of Supervision's chief medical officer and a famous expert in forensic medicine, whose report condemned such practices as the overcrowding of patients in wards and lack of sanitary facilities. Although external criticism was not always accepted with a good grace, reforms began to creep in both at Barnhill and the Town's Hospital – better diet, warmer and drier wards, cleaner patients and bed linen, the separation of difficult and restless cases.

The City Parochial Board, suffering from a restricted site, old and unsuitable buildings and financial difficulties, found these improvements more difficult to make than Barony and soon lost the lead it had once held in medical matters. Barnhill, on the other had, had the appearance of a general hospital by 1880, with accommodation for skin diseases; a children's ward and small cottage hospital for treating minor juvenile infectious diseases; maternity, venereal and consumptive wards; and general medical and surgical wards for chronic and acute cases.

By the 1880s Glasgow's parochial hospitals, in spite of the antipathy shown towards them by the poor, were treating substantial numbers of patients every year. The greatest number found their way to the Town's Hospital, whose 25 wards averaged 440 patients daily. Barony, with 380 beds, averaged over 300 daily, while the smallest, Govan, supplied a further 240 beds. No real improvements could be made, however, while the standard of nursing remained low. Here the parochial hospitals throughout Scotland were falling far behind the charity hospitals, and in the summer of 1879 the Board of Supervision circularised all parochial boards on the subject. The circular condemned the use of pauper nurses and recommended a system of trained nurses as adopted by many Poor Law hospitals in England, at a ratio of one trained nurse to every twenty patients. Barony Parochial Board responded quickly and, after investigating several Scottish and English hospitals already using such a system, particularly the large Poor Law hospitals in London as in similar circumstances in Barnhill, selected Miss Augusta Pigott of Guy's Hospital as Lady Superintendent. When on 1 July 1880 Miss Pigott entered Barnhill's wards, the influence of Florence Nightingale at last penetrated into Scotland's parochial hospitals.

Miss Pigott and her successors succeeded in achieving discipline, efficiency and dedication in their trained nursing staff, and in return they were given a freedom of action and even a deference from management and medical staff which was remarkable. In February 1881, with the appointment of six nurse probationers, a further important innovation was made, so beginning what was to develop into the Barnhill nursing school. Probationers were given a two-year training course with one further year as a staff nurse before being granted a certificate by the Board of Supervision. Their training included experience in all wards, including maternity, lecture courses and written and oral examinations. By the end of the century Barony had instituted midwifery training, the candidates taking the examination for the Certificate of Midwifery of the London Obstetrical Society.

The success of the Barnhill venture and the carrot held out by the Board of Supervision in the form of a grant for each trained nurse engaged, led first Govan and finally the City parochial boards to introduce similar systems. The nurses were in great demand once trained, particularly for poorhouses, where they were preferred to those trained in general hospitals.

Following the Local Government (Scotland) Act of 1889, the Board of Supervision was replaced by the Local Government Board and the parochial boards gave way to parish councils. With the new administration came a determination to make the deterrent aspects of the Poor Law work more efficiently, a decision at first sight at odds with parochial health care as it had developed. Whereas it might be possible to classify venereal cases and pregnant unmarried women among the undeserving poor, the majority of pauper patients were the chronically sick or those ill through no fault of their own. It was obviously necessary to separate the pauper sick, infirm and mentally ill from the general body of paupers, but this would require imaginative thinking and a great deal of money. By the mid-1890s both the Town's Hospital and Barnhill were unsuitable for any further extension, and it seemed inevitable that the Poor Law medical establishments would soon be left far behind the charitable ones.

Neither Barony nor the City could have built a new general hospital on its own resources, but in 1899 they amalgamated to form the Glasgow Parish Council. Almost at once plans were put in hand for a major general hospital which would divorce patient care from the management of paupers and so overcome the great reluctance shown by the outdoor poor for treatment in parochial hospitals. The buildings were to be equipped with every modern device and were to be no more than fifteen minutes' walk from public transport. In 1900 building began on the estate of Stobhill outside the built-up area, and the hospital that arose was in every way a fine and imaginative concept, destined to serve generations of the people of Glasgow. Its opening in 1903 enabled Poor Law health care to enter a new era where the stigma of pauperism was as far as possible banished from the wards.

How important was Poor Law health care before 1900? At no time did it come near to providing the medical aid given by charities, nor did it attempt to do so. Its role was primarily a service to the registered paupers (3·5 per cent of the population in 1875) and it is in this light that its efforts should be judged. On outdoor medical relief the parishes never succeeded in meeting demand, since surgeons working only part-time and for low pay could never provide an efficient service. The real constraints arose from the constant need to convince ratepayers that no money was being spent frivolously, and this prevented reforms from being introduced until long after they were established practice elsewhere in medicine. Nor could the parishes help more than a small part of their potential patients as long as admission to the hospital wards of a poorhouse carried a stigma.

Up to the general expansion of medical aid after 1874, Glasgow, as compared with other cities, was poorly served even by medical charities: the numbers treated by charity (either at home, at a dispensary or in hospital) in Glasgow by 1875 were seventy-two per thousand of the population compared with 200 per 1000 in Edinburgh and 236 per 1000 in Liverpool.[7] By the end of the century Glasgow was fairly well supplied with medical services, both parochial and charitable. Nevertheless, had the parishes not provided in early decades even a meagre service, the poor would have suffered immeasurably greater hardship, particularly during epidemics, when the operations of parochial officials in the worst districts were the only indication that the authorities cared. Between 1845 and 1900 many thousands of destitute people obtained medical attention through the Poor Law, inefficient as it might have been. This fact alone stands as evidence of its importance to Glasgow.

Notes

1 Unless otherwise indicated, all the information in this study has been obtained from the minute books of the parochial boards of Glasgow, lodged in the Strathclyde Regional Archives, Glasgow.

2 See ch. 10 above and ch. 13 below.

3 T. Chalmers, *The Parochial System without a Poor Rate* (London, 1848) p. 392.

4 *Vital Statistics of Glasgow*, annually, 1847–54.

5 See Appendix A to *Report of the General Board of Health on Epidemic Cholera of 1848–1849* (PP, 1850, XXI).

6 Although this was already accepted practice in most Glasgow and Edinburgh hospitals from the late 1860s, and had been adopted by hospitals in France and Germany following the Franco-Prussian war, the medical superintendent of the Town's Hospital in 1879 would have been gratified to learn that in introducing antiseptic techniques he was still in advance of most London hospitals.

7 J. B. Russell, *Report on Uncertified Deaths in Glasgow by the Medical Officer of Health* (Glasgow, 1875).

13 The Scottish Poor Law and Unemployment, 1890-1929

IAN LEVITT

It is one of the ironies of the present revival of modern nationalism in Scotland that historians are coming to realise that, while the dominant theme of the history of Scotland since the Union of 1707 has been the assimilation of Scottish institutions to English patterns, that assimilation was always incomplete. The development and peculiarities of the Scottish Poor Law are a testimony to this fact. While its origin before the Union of the Crowns owed much to Scottish statute imitating the Elizabethan Poor Law, the Scottish Poor Law was moulded in the next three centuries by the interplay of different needs and pressures in Scotland and different interpretations about how political administrators should respond to them. Thus arose one of the essential differences, confirmed by judicial decision as late as 1866, that no relief could be given to the able-bodied out of work.[1] Those that could receive relief included 'all persons disabled by age or by mental or bodily infirmity from gaining a livelihood by working and having no means of subsistence; widows or deserted wives burdened with children . . . and orphan children'.[2]

Freed from the necessity of applying a work test, the Scots could develop a different mode of administration. While industrial England in the first part of the nineteenth century directed its attention towards restricting relief in the interests of stimulating its market economy, Scottish attention was directed towards ensuring that all those entitled to relief actually received it. The uneven expenditure on relief between areas revealed the overall inadequacy of Poor Law relief and it was one of the explicit functions of the 1843-4 Scottish Poor Law Commission to secure adequate relief. Consequently, the Poor Law Amendment Act of 1845 was directed at improving the administrative structure by creating a central Board of Supervision, amongst other things, and ensuring the rights of the poor by an appeal system against refusal of relief (to the local sheriff) and against inadequate relief (to the Board of Supervision).

Given these peculiarities, outdoor relief continued to be the dominant vehicle of Poor Law provision. As a consequence, the poorhouse (significantly, never called a workhouse) remained a secondary instrument of policy. In addition to institutional provision, the poorhouse could be used to 'test' any dubious applicant: for example, any unemployed person who, in order to gain legal relief, could obtain a medical certificate of disablement testifying to at least temporary sickness might be asked to enter the poorhouse to prove the genuine character of his need. But the poorhouse was never intended for the unemployed, and unlike England, there was never any statutory authority to detain an inmate. With these fundamental differences of emphasis, the Scottish poorhouse never quite obtained the same notoriety as the English workhouse.

With these considerations in mind, the aim of this essay is to show how the Poor Law was transformed to meet new exigencies in a radically different social and economic context, and the extent to which the problems of unemployment became a perennial concern of social policy in Scotland.

The origins of this transformation can be traced back to the 1890s, when it was noted that the biggest group increasing its usage of the poorhouse was middle-aged men discarded by the labour market.[3] In Glasgow, the parochial boards had for a number of years been worried by an increase in the numbers applying for poorhouse relief. They felt that many were borderline able-bodied cases who came into the poorhouse when out of work or when homeless or when just plain hungry. All, of course, had a medical certificate. To control their numbers they attempted to introduce a 'test' labour-yard where work like stone-breaking could be performed. They also introduced a period of detention lasting seventy-two hours for this group.[4] The latter, though approved by the Board of Supervision, was of course quite illegal in Scotland. But these attempts soon failed, owing to the desire to use inmate labour for house duties (cheaper than non-pauper labour), the expense involved in building and staffing 'test yards', the lack of tradition for such stringent measures, and the continued increase of transient 'ins and outs', despite these attempts. The larger, mainly urban Poor Law authorities (those that bore the brunt of this type of applicant) had to look elsewhere for some solution to their problem.

In 1888, the Glasgow Police Board suggested some form of detention for habitual drunks, criminals and poorhouse cases. This was eagerly taken up by many groups, including the parochial boards, and, when a special survey of German labour colonies was undertaken in 1892 – which suggested a farm colony for the unemployed and possibly other types, such as inebriates – Poor Law authorities had a ready-made scheme at hand.[5] But as this scheme dealt with the genuine unemployed as much as the casual poorhouse 'in and out', in whom the Poor Law administrators were really interested, it took another two years for the Glasgow Poor Law Inspector to 'move from viewing the labour colony as a measure for assisting the ordinary unemployed, to demanding it as a place of detention for men of predatory habits and loose morals, who demoralise alike the casual and unskilled labour markets and relief works'.[6] With this change of orientation, and when a local Glasgow Police Bill failed to get some powers of detention for this sub-category of unemployed, local bodies moved to establish a voluntary labour colony.[7]

In 1893, owing to the onslaught of a trade depression, the Board of Supervision[8] undertook a survey of distress and its relief. Traditionally, such relief had been met by town councils and/or local charities initiating relief works or soup kitchens, but the survey uncovered the fact that some parochial boards did grant occasional relief, mostly medical, to able-bodied men and their dependants. This was permissible under a Board circular of 1878 which stated that relief could be given if other agencies had failed and it seemed likely that the unemployed would become physically disabled and hence entitled to perhaps even greater relief. But no relief could be given to a striker, and at no time does the circular mention dependants, as obviously their rights were subsumed under the person unemployed. The investigator was sufficiently impressed by the distress to recommend some relaxing of the law in periods of severe unemployment.

The problems associated with inebriates, habitual offenders and vagrants in the early 1890s, particularly with their control, had led to the setting-up of a departmental committee in 1895. In obvious difficulty with the preservation of the 'liberty of the individual', it sought to establish clear criteria for national and local assistance. Remedial reformatories, compulsory detention and town council relief works were amongst its major recommendations.[9] As a result, a rather weak Inebriates Act was passed in 1898 which failed to deal with the majority of poorhouse 'ins and outs'.

Thus, by the late 1890s, the thrust into the problem of the unemployed had produced few tangible results, as the reforms suggested required major alterations in the relationship of the State to the individual and the functions of the State and local authorities. Moreover, the nature of the problem was still at an elementary stage of analysis. Although more attention was now being paid to the groups below the respectable unemployed, the 'reformers' (Poor Law, local authority and philanthropic) were only just beginning to move towards a greater understanding of the types in this 'submerged pool'.

To do that, however, involved opening the floodgates to counter-explanations and to neutral causal factors, at least as far as the individual was concerned. Thus the poorhouse governor at Glasgow produced a breakdown of applicants by age, marital status, place of residence, addiction to drink, and so forth. He concluded that his poorhouse was rapidly becoming a habitat for single, middle-aged, homeless, alcoholic men, who were going in and out at an increasing rate. Elsewhere, at Dundee and Edinburgh, attention had been focused on the association of tuberculosis with applications for relief, and a long campaign to treat the disease in a modern fashion was begun. Other causes, obviously 'neutral', such as epilepsy and mental subnormality, began to receive critical attention: the scheme of preventive observation at Glasgow gained widespread acceptance.

The 'new mood' is best summed up by the Chairman of Glasgow Parish Council, a Tory, who stated in 1901:

Hitherto the administrators of the Poor Law have had to accept final results, and act without regard to causes; but the relief of this class [the unemployed] cannot be satisfactorily undertaken without breaking that ancient policy. Now the time would seem to have come when power should be transferred on Parish Councils to take causes of pauperism into account.[10]

To do that meant classification on a wider scale, a policy strongly recommended by the Local Government Board.[11] The result was the continual elaboration of the kinds of 'need' to be met, so that not only was more spent on paupers, but in addition more was spent on new and marginal areas. The Glasgow Inspector commented wryly that before 1894 the policy had been to discourage pauperism, but that the policy of the 1900s was to encourage it.[12]

Any orderly progression to a possible new policy was soon defeated by the unemployed themselves. Glasgow's Barnhill poorhouse, which in 1899 had a mere 1500 'ordinary' (i.e. non-hospital) inmates, had over 3600 by 1903 and 5600 by 1905. Leith's poorhouse had 370 such inmates in 1898, with an average of 125 on any one day, but by 1904 this had increased to 720 and 190 respectively. Other urban centres had similar rises, most of which were entirely owing to the trade depression of 1903–5. Thus, not only were daily numbers increasing, but also the numbers going in and out were increasing faster – as one commentator put it, 'to recuperate after their debauchery'.[13] The dislocation of the labour market was undoubtedly increasing the pressure on the weakest members of the class of unskilled labourers, who were probably increasing in real numbers in the urban and dockland areas.[14] Such men could readily play on any physical infirmity to acquire the necessary certificate of 'disablement', with backache or 'general debility' being the most favoured.

Faced with such blatant abuse of the system, the impetus for legislation intensified, but the conservatism of Lord Balfour, the Scottish Secretary, led to the withdrawal of two Bills on compulsory detention, in 1901 and 1902. Undaunted, by 1904 more ambitious schemes were being mooted. When the prospect of an Unemployed Workmen's Bill became real in England, the agitation increased and it was no surprise that some Scottish MPs rose to include Scotland when the Bill was presented to Parliament. Indeed, the only real opposition came from Lord Balfour, who had by then left office.[15] The Bill was accepted, and for the first time statutory aid to the unemployed in Scotland was legalised (though outside the Poor Law). A Scottish Department, the Local Government Board had direct responsibility for ensuring that any ensuing distress was met.

Further reform in this area was delayed before the First World War, however, partly as a result of the new act itself, which diverted the energies and attentions of the Poor Law and local authorities; partly as a result of the cumbrous succession of Government commissions and committees appointed between 1904 and 1909; and partly as a result of the trade boom after 1909.[16] Moreover, the arrival of State insurance and labour exchanges, and the general hostility of local Poor Law authorities to the 1909 Poor Law Commission still further obstructed any impetus for legislative change.

Thus, the problems associated with unemployment and its sub-categories forced administrators seriously to consider some form of action. At the same time, problems associated with other kinds of poor increased the pressure for the elaboration of separate categories of need, including children, the elderly and the sick. The reasons for the development of this have been studied elsewhere, in a UK perspective.[17] For the Poor Law, an important aspect of this categorisation lay in the growing acceptance of the need to treat each member of the family as an individual unit of public assistance – a direct reversal of the nineteenth-century legal and moral position where the family was held responsible for its own poor. This trend was reflected in official statements, which with time grew bolder. Thus, by 1917 the medical member of the Local Government Board could state,

If the family is the growing point of society, the child is the growing point of the family. If you cannot understand social institutions until you realise that they have their roots in the needs of the family, neither can you understand the functions of the family without realising that they have their roots in the needs of the child.[18]

Thus, from the early 1900s a steady stream of circulars and correspondence emanated from the Board, all of which stressed greater use of discretionary powers. This complemented the work of many parish councils, particularly the urban ones, which were already formulating new policies. But the medical member of the Board felt that even these were not sufficient and claimed in respect of the unmarried mother that 'the essential point is that the system does not provide for the individual treatment of each mother on her own merits as a person'.[19] Discretion, it seems, was not enough in the growing complexity of early twentieth-century welfare.

There was, moreover, yet another element, for the limits of Poor Law action was also determined by the judiciary (which, since the 1898 Poor Law Act included the Local Government Board itself). In a series of court decisions after 1900 there occurred a steady elaboration of able-bodied entitlement to relief.[20] A rather worried *Poor Law Magazine* commentator wrote,

The general result would seem to be that relief may be given to the dependant of an able-bodied man. . . . And this curious result follows – that the *dependant*, irrespective of age or sex or status, is a pauper in his or her own right. That is a contradiction in terms, but it is an inevitable result . . . in none of these cases was the dependant who became chargeable actually residing with the able-bodied husband or parent; but that does not seem to affect the principle, which no doubt, will soon be applied in cases where the parties live together.[21]

By 1914, therefore, there was some minimal provision for the unemployed man through the workings of the Unemployed Workman's Act (outside the Poor Law), and an admission that his dependants could under some still exceptional circumstances be relieved from the Poor Law if he was unable to support them himself. The history of the post-war years is of the sudden and total buckling, under the twin pressures of industrial militancy and structural unemployment, of the old resistance to relieving the able-bodied and their families from the Poor Law.

The first occasion when organised labour brought pressure to bear on the matter occurred during the miners' strike in April 1921. A call to relieve striking families from Poor Law funds came from a miners' union branch at Auchinleck, Ayrshire, and was transmitted through their local parish council along with similar representations from parish councils in the mining areas of Fife, to the Board of Health (which in 1920 replaced the Local Government Board as the commanding authority over the Poor Law). This resulted in a revised circular on the able-bodied poor which was issued by the Board to all the parish councils:[22]

> Parish Councils have no legal authority to grant relief to able-bodied persons and their dependants. Relief can be competently afforded only to applicants who are both destitute and disabled. It will be obvious, however, that Parish Councils, as authorities responsible for relieving destitution, cannot allow women and children to suffer undue hardship through lack of food. The policy which should be adopted by Parish Councils should be to refer applicants for relief on account of the strike to those administering any voluntary or other funds available for the relief of distress, but if no such funds exist, or if they are insufficient, or if they become exhausted, and absolute destitution threatens to cause physical injury to applicants or their dependants, Parish Councils may then afford such relief as, in their discretion, they think necessary. . . .

With such an ambiguous circular it is not surprising that virtually all mining parish councils held back from actually relieving strikers and their dependants, uncertain whether to obey the law as they knew it or the Board. Except for one parish, all relief was restricted either to the occasional cases or to cases where a medical certificate had been obtained. The exception was Newbattle, a mining parish controlled by the Labour Party, which saw very clearly that the circular gave an opening for the relief of able-bodied destitution on a wide scale. It was soon engaged in battle with the Board, which was able to resist Newbattle's generous interpretation of its circular, but only after its representative had admitted that 'the Board had gone a little way from the strict legal position out of sympathy with the people who were suffering and had given the Parish Councils a loophole to relieve really destitute people approaching sickness'.

The Board was therefore openly prepared to tolerate illegality, but only in individual cases where approaching sickness threatened, because it believed the parish was the authority 'responsible for relieving destitution'. Newbattle had indicated the illogicality of differentiating between individuals and a large number approaching sickness. The strike had indicated the intolerable position which the Poor Law faced.

But a single strike was one thing; the new structural problems of the inter-war depression were another. Early in 1921, Scotland yet again met a rising tide of unemployment with the traditional methods of relief, backed this time by the National Insurance Fund. Local newspapers ran distress appeals, linked in many cases to provost relief funds. Local authorities hastened public works. Firms went on short time, organised their own relief funds and remitted rent on employees' homes if owned by the firm. Savings were dipped into and shopkeepers, especially the Co-op, extended credit. School meals and child-welfare diets were expanded on a free or subsidised basis.[23] But, with the limitations on Unemployment Insurance and uncovenanted benefit from March onwards, the depth and extent of the depression and the allegation that, owing to a 'middle-class' belief that the 'working class' had had 'good wages in past years', appeal funds were insufficient, these methods proved inadequate. By July, the pressure in all industrial parishes was very noticeable.

At Wemyss on 21 July, the Parish Council, after representations from local unemployed miners and on reconsidering the April circular, agreed to leave it to their officials to devise a scheme of assistance. A scheme of loans, entirely illegal under the Poor Law, was instituted. On 31 July the *Sunday Post* stated that Wemyss Parish Council was giving unconditional relief on the Board's authority. Though incorrect, the Board was soon deluged with requests for similar authority from hard-pressed inspectors of poor. The inspectors at Govan and Glasgow did not wait for the reissue of the Auckinleck circular on 4 August, but began doling out relief to growing numbers of unemployed workers. The pressure was so great that half the cases in the Glasgow Sheriff Court were Poor Law appeals.[24] At Blantyre, the Parish, after reading an ambiguous telegram from the Board, promptly enrolled 300 miners. It thus became the first parish to agree on unconditional relief through the Poor Law to a large body of able-bodied men out of work.

By mid-August, between six and ten parishes had followed suit and were giving some form of relief to over 2000 unemployed, although the Board tried hard to explain that there was no such statutory right. At Dundee, the Town Council, in response to local pressure, asked Winston Churchill, their own MP and a member of the Cabinet, for assistance.[25] He expressed surprise that Poor Law practice in Scotland differed from that in England, where relief for the able-bodied was a matter of course, and immediately brought it to the Cabinet's attention on 19 August. The Scottish Secretary may well have raised the problem too, but the result can be seen in Churchill's telegram to Dundee:

> Government do not contemplate extension of Unemployment Benefit, but possibly of relief in other directions is under consideration, and the Secretary of State is discussing with the Scottish Executive means of ensuring that relief in Scotland is administered in a manner not less favourable than in England.

Within the next six weeks the Board of Health had surveyed the effects of the depression, but, with renewed pressure for a definitive statement from hard-pressed parishes and the Fife Miners' Union, the Lord Advocate issued a memorandum on 2 September. It stated that relief could be given and that the position of the parish councils would be protected by retrospective legislation.[26] The Cabinet agreed to this on 9 September, together with other proposals for unemployment relief.[27]

The Scottish Departments knew by early October that the Scottish economy was in a serious position, with surplus capacity and labour in virtually every traditional industrial sector. 25,000 miners were thought to be surplus 'for years to come'. An official investigator commented that,

> Distress is widespread and is especially marked throughout the steel and mining areas. As resources diminish and distress becomes more acute, these particular areas will have to be carefully watched. In them and principally in Fifeshire, Lanarkshire and Glasgow, there are very inflammable elements which, while subjected during ordinary times to damping down by the saner and much larger section of the community, will not improbably be fanned into activity as the endurance of that more sober section is broken by the continued tightening of waistbelts round empty bellies.[28]

What had been of rather peripheral concern for Scottish officials now became of central importance, as unemployment threatened not only to retard its social policies, but also to weaken the stability of democracy itself. The unequivocal decision to use the Poor Law to relieve the unemployed was helpful, because it resolved the previous ambiguity. But it still left the Board of Health with a need to devise acceptable policies to meet the new situation. Its prime aim was to ensure 'adequate' relief (as always), with no mass physical deterioration of the population and no breakdown of local and Poor Law administration through bankruptcy, for the consequences were unthinkable.

In September 1921, a conference of parish councils agreed on a uniform scale of relief. This scale remained semi-official as the maximum until 1926, when the Board reduced it to the Unemployment Benefit level. Only two parishes challenged the 1921 scale – Falkirk and Larbert (both Labour) – and they were speedily brought into line by threats of surcharge. Perhaps more important was the decision by the Board that no relief could be paid to those with earnings below the 1921 scale, because the new 1921 Act made no reference to such relief. Acting as an effective wage-stop, this policy was used by parishes that paid less than the scale to cut down on relief. Further, the relief given was intended as temporary assistance between periods of unemployment, unlike ordinary poor relief, and could not be supplemented for clothing, fuel or rent.

Many parishes, after an initial period on the 1921 scale, cut their own scale to that of Unemployment Benefit, a considerable reduction, especially for children (see Table 24). But any further reduction the Board was not willing to accept. Those that reduced their scales virtually avoided financial drain on their resources, because Unemployment Benefit disqualification and hence Poor Law applications in most areas did not become a serious problem until

TABLE 24   Scales of poor relief in Scotland, 1920s

	Agreed parish relief, 1921 £ s d	Unemployment Benefit, 1921 s d	Unemployment Benefit, 1924 s d
Man	12 6 (57½p)	15 0 (75p)	18 0 (90p)
Wife	10 0 (50p)	5 0 (25p)	5 0 (25p)
Child	3 6 (17½p)	1 0 (5p)	2 0 (10p)
Maximum	2 0 0		

1926.[29] Some parishes which were also landward authorities were able to offer relief work on burial grounds or footpaths, often with the concurrence of local unemployed committees. As the Clamour for 'work not doles' grew, legislation was passed in 1923 and 1925 for parish councils to engage in relief works on a grander scale. Although never legally a condition of relief until 1934, parishes could now offer a 'work test', at which point the local unemployed committees soon took offence.

By early 1922, policy was becoming clearer, but the Board of Health was aware that, while councillors elected in 1919 were not elected on an 'unemployment ticket', the experiences suffered by the unemployed in 1921–2 would produce a crop of more militant ones at the 1922 elections.[30] Fortunately for the Board, the employed ratepayers, many of whom were on reduced wages through wage cuts and short time, prevented any large leftward drift. Most parishes had sizeable groups dedicated to assisting the unemployed and other poor persons, but only two, Bonhill (Labour–Communist) and Old Kilpatrick, moved to challenge the Board's policy in any direct manner, and in both cases the parish did not press the contest to a decisive conclusion.[31]

Throughout most industrial parishes from mid-1921, the local unemployed had some semblance of organisation, often led by local trades councils. Generally, the leadership of these committees passed into left-wing or Communist hands; parish councils and the Board became aware of the difficulties of meeting this local and usually vociferous challenge to policy. The fact that riots and disturbances were so few (occurring at Dundee, Port Glasgow, Greenock, the Vale of Leven and Motherwell in 1921 and 1922) is no doubt an indication of the willingness of parishes to moderate any of their more extreme policies.

The failure of the Scottish economy to return to 'normality' in 1922–3 not only created political problems at local and national levels for the Board, but also affected its ability to satisfy its statutory aims, which included, 'the effective carrying out and co-ordination of measures conducive to the health of the people'.[32] It frankly admitted that, with mass unemployment and the financial restrictions on expenditure imposed by successive Governments, these aims 'were not destined to be fulfilled' and more 'could undoubtedly have been achieved'. Moreover, as Scotland fell behind England on social indicators of well-being, the Board of Health was keenly sensitive to the jibe that it could be renamed the 'Board of Deterioration'. This hypersensitivity to its own reputation resulted in an increased willingness to become involved in new areas of welfare, particularly if they came within the ambit of preventing physical deterioration. This involvement meant widening the scope of Governmental commitment, even if that only included co-ordinating the activity of others.[33] The expectation of such involvement and commitment would as a consequence increase, and the Board would be drawn further and further into social and economic affairs. Structures, such as the Poor Law, with rather restrictive organisational and legal elements would, as the last statutory bulwark to mass physical deterioration, automatically come under Board pressure.

This can be seen when strike relief again became a matter of contention. When the engineers' strike of 1922 loomed, Govan Parish Council asked the Board for clarification of the legal position. Its first reply was 'vague and indefinite if not contradictory in terms'. The next reply was more specific, stating that the 1921 Act did not cover strike relief, and quoted the English Poor Law case of Merthyr Tydfil in 1900, the men there being able-bodied and out of work owing to a strike. The Board further stated that 'any application for relief on behalf of themselves or their dependants should be dealt with as applications for ordinary poor relief under the Act of 1845, and disposed of in accordance with the practice which has obtained in the administration of that Act'.[34] Govan pressed further, wanting to relieve those without income. This the Board refused, stating that they had 'no statutory right to relief', but 'in any particular case . . . in order to prevent hardship through lack of food' they could relieve under the 1845 Act. This meant little relief, because Govan sent all applicants to the Sheriff, to avoid illegality. Out of 200 applicants only 7 were successful.

Further pressure came from an MP, F. Rose (Labour), and the matter was referred to the coalition administration's Conservative Scottish Law Officers, C. D. Murray (Lord Advocate) and Briggs Constable (Solicitor General). They stated, 'there is no difference, so far as the Poor Law is concerned, between men on strike and other men who can, but will not, support themselves'.[35] But, whatever the opinion of the Law Officers, there was no reference to the 1845 Act, and discretion according to the Board remained available under that Act.

However, in 1924 the Labour Government added to the Law Officers' memorandum a paragraph specifically stating that discretion was available under the 1845 Act – an action deprecated by the Board's chairman, who felt that 'it gave the whole show away', tending towards indiscriminate relief. In 1925, the Board began to reconsider its policy in view of the possibility of a general trade dispute and asked the Scottish Secretary of State for guidelines in respect of an all-UK position. The existing position was reaffirmed as being in line with that of the Ministry of Health. That policy was soon tested, for in November a dispute flared up in the shale-oil districts of West Lothian. The parishes, twelve in all, defined it as a lockout, promptly decided upon a scale and enrolled 5000 persons. The Board could not agree and, worried about the financial position, called a conference to declare that no strike relief could be given under the 1921 Act, but that relief could be given under the 1845 Act to destitute women and children. The Board's chairman remarked that:

they had not any wish that any man should suffer any unnecessary hardship whatever. Those in authority over them [the Scottish Secretary] had permitted him to authorise Parish Councils to stretch the law to the extent he had indicated to prevent people suffering. They were satisfied that if Parish Councils used the 1845 Act properly there would be no undue suffering.

The head of the household (the striker) was to be the applicant and settlement was not to be pressed. Uphall Parish Council considered that he had simply brushed aside difficulties. The dispute was settled soon after and the policy never became contentious.

At the same time as the Board was agreeing to the use of the 1845 Act, the Court of Session completely overturned the decisions of the lower courts, 1903 to 1918, on the rights of dependants to receive relief.[36] A *Poor Law Magazine* commentator was very alarmed, because this meant in some cases that no interim relief could be given to any dependant in need, pending investigation. He considered it against the spirit of the 1845 Act. By 1925, law and practice were at variance.

The beginning of the General Strike in 1926 led to further pressures: the Cabinet agreed to a Ministry of Health memorandum on relief and a circular was duly issued on 5 May.[37] Three days later, after repeated requests for guidance from parish councils, the Board issued a similar circular, which stated that, where relief could not 'lawfully be given to the man' and 'where acute destitution and suffering on the part of the man's dependents is immediately threatened, temporary relief in respect of such dependents may have to be afforded'.[38] It went on to state that relief could be given under the 1845 Act to a man unemployed or otherwise if he was physically unable to perform work, and then gave the same scales of relief as were operating in England. Great stress was put on ensuring the parish council's financial position, and all unemployed relief was recommended at the Unemployment Insurance level. The miners' strike of 1926, however, turned out to be far from 'temporary' and the circular was at best a reasonable attempt to reconcile practice with law.

With small units of administration on low rateable values, the Board rarely had trouble from parishes seeking to pay relief over their recommended scales.[39] Labour-controlled parishes in Fife, a 'red' area, tried to pay extra relief, but soon ran into overdraft difficulties, and consequently accepted the Board's recommendations. Two parishes, Beath and Culross, that had paid relief to single miners for a short time, were at first surcharged, but this was subsequently withdrawn.

When pressed for the legal authority for relief, the Board frankly admitted that it was illegal. A letter to Bo'ness in August, similar to one sent to Dunfermline in May, stated:

as you are aware, the primary duty of a Parish Council is to relieve destitution where it is found to exist. Moreover, it has been the long-established practice of Parish Councils in cases where actual physical suffering is immediately threatened, not to await the actual emergence of such suffering but to grant relief to prevent it. . . . It was having regard to these aspects of the situation that the Board, while recognising that on strict interpretation of the Law it might be held by the court that there is no power to grant relief to the wives and children, as a class, of unemployed able-bodied men directly concerned in a trade dispute, felt justified in issuing to Parish Councils the recommendation. . . .

Initially, no parish council refused to give relief to miners, but, as costs soared and the 'lockout' became a strike in July, many began to have second thoughts. Scales were cut at first, but, when local ratepayers began to object to the continuance of relief, large numbers, particularly the smaller parishes, stopped all relief. The refusal of Lord Moncrieff in the Court of Session to grant interim interdict against Hamilton Parish on grounds that 'the balance of convenience' lay in the continuance of relief, seemed to have little effect.[40]

With increasing concern voiced in the House of Commons, the Board drafted a letter to these parishes. It said, 'the Board view the Councils' attitude with grave concern, as it practically amounts to the Councils refusing to perform one of the main duties laid on them by statute, viz., the duty of ensuring that relief is afforded out of the Poor rates to prevent injury to health through the effects of destitution'. These parishes were asked to reconsider their decisions. Out of about 100 mining parishes, some 33 stopped relief. Early in August, the Board was forced to utilise Government loans for those parishes whose banks were stopping overdraft facilities, even though Baldwin had agreed 'to protect the position' of the parishes.[41] By the end of the strike, forty parishes were receiving these loans.

Whatever the pressure from the Board, parishes had also to contend with local pressure. Riots, though few, were a continual fear and those parishes with weak constitutions found it easier to continue relief on lower scales than to stop it altogether.[42] The declaration by the Court of Session in December, when the strike was over, that dependants' relief was illegal, was, however, no surprise and the Scottish Secretary of State, who had already a draft of a retrospective Bill, quickly introduced the necessary legislation.[43] The message of the strike was clear: the Government was unwilling to accept widespread physical deterioration of the population, no matter how abhorrent the causes.[44] This opinion was shared by many at the local level, because most parish councils had unfailingly followed the Government's instructions. It was a major reorientation of social policy in the interests of ensuring stability.

Once the smoke of the retrospective legislation had died down, it soon became clear to most observers that the Poor Law's problems had been compounded. Many industrial and mining parishes were so highly rated (despite a grant to offset the relief to miners on strike) that, for some, bankruptcy seemed almost inevitable. The Board was forced into recommending such extreme policies as the cutting of scales of relief and the stopping of all relief to the long-term unemployed in Central Clydeside, to force them to migrate. Both policies aroused strong local emotions. But the Board felt that there was no alternative to this stern action, because any bankruptcy and the default on loans given to parish councils could herald a complete breakdown of public order.

Whatever the political acrimony over the reform of local government in the years before the 1929 Local Government Act, few believed that parish councils should continue to administer poor relief, either to the unemployed or to anyone else. Under the new Act, control of Poor Law affairs was vested in the large burgh and county councils, but unemployment was increasingly seen to be a question demanding not the alteration of local social and economic policies, but national initiatives. By 1934, with the creation of the Unemployment Assistance Board, the bulk of the unemployed finally ceased to be the concern of the Poor Law. But, because the Government had been successively drawn into alleviating the plight of the unemployed, it also found itself increasingly under pressure to provide some direct economic aid to the depressed areas.

In conclusion, this essay has sought to indicate the causes and the processes of this change. The context in which the Poor Law operated altered, causing it severe administrative problems. The first reactions of the mainly urban authorities were to control or divert the consequences elsewhere. But this failed, owing to the unresponsiveness of the broader institutional complex. This resulted in renewed attempts to understand and explain the nature of the phenomenon, in order to convince the more conservative, the more radical and the more sceptical of the necessity of reform. Once involved in analytical understanding, it became impossible to prevent conflicting interpretations and alternative remedial actions (there being no monopoly of knowledge) through the political activities of others. Hence administrators were forced slowly to abandon their previously held principles, because they had admitted the existence of a problem. Moreover, the Poor Law, the statutory aim of which was the prevention of destitution, had to become involved in newer welfare institutions, the function of which conflicted with their own activities, in order to prevent criticism of neglect of their aims.

However, the degree of institutional penetration of old doctrines was so great that total reform at the local level remained incomplete. As a result of this failure, initiative was increasingly dominated by other welfare institutions and higher-level policy-makers. Thus, the unemployment problem progressively moved from the locality to the wider community. The agents of this community, the national administrators, became increasingly aware that, in order to satisfy *their* statutory aims, they had not only to increase welfare *per se*, but also to broaden the categories of assistance to newer groups or areas in 'need' or poor.[45] They therefore moved to an extended view of social welfare and the progressive involvement of the wider community in social problems and affairs.

Notes

1 *Jack* v. *Isdale*, 2 M978.

2 For a good summary of the Scottish Poor Law, see the evidence of the Local Government Board to the *Royal Commission on the Poor Laws* (PP, 1910, XLVI); also R. Mitchison, 'The Making of the Scottish Poor Law', *Past and Present*, no. 63 (1974), and A. Paterson, 'The Poor Law in Nineteenth Century Scotland', in D. Fraser (ed.), *The New Poor Law in the Nineteenth Century* (London, 1976).

3 *Poor Law Magazine*, 1891, p. 393.

4 Parish-council references are taken from their respective council minutes, now held by the regional councils. Newspaper references are to be found in local libraries. About 120 parish-council records have been searched in central and southern Scotland.

5 AICP, *Report on Labour Colonies* (Glasgow, 1892).

6 J. C. Pringle, 'The Effects of Employment or Assistance given to the Unemployed . . .', *Royal Commission on the Poor Laws* (PP, 1910, LII).

7 *Poor Law Magazine*, 1893, p. 567; 1894, pp. 6 and 142; and 1895, p. 177.

8 *Report by the Board of Supervision on the Measures taken by the Local Authorities for the Relief of Able-bodied Unemployment* (PP, 1894, LXX): The Board of Supervision was superseded by the Local Government Board in 1894, which in turn was superseded by the Board of Health in 1920.

9 *The Departmental Committee on Habitual Offenders* . . . (PP, 1895, XXXVII).

10 *Poor Law Magazine*, 1902, p. 1.

11 *The Departmental Committee on Poor Law Medical Relief (Scotland)* (PP, 1904, XXXIII).

12 See evidence of J. R. Motion to the Royal Commission on the Poor Laws (PP, 1910, XLVI).

13 *Poor Law Magazine*, 1904, p. 253.

14 See evidence of R. H. Tawney to the Royal Commission on the Poor Laws (PP, 1910, XLIX).

15 *Hansard* (Commons), 4th ser., CLJ (1905) 299.

16 *Departmental Committee on Vagrancy* (PP, 1906, CIII); *Royal Commission on the Feeble-Minded* ... (PP, 1908, VII); *Departmental Committee on Inebriates* ... (PP, 1909, XXVI).

17 J. R. Hay, *The Origins of the Liberal Welfare Reforms, 1906–14* (London, 1975).

18 L. McKenzie, *Carnegie Trust Report on Physical Welfare (Scotland)* (Dunfermline, 1917); D. N. Paton, *et al.*, 'Poverty, Nutrition and Growth', *MRC*, 1926.

19 McKenzie, *Carnegie Trust Report*, p. 115.

20 *Poor Law Magazine*, 1904, pp. 14 and 46.

21 Ibid., p. 418. Court cases subsequently elaborated these decisions to cover a wide range of able-bodied entitlement.

22 *Board of Health Annual Report*, 1921. The Scottish circular predated one sent by the Ministry of Health.

23 SRO, HH31/36, 'Reports and Memorandum by the Board of Health into Industrial Unemployment and Distress, 1921'.

24 SRO, SC36/7/30.

25 *Dundee Advertiser*, Aug and Sep 1921; PRO, Cab. 23/27, Cabinet meeting 71 of 1921.

26 *Board of Health Annual Report*, 1921.

27 PRO, Cab. 23/27, Cabinet meeting 74 of 1921.

28 SRO, HH31/36.

29 SRO, HH40/123–40 and DD10/192–3.

30 SRO, ED7/7/7.

31 Bonhill initiated rebates on war disability pensions, increased the maximum payable and gave a number of other allowances. Some of the Labour councillors got cold feet when the funds ran out. At Old Kilpatrick, allowances were increased by up to 25 per cent, with no 'wage stop', but after a year were unable to raise the necessary money from the local rates. A surcharge on Bonhill, imposed in 1923, was subsequently withdrawn.

32 *Board of Health Annual Report*, 1928; SRO, DD10/363, 'Report by the Board of Health on Unemployment in the Glasgow and Clyde Area, 1923', and ED7/7/7 'Report ... on the Physical Condition of Children in the Clyde Valley 1924'. In 1923, James Maxton made his notorious House of Commons speech in which he called the Board, the Government and their supporters 'murderers' on account of the policy of financial entrenchment.

33 This policy can be seen when a famine threatened the western Highlands in 1923–4. The Government anticipated the crisis and then skilfully coordinated voluntary effort to supplement its own schemes of assistance (SRO ED/7/7/6).

34 SRO, HH56/15.

35 SRO, SC36/7/31.

36 *Poor Law Magazine*, 1925, p. 3.

37 PRO, Cab. meeting 24 of 1926.

38 *Board of Health Annual Report*, 1926.

39 In Scotland this problem was endemic amongst all forms of local government. See Scottish evidence to the Royal Commission on Local Government (1925–8).

40 *Poor Law Magazine*, 1926, p. 225.

41 SRO, DD10/242–3.

42 A riot occurred at West Calder, and St Ninians (Bannockburn) was besieged by hungry miners. Both reversed 'no relief' decisions. At Cumnock, the parish held a referendum of ratepayers, who agreed that relief should continue on loan (which was illegal!). Overall, the scales dropped from about 10s (50p) and 3s (15p) for a wife and child to 8s (40p) and 2s (10p) per week. The Board had recommended 12s (60p) and 4s (20p). Fife and Lanark were the most generous areas, with Ayr and Clackmannan the meanest.

43 PRO, Cab. 24/181; *Poor Law Magazine*, 1927, p. 1.

44 The Board noted with some relief that the mining population showed few outward signs of deterioration once the strike was settled (*Annual Report*, 1927).

45 G. Simmel, 'The Poor', trans. in *Social Problems*, XIII (1965–6); P. Blau, *The Dynamics of Bureaucracy* (Chicago, 1955); J. Child, 'Organisational Structures, Environment and Performance – The Role of Strategic Choice', *Sociology*, VI (1972).

Index